HINDU

by

Chitralekha Singh

Prem Nath

CPH

Crest Publishing House

(A JAICO ENTERPRISE)

G-2, 16 Ansari Road, Darya Ganj

New Delhi-110002

HINDUISM
ISBN 81-242-0089-0

First Edition: 1996
Reprinted: 1999

Published by:
CREST PUBLISHING HOUSE
(A Jaico Enterprise)
G-2, 16 Ansari Road, Darya Ganj,
New Delhi-110002

Printed by:
Efficient Offset Printers
215, Shahzada Bagh Industrial Complex,
Phase II, Delhi-110035

CONTENTS

PREFACE

HINDUISM, the most ancient as it is, the published literature on it is as large. Its mythology, traditions and philosophy are so wide, that the more it is written on, the less it is. No one book can describe it, so as to bring home to the mind of the reader as what it is.

This book, an attempt to explain Hinduism, in brief, has been written in simple and easy language, which is easily understandable. Illustrations, a minimum possible in number, have been added to picturise some aspects in the description.

At the very outset, the reader will appreciate that Hinduism, is not a religion, it is a system of living, to which religious sanctions have been accorded from time to time. Changes have been affected, reforms introduced, so that it is a continuous living system and not a rigid orthodox religion.

Keeping this in mind, one must understand as to what religion is? What are its different aspects and what is its relation with other branches of literature. Therefore, the introductory chapter has been devoted to this basic need.

As the main source of a book is the knowledge contained in the previously published and available books, an introduction to the basic books laying fundamentals of Hinduism, needs to acquainted with. Hindu scriptures, sacred books of the Hindus, are so rich that though centuries have passed, yet the knowledge contained in them, about 2000 years old works, has no match today. They are as useful today, as they ever were.

Having prepared the mind psychologically about a religion, a religious system, the actual system of Hinduism, as it ever existed then and now has been attempted. Of course, this subject is so wide, that any paragraph in this book, could make an independent book, so brevity had to be maintained in the writeup. Only broad outlines, in brief have been incorporated.

Out of Hinduism, many sects and cults have arisen and some of them viz Buddhism, Jainism and Sikhism have since been recognised as separate religions. Reference to these have been made only, when it could not be avoided. Tantricism, though a Siva cult, yet it has so developed and deviated from main Hinduism, has become so complicated, that a greater description in this small book could not do full justice to the topic.

The development and progress of Hinduism, through the ages, has been attempted in the sequence order, through different periods in history, sythesising the concept of a particular doctrine in one chapter, though scattered references could not be avoided. Commencing with the Prehistoric age, one reaches the modern period of Hinduism, till the end of the book.

Vedas, Gita, The Cow, OM and Gayatri, are the pillars of Hinduism, its religious doctrines of life; so a greater, not exhaustive, interpretation of these aspects, has been given.

When one is lost in the complicated theories of Hinduism, one can appreciate it, in a 'NUTSHELL'.

The previous attempt on 'HINDU GODDESSES', published by Crest Publishing House has met with great success and the appreciation has been so much, that the authors were encouraged to venture on writing this book, which will be found a unique one, among most of the other books on this topic.

We are very grateful to Shri S.C. Sethi, who has given us the initiative and a continued encouragement to write another book on Hindu mythology, religious system Hinduism.

The authors do not claim, that this book contains 'all', but assure the readers that it contains 'Much' in brief about Hinduism.

Any suggestions for the improvement of the book in its next edition, are welcome and solicited.

Chitarangan
Krishnapuri
P.O. Barauli Ahir
Agra (India) 282003

Chitralekha Singh
Prem Nath

List of Plates

INTRODUCTION

In this advancing world, where we study political and economic systems, world history, literature and art, scientific and industrial developments, the role of the religion plays a great part, since it is faith and devotion that brings results. Problems of world hunger, patterns of family life, state reaction to religious bodies, cannot be faced intelligently without an understanding of the religion that motivates and affects the lives of the people, society and the community. Study of religion provides basic information, an appreciation of cultural contexts, and an awareness of personal feelings, all of which are essential for intelligent and responsible action.

Hinduism, the religious system of the majority in India, has the longest, unbroken span of ritual practices in the world and is nearly as old as mankind. In this book, Hinduism since Vedic ages is the focus. Hinduism through the ages, in its various aspects has been described in simple and commonly understood language. Jainism, Buddhism and Sikhism have been only referred to wherever necessary for the understanding of the development of Hinduism.

Before we proceed with the various developments in Hinduism; it is essential to learn about religion in general. What is religion? How it is related to philosophy, sacred literature, society, mortality, culture, seculiarism and science.

Religion is, in fact, a code of conduct for man in his society. It is the social system. As such Dr. Radhakrishnan holds communism also as a religion. But there is a difference. Religion is a social system in the name of God, for the benefit of human society. Religion is a social theory or doctrine declared in the name of God. Hence God's name is the central point in religion. Prophets, in fact, do establish social orders, as religions, in the name of God. Buddhism, initiated as a social order to combat against social evils, became religion with the evolvement of Mahayana and Buddha as God.

God, soul, nature are three different entities which form the basis of religion. According to Dr. S, Radhakrishnan[1], 'the endeavour of Religion is to get rid of the gulf, between man and God and restore the lost sense of unity'. Religion is an insight into the nature of Reality and it is also a personal experience. It is an experience in which the seperation between God (Reality) and man is eliminated. 'The man's being is entirely derived from that of God by some sort of emanation'[2]. The Absolute (B'rhma) is the self (Atman:Soul) and every subject and object is ultimately identical. The basis of religion is therefore this coexistence of man's self with the Absolute. The roots of religion lie in the spirit of man, deeper than feeling, will and intellect[3]. Radhakrishnan believes that as long as man is man and continues to reflect on the meaning of existence, we cannot get rid of religion. There is an incessent need in the human soul, to come to terms with the unseen Reality[4]. The inborn tendency of every religion accounts for the presence of religion in every culture.

Religion is a way of life in India and lives in the centre of the lives of the people. It is an experience of Reality (God) which concerns itself with inner life. The goal of all religions is a spiritual life[5] and spiritual life means a life of transformation. It is an unending

---

1. Radhakrishnan Dr. S. : An Idealist view of Life (1932)
2. Ibid The Bhagvad Gita (1948)
3. & 4 Ibid My search for Truth.
5. Radhakrishnan Dr. S. : Religion & Society (1947)

search, an evolution from the unknown to the known. Religion is the cultivation of the interior life. It is the attainment of spiritual freedom and is essentially the private achievement of the individual[1].

'Without religion, morality becomes an eternal striving, a perpetual progress, an endless aspiration, towards something we do not have. In religion, all this is turned into realisation, enjoyment and fruition. Then is the weakness of finite endowment and fruition. Then is the weakness of finite endowment overcome, and the finite self becomes endowed with a meaning and mission'[2].

'Religion is a configuration of doctrine and practice related to that which a community regards as sacred or holy.'

RELIGION AND HUMAN RACE

RELIGION is as old as the Human race itself. There are no people, however primitive, without some sort of religion. All anthropological studies have failed to search primitive people, without religion. All efforts at substantiating the preconceived idea that the 'origin' of the primitive idea of GOD must be very crude and simple and different from the 'developed forms', has been a failure. simple evolutionary progression in religion has been disapproved by the great anthropologist Father Wilhelm Scmidt.

Etymologically, Ciccro derives the word from 'Relegere'[3] which means 'to gather, count or observe', that is to observe the signs of a divine, communication or 'to read the omens'. Lattanzius[4] derives it from 'religare' meaning ' to bind ' so that religion meant relationship. Therefore religion means a relationship between a superior being and man. In the East, religion is

1. Radhakrishnan Dr. S : East & West in Religion
2. Quoted by Ayachit S.M. 'Aspects of Religion'.
3. Encyclopaedia Filosofica (Roma) 1957 PP 43
4. Maschetii A.M. : `Religione' in Encyclopaedia Filosofica.

described in terms of 'Movement' as a 'way' as against 'fixed relationship' in the West. Hinduism depicts religions as rivers which take men to the ocean of GOD. In religion, we are on another plane - the world of the supernatural, the world of God. 'GOD', an anglosaxon word, ultimately derived from Sanskrit, 'HU' , to invoke, or 'Hu' to sacrifice to[1]. Among all people, in all times, in all places, the idea of and the faith in, a Supreme Being, creator and Lord of the universe, and of the man especially, has always been existent[2]. This belief in 'ONE SUPREME BEING', in the history of religion was so widely spread since 5,000 B.C. that its discovery in the R'gveda became an incontestable proof to the advocates of Hinduism (Vedism).

RELIGION AND PHILOSOPHY

Sankaracharya while acknowledging the fundamental difference of the intellectual approach and the popular approach distinguished between philosophy and religion. Philosophy, though it is to be realised religiously, has to suffer in order not to distract the great majority, which it has to serve. Religion is the more important, considering the large interests of the society. Philosophy stops short half way, otherwise experience of the pluralistic realism will be inexplicable. If subjectivity is overcome, there will be no trace of the world of objects. All individualism is the result of the confusion of subjectivity. Are we to give more importance to individual experience dependent upon senses or to infrential knowledge leading to some kind of 'idea' only. The faith meant by the Bhagvad Gita is the combined force influencing the temperament of the thinker and is the result of the environment and the sanskaras counteracting and influencing each other if, therefore the higher problems of philosophy, as also that of science, involve the character of the subject in their

1. Encyclopaedia Brittanica 1960
2. Dictionary of Dogmatic Theology 1957 PP 12.

objective knowledge, it is worthwhile considering the developments of the group psychosis, in the considerations of the religious institutions, where there is the free growth of personality on the right path. The fact that all great preachers and saints have made their greatest efforts to create and foster the spirit of spiritual development and not to confuse the masses, cannot be contradicted.

At any rate Hinduism bases firmly its Morality on metaphysics. Gita says, 'who sees God in every being realises the essential unity of the universe, he is the perfect Being; God never fails him in blessing'[1]. Under the structural and doctrinal aspects of philosophy & Sociology, the upanishads did well in bringing the Brahmanical religion in line with popular aspirations, but there the philosophical issues went too far and the common man had to find the culmination of his aspirations in the epics, particularly Mahabharatta and Srimad Bhagvad Gita. The Gita represents a compromise between the purely intellectual speculation and the emotion of faith. It incorporates popular methods of finding spiritual perfection into the frame work of highest thoughts. The religion of vedas traverses the whole gamut of deism, and represents intense thinking in religion and philosophy.

Goethe opines 'The Christian religion has nothing to do with philosophy' [2], yet it progresses; but in India, philosophy and religion i.e. knowledge of truth and its realisation, are one and the same. Philosophy deals with the theoritical principles of ultimate Reality, whereas Religion is the practical application of those principles in our daily life.

Dr. S. Radhakrishnan in his 'Indian Philosophy' says :- 'Philosophy in India is essential spirituality.' [3] and 'To those who

1. Gita XIII 28 & 30
2. Goethe quoted in Hibbert Lectures for 1931 (Published 1937)
3. Radhakrishnan S. Indian Philosophy Vol I PP 24

realise the true kinship between life and theory, philosophy becomes a way of life, an approach to spiritual realisation'[1].

Max Muller says, 'we keep religion and philosophy in different compartments while with men such as Ram Mohun Roy, the two were one, and the religion of the vedas led naturally on to the philosophy of the vedanta (Neo Brahmanism), which became in turn the firm foundation of their religion. The vedanta philosophy was so brood that it could well have served as a common ground for religions[2].

Religion : Sacred Literature

Literature in religion has been of a varied nature. Nothing at all has been written down about tradition in some viz. Nature American, African and some others. Oral tradition, enactment in ritual for the meaning in sacred texts. The constant repetition of myths and rituals has resulted, in a remarkably exact preservation of stories, myths, legends, laws and stories, almost a word by word transcription. Identifiable texts as Quran for Muslims, Tripitaka for Buddhists, prescribe the words of the text to be regarded as divine commands that may not be questioned, and the quoting of a verse may settle all problems in any succeeding age. Five classics of ancient China are authoritative books for the community because the words of the text have been handed down from wise men of old.

In Hinduism, sacred literature consists of one book (Vedas) held of supreme importance, but also supplemented by commentaries that spell out in greater detail what may be stated generally or cryptically in the supreme text. It includes 'Sruti' (which is heard) and Smriti (which is remembered).

Sacred literature is an important aspect of religion. Myths may be approached as literature, where scholars analyze, interpret

1. Ibid P 26
2. Max Muller : Biographical Essays (1884)

and compare side by side the writings of very different peoples and cultures. The techniques of literary criticism have proved most helpful in the critical study of religions texts, although there are persons in any religion who object to a 'critical study of a text held to be sacred. Critical study leads to exhaustive and vivid interpretation of the doctrines in the sacred texts. For instance R'gveda, in original Sanskrit could not be followed as a common man's hymn for prayer. Its interpretations were made by as many as 300 rishis (saints) and presented in form of Samhitas. Similarly the hymns in other three vedas have also been spelled out (incantated) by as many rishis.

Vedas gave birth to Brahmanism, vedanta, Neovdeism and such other Isms' in Hinduism.

Religion and Society

In a situation, where a religious society is almost synonymous with life itself, it is very difficult to separate the religion from the social, because then religion is just the way of Life. Where there is close interrelation between religion and society, religious sanctions support family life, the world of work, and the Government, and thus authenticate the existing social order. In traditional societies like Hindu, Muslim, Medieveal catholic, the social order in turn supports religious structures. Any change is resisted and the individual (reformer) is pitted against the inertia that tends to prevail in any society e.g. Ram Mohun Roy's abolition of suttee. Philosopher Chuang Tzu was considered a social rebel against orthodox confucian society. Durkheim expressly stated that the function of religion is mainly to achieve the solidarity of a society. He says, 'The function of religious rituals is to affirm the moral superiority of the society over its individual members and thus to maintain the solidarity of the society. The God of the clan can be nothing but the clan itself, and that religion is

Universal and cannot be illusory[1]. Liebman[2] says, 'The faith hungry heart, beating plaintively in a world of confused struggle and fight, no longer asks 'what shall a man believe?' So enormous and critical is the problem that mere intellect has been transcended; we seek not a crado or a doctrine, but a reality that will sustain us in the battle. We wish to discover, if possible, a core of being around which we may integrate ourselves, an armateure on which we can wind the immortality charged threads of personality and character.' Tradition (religion) is upheld mainly due to such an inelastic attitude. Religion is a prime mover, so far as emotional compactness is concerned. It is the cement of cohesion. Religion is the very life blood of society. Hinduism attempts at comprehending and actualising religious and social reality as a correct approach. They are not despondent and gloomy but always hopeful. Gita in X. 10-11[3] says :-

> 'And Unto these, thus serving well, thus loving ceaselessly
> I give a mind of perfect mood, whereby they draw to Me;
> And, all for love of them, within their darkened souls I dwell,
> And, with bright rays of wisdom's lamp, their ignorance dispell'.

Hegel concludes, 'Strenuous and honest effort ot understand the world (society) will be rewarded by an assurance, not otherwise to be won, if its ultimate rationality and goodness' (religious).

Religion and Morality

The world is a purposive moral order, where individuals obtain what they desire, atleast they attempt to do so, as a matter of faith. What do the people do in order to express their faith and devotion. They undertake religious rituals and ceremonials and

1. Bottomore : sociology : A guide to problems and Literature (1962) PP 222
2. Liebman J.L. : Peace of mind (1946) PP 139
3. Arnold Sir Edward = The Song Celestical

conduct their life with morality. Whereas rituals comprise of worship, prayer, chants, songs and dances; Moral conduct includes righteous deeds, acts of duty and charity, which they practise by action, practice and deeds. Religious community's commitment to a moral standard, as exemplified in the lives of certain individuals (saints and such like) is often the most attractive feature of a religion (Abolition of child marriage and suttee in Hinduism).

All major religious teach that personal service of a mankind is itself service of the Lord. Man is asked by religious to do something to please God, something else for the betterment of the community in which he lives, this and that for someone or the other. He cannot help doing this if he wants to get on in life. These are restrictions, but restriction is merely a discipline conducive to general welfare, just like certain conditions and restrictions on pleasure (promiscuity, Gambling and such evil deeds). Rules of diet, exercise (yoga) which aim at physical strength lead to the growth of Moral power (will power). On the aspect of religion asking men to exert for his fellow beings, J.S. Mill, the utilaitarian philosopher says,' I do not mean to assert that the promotion of happiness should be itself the end of all actions or even of all rules of action. It is the justification and ought to be the controller of all ends, but it is not itself the sole end. It can be shown that, on the whole, more happiness will exist in the world if feelings are cultivated which will make people, in certain cases, regardless of happiness'[1]. Religion only encourages social service and does not put restraints. In Hinduism, the path of Disinterested Action (Karma Yoga) is more favourable than the purely intellectual approach. Gita (IX-30-XI 32) opens the door of spiritual perfection to all men irrespective of caste, creed, age and mental progress. In all religious history, appeal to

1. Mill J.S. Philosophy of Scientific Method (1950)

sentiment has been more powerful than an appeal to the intellect. Society accepts that form which it can easily practice. Religion as a social institution is a tie binding man to the society and to God. Social mind, by nature, finds itself in element when the same ideals are put before it in the more attractive garb by appealing to the sentiments. Love and faith (Morality and religion) work wonders where reason fails. Trend has openly accepted the actual achievements of religion, which according to him is the product of the wish world.

There is a close relationship between religion and morality. Hinduism morality is based on metaphysics. Gita (XIII 28 and 30) puts it 'Who, sees God in every being, realises the essential unity of the universe, he is, the perfect being; God never fails him in blessing.'

The people, affirming particular beliefs (Religion) and undertaking certain responsibilities (morality), bind themselves together. This 'binding' is actually one of the root meanings of Latin word, 'religion', which is the source of the word 'religion'. The word 'religion' is said, to have been derived from 'religare' which means 'to bind'.

Religion : Culture

Pictures that can be seen on cave walls (Rock Paintings) and objects excavated from ancient sites (from tombs in some countries) in various parts of the world indicate that religious experience has been an integral and vital part of our total human experience through the ages. T.S. Eliot[1] states, 'No culture has appeared or developed except together with a religion. To the observer culture will appear to be the product, of the religion, or the religion the product of culture.' Indian culture, which is rich,

1. T.S. Eliot quoted by Majumdar in Caitanya : His life and doctrine.

complex, dynamic and growing, rests upon its spiritual foundations. The great seers, sages, and saints have not only 'seen' the truth directly, they have also lived it in actual practice. Hegel calls religion as the 'bearer of culture'.[1] Tillich defines culture as 'lived religion'[2] .

Any doctrine, ritual or organisational pattern (religious) should be considered in view of its cultural context viz. historical background, the personalities of the teachers (Gurus), their methods and such other factors. Findings of Historians (religious personalities and events), philosophers (analysis and interpretation of ideas of a tradition), psychologists (phenomenon of human behaviour), Sociologists (grouping and organisation of religious communities, religion as a force in society), Anthropologists (religious rites, ceremonies, myths, role of chief in a tribe) are useful in the study of religion in the cultural context.

In the contextual frame work of religion, the appreciation of the arts vis. painting, sculpture, architecture, music, theatre and dance is intimately related. A work of art is an expression of the artist's feelings, the meaning of which can seldom be expressed adequately by logic or reason. To understand an artist, one has to try to feel or be sensitive to what the artist feels. Arts provide assistance in understanding the major problem in the study of religion. Religious ideology is almost a permanent feature and can be traced back into endless time (its culture). Religious experience from culture can only be explained in part by reference to the historical and cultural setting of the age. Visions of the divine have been referred to by Hindu and Muslim Mystics, Gautam Buddha found enlightenment; but what divine really is or what enlightenment really is, has not been explained. Still the religious experiences from cultural setting have never lost roots in the community.

---

1. Hicks G.D. 'The philosophical Bases of Theism (1931/1937) P 33
2. Jour : His of Philosophy Vol III No. 2 (1965)

Religion : Seculiarism

In Modern thought, the most influential trend is towards secularism. In seculiarism, nationalistic spirit predominates, universalism comes later. Nationalism also means revival of traditional culture. It has therefore to be evaluated how far the revival of traditional culture may harm seculiarism. Seculiarism is based on Materialistic welfare and has pushed religion out of life of may persons in growing discontent and frustration. Man has been enslaved in the machinery of production (industrialisation) and his attention is diverted by the secular idealism, secular entertainments and thus leading to a certain loss of balance. This imbalance, dissatisfaction and tension can only be removed by effecting a radical change in the outlook in life of the people. Therefore there is a need for just distribution of moral, religious and other secular pleasures.

Religions are caught between tradition (culture) and change (Modern thought in politics). This resulting tension has affected the interpretation of sacred texts, doctrinal statements, patterns of worship, the moral life, organizational structures, the relation of religion and society and even the goals towards which the lives of the believers, nationalists, are directed. Fundamentals of religion and morality are nor inconsistent with the strife for change for material prosperity (seculiarism). Can we confidently state that the purely secular way of life would be satisfactory to our needs; in a country, particularly in Hinduism, where religious instinct is steeped in the permanent. Religion is nor an expression of desires in response to temporary needs of an inner life, but is the outcome of our thought world. We have to take into consideration, the values which the past generations strived to achieve. Individuals may be satisfied with mere intellectual and secular pursuits; but for the nation. Religion may not have fully established itself as a convincing way of life for an intelligent human being; but neither are democracy and other social patterns so established in their respective spheres. We can not put aside the religious experience as such and the great religious movements for the emancipation of mankind from ethereal bondage.

RELIGION AND COMMUNALISM

In the book 'MEIN KAUN HOON' (Who am I), by Ramesh Dutt Misra, he has differentiated the two aspects of communalism and religion. According to him Communalism is a special action of adoration and a worship system, but in religion there are and can be numerous systems of worship. Religion is not an adoration for a special community. It is eternal, ancient, time honoured and universal. Sceticism is a particular action or a process of prayer (devotion), whereas in religion there are many innumerable processes of prayer. Religion is not for any particular thought, prayer or for any community. Religion spreads from Neitherlands to the universe, the cosmos. Religion is the soul of the body, an exercise to keep a mortal body in health. The religion of humanity is one and not a personalized thought. Religion is only one and nothing more, if so those are sects, cults or creeds. To accept these or to bring in a change in these, an individual is absolutely free, but if he changes his sect, there is no effect on religion. A dogma or a doctrine is the body but the religion is the soul. Any attempt to remove the soul from the body will make it lifeless. Those people who consider religion is an obstruction in their life, are making an easy approach to death. Giving up religion amounts to the acceptance of death.

Religion and Science

Bernard Shaw once wrote, 'There is nothing that people will not believe if only it be presented to them as science and nothing they will not disbelieve if it be presented to them as religion. I myself began like that, and I am ending by receiving every scientific statement without suspicion whilst giving every respectful consideration to the inspirations and revelations of the prophets and the poets.'

(Quoted by Majumdar: Caitanya : His life & Doctrine P VII)

In Hinduism, there is a settled view of things religious and secular, they do grasp the importance of the respective spheres of religion and science; but they openly accept that they may be called averse to science but never irreligious. They have realised the importance of being religious, in whatever form rather than rairing a so called scientific view of the world and life. they are fully aware that this 'scientific' view is not going to give them the solace and peace of mind they need so much, whatever be the merits of that view in other ways. It has been alleged that religion interfered in science and humanities and led to the growth of blind faith. Magic, sorcery, inhuman practices of human sacrifices, as cause of blind faith exist no more. Religious history distinctly shows evolution in this direction.

Thomas Hoult expresses, 'Scientists everywhere have proclaimed that the way to 'Trugh' lies in questioning every conclusion, conducting careful research and keeping an open mind.' Science has succeeded in giving the men the means of controlling many processes once thought to be 'in the lap of the gods'. This has led many people to doubt the reliability of the traditional religious use of intuition, sacred literature and established dogmas, but it is necessary to examine the essential character of religion and the influence of Modern concepts (science) on the religious sphere. In this connection Freud remarks 'From the pint of view of science, we must necessarily make use of our critical powers in this direction, and not be afraid to reject and deny. It is admissible to declare that science is one field of human intellectual activity, and that religion and philosophy are others, at least as valuable, and that science has no business to interfere with the other two, that they all have an equal claim to 'Truth', and that everyone is free to choose whence he shall place his belief. Such an attitude is considered particularly respectable, tolerant, broad minded and free from narrow prejudices, Unfortunately scientific research looks on the whole field of human activity as its own, and must adopt an uncompromisingly critical attitude towards any other power that seeks to usurp any part of its province[1] .

Both science and religion believe in faith .science proceeds on definite hypotheses of an assumption and with the faith in that ,it adopts reasonable methodology whereas the faith in religion (Gita) is the combined force influencing the temperament of the thinker and is the result of the environment and the sanskaras counteraction and influencing each other .The teachings of all great preachers and saints and their greatest efforts to create and foster the spirit of spiritual development and not to confuse the massases, cannot be contradicted.

Astrophysics in ultra modern thinking in the expanding universe theory states that the universe originated at a certain moment as a dense lump of matter which exploded with the emission of the galaxies in all directions. The 'Steady State'. Theory (continuous creation theory) holds the universe as homogeneous and in a steady state, assuming that the matter should be continually created. Klein assumes that the initial state' was as extremely dilute cloud consisting of electrons and protons, a part of which contracted under gravitation and later formed Metaglacial system and thin plasma consisted of homogeneous mixture of equal amounts of particles and antiparticles, symmetric and equivalent, with extremely low density. Eddington[2]

1. Freud S : New Introductory Lectures on Psychoanalysis (1957) Sprott J.H. (A Philosophy of Life PP 202-233
2. Alfven H : Reviews of Modern Pysics Vol. XXXVII No. 4 P 653.

acknowledged that 'a cosmology can never avoid making assumptions about the initial state'. In religion the conception of 'Initial State' and the origin of universe is the primeval Golden egg whence B'rhma (Narayana) is explained as matter (Prakriti) in an unmanifested stage. So scientists rightly say that 'Theories depend to a very considerable extent upon assumptions and hypothesis' but religion does not insist on theories. It emphasizes religious experiences, the practical side; its practical importance of actual experiences.

A daily phenomenon to remind us about the existence of God and his immanence is the sun, which is so vital for all life on earth and without which this world will cease to exist. To mention only one aspect, the sun regularly rises and sets everyday and all through the year, it has been doing so for millions of years without any break. It is known that it is not the sun that moves, but it is the earth that goes round the sun revolving itself all the way. Its speed being constant and orbit a fixed one. It is inconceivable how the sun or the earth by itself without any outside agency can perform these functions so meticulously and perpetually. The sun, also, transmits enormous heat and light and other rays, reaching not only the earth but also very distant planets. This has been happening for centuries and the sun still continues to burn and radiate heat and light. In nature, anything that burns will soon burn itself out after the material in it is exhausted. The sun has not shown any signs of burning and its intensity of heat and light has shown no change. Scientists have endeavoured hard to find out the substance that burns in the sun, but they are no where near finding the original cause behind the apparently inexhaustable source of energy that is the SUN. One of the many mysteries, yet to be resolved by scientists, is the discovery of densites and temperatures between the various layers and the enormous heat of corona of the sun. Scientists are at a loss to answer why this is so and who is behind all this phenomenon

.. To explain this, the existence and immanence of the Supreme Being has to be admitted , and science has no solution.

The ultimate source of the entire creation, including all matter, all forms of energy, all the dimensions of space and time and all the laws of nature, as well as all the souls, is the Supreme Being. Even on the assumption that God is an entity is unreal, His existence cannot be denied. A mathematician deals with what is wholly unreal in human understanding like the square root of minus one (called I), infinity and zero. There is a whole field of mathematics based on these unreal entities, used not only in research but also in actual application in the field of science, technology, engineering and industry. Without these imaginary entities, no real progress would have been possible in those fields.

Formulae of nature given by science, cannot explain the appearance of consciousness, self consciousness and conscience. Vyasa supports Plato's view of regarding GOD as the artisan. God, the supreme artist, is then the intentionality or direction of all phenomenon. 'It is implicit that action rather than matter is basic, action being understood as analogous to human decision.' Krishna concedes autonomy to nature, 'Know that nature and thc person are born without beginning', and 'Under my presiding nature generates things inanimate, and by this instrumentation the world functions'.

God, the supreme artist, is then the intentionality or direction of all phenomenon and that intentionality (Jivabhuta) generator and sustainer of life, was envisaged first and then the instrumentality steadily perfected in evolution.

The primary principle of Indian aesthetics, upheld by Vyasa, considers artistic creation, great procession of the splendid forms of nature's evolution, as the supreme means of realising the Universal Being.

Evolution and involution of bodies, cannot, of its own power regulate itself or work for the good of others. Anything that is evolved and involved, whether it be an atom or the world, has been designed to serve the great ends of uplifting souls from their fallen condition, wherever they may have been placed, on earth or in another or projected in space. Evolution and involution are conducted in order by succession according to cause and effect relations, which hold sway throughout the universe, and are knowable in terms of the Divine power called TIME (Kal) Space of place (Desh) and cardinal direction (Disha). Of all the divine gifts, Karma Chakram (Bhog-activity) or the ordained course of works of the Supreme deity, where in works of love cause joyful effects and works of hate cause sorrowful effects. This is the true meaning of the phrase 'Causation reigns in the universe'.

It is in accordance with Sanatan Dharma that all things are evolved and involved for the ulterior and of converting bad souls into good ones. It takes ages to bring about the freedom (Moksha) liberation or extraction of the spirit from evil. By the design of GOD, conceived long before creation, the system of eternal laws, called SANATAN DHARMA, has been regulating the course of things, physical, mental and moral, for the fulfilment of the work of purifying every soul in due time, place and order.

CHAPTER - 2

Hindu Sacred Literature

The Vedic sages were the first harbingers of knowledge opening several avenues of wisdom and learning. They presented glorious glimpses of several sciences closely related to human life, spirit and culture. Their multifarious lusterous compositions exposed to us the meaning of the real knowledge, the context of superb human culture and relevance of magnificent moral and ethical values in our society. The literatures, scientists and thinkers all over the world would ever remain grateful to the vedic sages, upanishadic philosophers, exponents of subtle scientific principles, poets and playwrights presenting in charming diction the sublime tapestry of human life. Atri, Vashishta, Badarayana, Vyasa, Yagnavalkya, Yaksa, Manu, Isvarakrishna, Kanada, Gautama, Panini, Patanjali, Bharata, Jaimini, Shabara, Bhaskara, Varabamihira, Arya Bhatta, Chanakya, Shankara, Ramanuja, Madhava, Vallabha Chailanya and Prominent poets like Valmiki, Bhasa, Kalidasa, Bharavi, Megha, Banabhatta, Shriharsha, Jagannatha Pandita, and others. The whole of vedic literature consists of the four vedas (Samhitas) several exposing ritual texts attached to each of these vedas called Brahamanas and speculative treatises of upanishads concerned chiefly with a mystical interpretation of vedic ritual and its relations to man and to the universe.

Dr. S. Radhakrishnan considers that the main body of the scriptures contains the essence of Hinduism in his mind. He has commented on Prasthanatraya upanishads, Brahmsutra and Bhagvad Gita. These three writings provide the basis for Hinduism. These form together the absolute standard for the Hindu religion[1].

1. Dr. Radhakrishnan S : The Hindu View of Life P 18

The Vedas

'Let us remember, first of all, that the Rigveda is the older book of the world. It is older than any thing in Greece and Rome; older as a book, than any book in China, older than the old Persian Avesta, older than Buddhism and its sacred canon, older than the old testament.'[1]

The vedas are authorless and eternal, divinely inspired by Lord B'rhma, revealed through vedic sages who were greatly intellectual and intensely spiritual persons who in their mystic moments came face to face with Reality and this mystic experience, this direct intuitive spiritual insight over flew in literature as the vedic hymns. The keynote of the vedic hymns is the same spiritual monoism, the same immanent conception of the identity in difference which ultimately transcends even itself, the same indescribable absolutism which holds both monoism and pluralism within its bosom and which ultimately transcends both, which was so beautifully and poetically developed later in the upanishads, In vedas, the gods are praised; yet nor the Gods, but God is praised through them. There is monoism in the vedas right from the first hymn/mantra. The mantras sung by the priests and hymns sung by the bards have been preserved in form of collections; (Samhitas) the vedas. They are four; the Rig Veda, Samaveda, Yajurveda and Atharvaveda.

The Rigveda (RIK Samhita)

The Rgveda (veda of hymns or knowledge or verses) dated 2000 - 1600 BC was the first and the earliest, a collection of 1017 hymns, arranged for mere reading or reciting. This was the first bible of Hinduism and the first special book in the Vedism period of Hindu religion. Its hymns are addressed to various

---

1. Max Muller : Ram Mohan to Ramakrishna 1898, 1952 P 28-29

Gods and Goddesses. R'gveda is in ten books[1]. The earliest part of R'gveda to be collected was the group of hymns in Book II, though VII, I, VIII, IX and X were added by stages later. Since Agni was a dispenser of all that was desired and expected in Vedic religion (riches, happiness, long life, and many heroic sons) there are more hymns to Agni than any other God" in R" gveda. Next to Agni, Indra was honoured in R' gveda. R' gveda is aimed, in general, at 'Universal brotherhood'. 'If one has to study the origin of religion (Hinduism) of the Aryan race, to which we ourselves belong by language and thought, one has to study R'gveda. No one doubts now that the Gods of the Ancient Hindus were representatives of the great phenomenon of nature, conceived in the only way in which, in the then state of language and thought, they could be conceived, that is as active and personified. What we should have anticipated, and what in fact was anticipated by philosophers ', was fully confirmed by the hymns of the R'gveda'[2] (addressed to Dawn, morning sun, bringer of light, life, blue sky, clouds, river, rain, fertility, (Earth), fire, storm, diseases and their healing). There are some portions vis. song of the gambler, dialogue between Lopamudra and Agasteye, between Yama and Yami, between Puruvas and Urvasi, of which there is no connection to religion, but they are interesting as relics of antiquity.

2. **Yajur Veda** (Veda of sacrificial formulae : Knowledge in ritual forms. Yajur Samhita). It was a liturgical arrangement of part of the same collection of hymns, with additions (Yajus - prose passages) for intoning in a peculiar low tone at sacrificial ceremonies. It is a handbook for those priests who were responsible for directing any ritual. It provides a great deal of information on the actual performance of rituals, little of which is found

1. Bush R.C. The Religious World (1982) PP 57
2. Max Muller : Ram Mohan to Ramakrishna (1920) PP 29-30

in R'gveda. It not only deals with rituals and worship, but contains everything which man does in the path of life, progress and welfare of human society, political, social, economic and commercial development, as well as art and crafts.

3. **Samaveda** (knowledge in sacred melodies : Veda of Chants : Sama Samhita) includes the chants. This is believed to be the origin of the music. It is the handbook of special chanter priests, containing those hymns or parts of hymns from R'gveda, for which the chanters were responsible during the ceremonies and that they had to know. It adds little to vedic religion. Out of 1875 chants in Samaveda, only 69 are different, or else the rest are all from R'gveda except 17 from Yajurveda and Atharvaveda. A study of this veda, smallest of all the four, reveals the path of religious thoughts as expounded by vedic rishis (priests) and also their teachings for Humanity. Samveda Teaches :- Be generous, Do good deeds (15.3.1), Be ambitious for salvation (1.1.1),(15.1.4) Gain knowledge for control over the senses and do Good work (1.25.1), Be imparter of knowledge (1.3.103), benefaction of others is a prime duty (10.11.4.3). Devotion is the source of knowledge (5.6.19.1), true devotion from inner conscience (1.3.3) Good to others leads to salvation (1.7.7) Stick to truth (10.10.14.2), Do your duty with the vedic morals in mind (3.7.8), God will punish those who obstruct your truthful path (16.4.20.3).

4. **Atharvaveda** Spellveda or (Knowledge of the Atharvans, from the name of a family of priests who possessed particularly magical powers Atharva Samhita). This veda, which was added as the fourth to the three basic vedas (Trayi : triple science), comprises of all the sciences. It contains tantra, yoga, medicine, surgery, herbology, minerals, archery, sexual science and all such topics. It contains charms against disease and danger, megical formulae for cursing personal enemies and philosophical hymns. It is essentially a prayer book of the people, rather than of the

priests. Folk hymns were recognised in order to absorb folk cults in the fold of Hinduism.

Vedas : R'gveda, Yajurveda, Samaveda and Atharvaveda impart knowledge identical with or derived from the vedic hymns, which form the basis of most Hindu philosophical (upanishads) and religious systems.

Samhitas

The four vedas, as they exist at present, forming a veda tree has three branches each viz. The Samhita, the Brahamanas and the Sutram. These are the manuals of the Brahamanical priests (ritvij) providing them with the materials of hymns and sentences necessary for the sacrificial cult, as well as teaching them with their right use. Four chief priests, according to their courses of studies and functions, have been recognised as Hotar, Udgatar, Adhvaryu and Brahman. The canonical books for Hotar was R'gveda, Udgatar (Samaveda), Adhvaryu (Yajurveda) and Brahman (all three vedas and to dignify him Atharvaveda). Each of the priests required a collection of prayer formulae (mantras) and directions for the right liturgical and ritual application (Brahmanan) for the efficient performance of his duties. The manuals containing these were called Samhitas;* which are mantras sung by the priests and hymns sung by the boards based on a particular veda. Samhita is a collection of the mantras (verses or chants or sacrificial sentences) belonging to that veda.

R'gveda Samhita contains 1017 hymns in 10580 verses, as selected by Hotar.

Samaveda Samhita has 1549 verses, either from Samveda or from R'gveda. In this only 75 are such which do not exist in R'gveda material.

Atharvaveda Samhita has only 760 hymns, a small portion based on R'gveda, but mostly independent and quite peculiar in the vedic mantra literature.

Samhitas are the second division of vedic literature.

Sruti (Cruti)

Means revelation holy scriptures. The Samhitas, Brahamanas, Aranyakas and upanishads are of prime importance to the Hindu tradition. They constitute prime importance to the Hindu tradition. They constitute the sacred scriptures. Sruti corresponds to the revealed scriptures of other religions. An orthodox Hindu is one who accepts the Sruti, as revealed. Vedic crauta sutra dealing with public worship is based on sruti (Divine revelation). Older upanishads, (Brihadaranyaka, Chandogya, Kathaka, Kaushtaki, Aitareya, Taittiriya and the rest); Mundaka, Prasana, late originated cvetacvatara and even Jabala upanishad, Rest on sruti.

The holy scriptures, in the narrower sense the Brahamanas and upanishads, but also the mantras presupposed by them (hymns and formulae) are sruti, revealed for Badar-ayana are self evident and need no further authority. However Shankaracharya stresses on confirmation of sruti (Perception) by Smriti (inference)[1] .

Smriti (Tradition Human) means that which is remembered. The smritia are auxilliary to srutis. It also includes six vedangas (additional members or limbs) of the veda. Traditionally they were grouped into five classes : the vedangas (limbs of the vedas), Dharamsastras, Nibandhas (rituals), Puranas (religious stories) and epics (Ramayana and Mahabharatta). The Grihya Sutras dealing with domestic ceremonies (at birth, marriage and the funeral) rest on Smriti. Shankaracharya understands Smriti as the source of knowledge, Sankhya and Yoga systems, the Mahabharatta especially Bhaveda Gita, the law book of Manu and perhaps some other books. He considers that Smriti has only the force of proof is only so far valid as an authority, as

1. Devsen P : The System of Vedanta (1987) PP 23, 90

it confirms the Sruti by its testimony and completes it by right inferènce. Therefore it is frequently quoted in confirmation, but its ideas are rejected as far as they are in contradiction to the Sruti (Bhagvada Gita 8, 23).

The most famous is the Dharamsastra (Smriti) of Manava, known as Manu Smriti. Similarly there are Narada Smriti, Vishnu smriti, Yajnavalakya smriti. Vishnu Smriti is in prose and others are in verse. Basically the Smritis are concerned more with moral and civil laws rather than ritual or philosophical speculations.

THE MANU SMRITI

The Manu smriti is the most authoritative work on Hindu law. It was adopted in British courts in India. There were old sayings of MANU, which were collected together as MANU SMRITI or Manav Dharmasasatra. 'AJODHYA claims to have been the capital of the Solar race of kings, of whom, MANU, the law giver, was the first'[1] , The Manu Smriti refers to the Dharmasastras of ATRI, Gautama, Shaunaka and Vashishta. The Manu Smriti divides the society into two Aryans (Arya Varna : Fair complexioned) and Non Aryan (Da Varna : Drak skinned). Non Aryans were called Anarya, Dasyu and malechha ; which included Chandalas, Shvapakas etc. Aryan society was divided in Dvijatas and Ekajatic. Thus there were four varnas (classes or orders) among the Aryans; Dvijatis were Brahmins, Kshatriyas and Vaiseyas and ekjatis were Shudras. The division was according to functions allotted and had no base on birth. Manu Smriti mentions about 60 castes but refers to only four varnas[2]. Varna was a common name of all castes based on colour of garments viz white for brahmins, red for kshatriyas, yellow for vaiseyas and black for Shudras[3]. Verna (class) served political ambition while

1. Blackham R.J. : Incomparable India PP 133
2. Smith V.A. : Oxford History of India
3. Shamashastri quoted by Mahajan V.D. Ancient India

caste obeyed strict scruples and traditional customs. The class of Dvijatas, who performed the function of learning, teaching and religious ceremonies were classified under Brahmin Varna; rulers and warriors under Kshatriye and so on. It was not caste distinction. This change of Manu's varnas (class or orders) was later changed to the present Brahmin, Kshatriye, Vaish and Shudra caste, under Hindu Brahmanical period.

A few quotations from Sacred books of the East[1] , give a few laws of Manu :-

'To act solely from a desire for rewards is not laudable, yet an exemption from that desire is not to be found in this world (ii, 2) '

' Desire is never extinguished by the enjoyment of desired objects. It only grows stronger, like a fire fed with clarified butter (ii, 94)'

' By honouring his father, his mother, and his teacher, all that ought to be done by man is accomplished; that is clearly the highest duty; every other act is a subordinate duty' (ii.237)

' Where women are honoured, there the Gods are pleased, but where they are not honoured, no sacred rite yields rewards.' (iii.56)

' A guest, who is sent by the setting sun in the evening, must not be driven away by a householder. Whether he has come at supper time, or at an inopportune moment, he must not stay in the house.without entertainment.' (iii.105)

' Let a man not, even though in pain, speak words cutting others to quick; let him not injure others in thought or deed; let him not utter speeches which make others afraid of him, since that will prevent him from gaining heaven. '(ii.161)

1. Buhler G : Books of The East : Laws of Manu.

'Let him say what is true, let him say what is pleasing, let him utter no disagreeable truth, and let him utter no agreeable falsehood; that is eternal law. ' (iv.138)

'Let him not insult those, who have redundant limbs, or are deficient in limbs, nor those destitute of knowledge, nor very aged men, nor those who no beauty or wealth, nor those who are of low birth. ' (iv.141)

'Let him, though suffering in consequence of his righteousness, never turn his heart to unrighteousness, for he will see the speedy overthrow of unrighteous wicked men. ' (iv.171)

'Unrighteousness practised in this world does not at once produce its fruit, but advancing slowly, it cuts off the roots of him who committed it. ' (iv.172)

The emphasis with which the results of unrighteousness are pronounced, to be inevitable reveals a deep moral insight, while the tender considerations for others shown in many of the ancient laws is a highly commendable feature.

'Giving no pain to any creature, let him solely accumulate spiritual merit, for the sake of acquiring a companion in the next (iv.238)

'For in the next world, neither father nor mother, nor sons, nor relations, stay to be his companions; spiritual merit alone remains with him. ' (iv.239)

'Single is each born, single it dies; single it enjoys the reward of its virtue, single it suffers the punishment of its sin. ' (iv.240) These allusions to future state appear to embody the doctrine of KARMA, that by the practice of good deeds , a degree of spiritual merit is acquired, which will reduce the chances of future, and most probably rebirths.

THE BRAHAMANAS (1200-800 B.C.)

B'rhma originally means 'Prayer', whereas the Rishis were the seers of the Mantras Hymns) in the vedas, the Brahamanas were written in prose. They are elaborations of the complicated ritualism of the Vedas. They deal with the rules and regulations laid down for the performance of the rituals and sacrifices. These were mere explanatory with little philosophy. BRAHMANAS were explanations, applications and ritualistic commentaries produced for the guidance of the priests, who used the hymns for the rituals.

The Brahamanas were composed by arrogant Brahmins, who had become powerful and the purpose of the Brahamanas was to assert Brahmin superemacy through emphasis on ritual, which only Brahmins could perform. Towards the period of later Brahamanas, earlier Upanishads Grammar of Panini were composed.

While the Brahamanas (product of Law-Culture) were being composed, highly intellectual, the UP ANISHADS, GRAMMAR of Panini and a little later THE EPICS were also composed.

Dr. S.K. Ghosh[1] states, 'That all that is noble and beautiful in Hinduism was foreshadowed by the R'GVEDA, and all that is filthy and repulsive in it, by the Brahamanas' for example, 'A Brahamana author has declared that a 'murder is no murder if the victim is not a brahmin.'

R'gveda to the Samaveda marks a trend towards ritualism, which trend continues in the next two vedas (Atharva & Yajur) and the Brahamanas, until we have a reaction against ritualism in the upanishads.

---

1. DR. GHOSH S.K. BHAVAN's Series Vol. I PP 422.

Aranyakas (Forest meditations) Aranyakas mean belonging to the forest. It is therefore intended for study in the forest by Brahamins, who had revised from the world's distractions. They are the chief content of the appendixes to the Brahamanas and whose original purpose was to serve for the life in the forest (aranyam) which was enjoined on the Brahamins in old age. to serve as a substitute for ritual, which was very limited. Aranyakas mark the transition from the ritualistic to the philosophical thought. Certain philosophical enquiries and upanishads, flowering Hindu philosophy, developed out of Aranyakas. There is a mystic interpretation of the vedic sacrifices in them. In them, we meet abundantly a wonderful spiritualising of the sacrificial cult, in place of the practical carrying out of the ceremonies, comes meditation upon them and with it a symbolical change of meaning, which then leads on farther to the loftier thoughts. The Aranyakas in mystical tone explain the deeper meaning of the sacrifice, its symbolism and its philosophy.

Opening passage of Brihad Aranyakam (which is intended for the Adhvaryu) in which the House sacrifice is treated, is an example[1]:-

Om : Dawn verily is the head of the sacrificial house, the sun is his eye, the wind his breath, his mouth is the all pervading fire, the year is the body of the sacrificial house; heaven is his back, space is his belly, the earth is his foot stool. The poles are his loins, the intermediate quarters are his ribs, the seasons are his limbs, months and half months are his joints, day and night are his feet, the stars are his bones, the clouds are his flesh. The deserts are the food which he consumes, rivers are his entrails, the mountains his liver and lungs, plants and trees are his hair, the rising sun in his forequarters, the setting sun

1. Deusen P. The system of vedanta (1987) PP 8 Quoted.

is his hindquarters; when the yawns, that is lightening; when he neighs, it is thunder; when he waters, there is rain; his voice is speed. Day verily arose after the house as the sacrificial vessel, which stands before him; its cradle in the eastern ocean; night verily arose as the sacrificial vessel, which stands behind him; its cradle is in the western ocean; these two sacrificial vessels arose to surround the house. As a racer he carries the Gods, as a warhouse the ghandaravas, as a steed the demons, as a horse the mankind. The ocean is his companion, the ocean his cradle.

(House refers to universe i.e. the ascetic has to renounce the world).

The most important part of these Aranyakas were later detached from them in the formation of the upanishads.

Since the Aranyakas and the upanishads come towards the end of the vedic literature, they are called 'Vedanta' (concluding part of vedas)

Upanishads are intensely philosophical, spiritual and the essence, the cream, the height, of the vedic philosophy. A collection of philosophical texts believed to number between one and two hundred, but most interpreters deal with slightly more than the ten on which Sankara commented. Radhakrishnan follows Sankara's suggestion that 'Upanishad' means B'rhma knowledge by which ignorance is loosened or destroyed.

Since the upanishads, were a protest against Brahamanas, it has been presumed that most of their authors were Kshatriyas. As a positive evidence of this, in Chandogya upanishad, a king named Pravahana explains to the Brahmin Gautama, the concept of transmigration, while King Kaikeya teaches five Brahmins the concept of 'Atman'. The upanishadic philosophers are deeply concerned about the ultimate reality. They speak of B'rhma (God) and Atman (Soul) and in their relationship, they declare the two as one. The upanishads developed out of the Aranyakas and certain philosophical enquiries which led to the flowering of Hindu philosophy. This literature is closely connected with the Brahmanas. The Hindu seers in the tropical forests meditated on life and death, the world and men. God and his universe. This knowledge was considered the most important part of the 'Divine knowledge'. The teachers answered profound questions on Truth. The character of the intellectual research recorded in the upanishads leads oriental scholars to believe that those speculations must have preceded the rise of Buddhism by some centuries. These must therefore belong to earlier than 600 BC. The whole of the upanishads section of the Vedas forms a kind of philosophical patrology for the Hindu tradition and is regarded with special reverence.

Bloomfield remarks : 'There is no important form of Hindu thought heterodox Buddhism included which is not rooted in the upanishads'. Dr. Radhakrishnan says 'Later systems of philosophy display an almost pathetic anxiety to accommodate their doctrines to the views of the Upanishads, even if they cannot father then all or them'. According to him, the upanishads contain the religious experiences of the Indian sages, The perception that the ultimate and supreme as it is in itself , is impersonal, for a personality is a form of limitation, such as may not be attributed to that which by definition is unlimited. This humility of approach is expressed better than anywhere else, in the upanishads and in Hindu wisdom. Prof. R.S. Ranade says 'The upanishads constitute that lofty eminence of philosophy, which forms its various sides, gives birth to rivulets of thought, which as they progress onwards towards the sea of life, gather strength by the inflow of innumerable tributaries of speculation which intermittently join these rivulets, so as to make a huge expanse of waters at the place where they meet the ocean of life.

The Gita is the milk milched out of the upanishad cows, particularly influenced by the Katha and the Isha.

Shankara, Ramanuja, Nimbarka, Madhava and Vallabha acharyas have always regarded the upanishads as the sacred texts and have interpreted them so as to make them suit their theories. Upa (near) ni (down) Shad (to sit) i.e. sitting down near. Groups of pupils sit near the teacher to learn from him the secret doctrines in the upanishads which illustrate the mexim that 'truth is one though it is glorified in many forms'.Upanishads are splendourous world of spirit.

C.Rajgopalachari says, 'The spacious imagination, the majestic sweep of thought, and the almost reckless spirit of exploration with which, urged by the compelling thirst for truth, the upanishad teachers and pupils dig in to the 'open secret' of the universe, makes this most ancient of the world's holy books still the most modern and most satisfying'.

Out of the 108 or more than 200 unanishads. 10-12 considered most important are:-

1. Isaupanishad — (Teaches essential unity of God and the world, being and becoming it. Perfect understanding of infinity was conceived in this, centuries before Christ. Based on Yajur veda).

2. Kenaupanishad — (The salvation is that of being 'firmly settled' in the universal place, 'in the infinite place of Heaven'.)

3. Katha upanishad (Based on Yajurveda. The Atman(Soul) is said to be the ultimate Reality. The objects are the roads, the body the chariot, senses the horses, mind the reins, intellect the Charioteer, ego the enjoyer and the Atman is the lord sitting in the chariot'.)

4. Prasna upanishad (Based on Atharvaveda.'Food indeed is the lord of all creation, from that verily is semen, from that are all creatures produced (1.14)

5. Mandukya upanishad (Based on Atharvaveda. Four states of consciousness viz. wakefulness, Dreaming state, Dreamless sleep and Transcendental consciousness, have been dealt with).

6. Mundakaupanishad (Also based on Atharvaveda. Two kinds of knowledge must be known, the higher and the lower. The lower knowledge is that which the R'g. Sama and Atharva, ceremonial, grammar give, but the higher knowledge is that by which the Immortal B'rhama is known'.

7 Taittariya upanishad (Based on Yajurveda, it deals with vedangas, knowledge of the supreme self, Parmatma - jnana. In this B'rhma is defined as that from which all these beings are born, by which they live, and into which they are reabsorbed'.)

8. Aitareya upanishad (Based on R'gveda. Deals with sacrificial ceremonies and their interpretations). It belongs to Hotar, has transformation

of meaning of 'OM' as a symbol of Parmatama.

9. Chandogya upanishad (Describes Tajjalan as that (tat) from which the world arises (ja), into which it returns (la) and by which it is supported and it lives (an). the teaching blends the subject with the object, the inhabitable with the infinite, the microcosm, the self with the netself. None of them can be taken as independent and separate. Both are manifestations of the same Sat.) This upanishad intended for udgatar teaches recognition and honour the syllable 'OM' which is a symbol of B'rhma (Parmatama-Pratikam).

10. Brahad aranyakaupanishad (Dr, S. Radhakrishnan considers this to be the most important upanishad. Basic identity of the individual and the universal self, certain models of worship and meditation, hearing, logical reflection and Meditation).

11. Svethasvathara upanishad (Based o;n Yajur veda 'Time' inherent nature, necessity, chance elements. female womb or male are to be considered as the cause 1,2 Dr.Radhakrishnan considered some more upanishads as very important:-

1. Kaustitaki Brahma upanishad (Based on R'gveda)

2. Maitri upanishad (Based ;on Yajurveda. Stresses the positive content of the notion of liberation, meditation on the sacred fires).

3. Subala upanishad (Based on Yajurveda)

4. Jabala upanishad (Based on Atharva veda.; Life in heaven, being the reward of merit, is finite; just as the effects of work here below are finite).

5. Paingala upanishad (Based on Yajurveda;)

6. Kaivalya upanishad (Based on Atharva Veda; absolute independence. eternal and free life of Purusa, free from Prakriti.)

7. Vajra Suchika upanishad

Sutras : Literally Sutra means a 'string'. Hence sutras were a string of sentences which were short and pithy condensations or formulae, composed for the purpose of memorisation, When ancient sutras began to be treated systematically in the schools and universities of Medieval India (500 BC.-1000 AD). concise sentences or Sutras were selected from the Hindu Patristic literature and included in a compendium for scholastic purposes. The sentences themselves date from very early times down to the 3rd C.B.C. and since they contained the distilled lore of the previous ages, the teachers commented on them in the schools. The scholastic production of the early days (500 BC-AD 500) are in the style of aphoristic formulae drawn from every conceivable subject found in the veda).

As the Aryans penetrated further and further, their literature increased in volume, as also its scope, Besides sacred works, secular works were also composed on various aspects, Since the disciples were expected to memorize this literature, it became necessary to put it in a condensed form. A whole idea was condensed into a short formula (Sutra) and thus a string of formulae Aranyakas and upanishads were supposed to be revelation

(Sruti), the sutras were supposed to be Tradition (Smirit). Once the idea of composing sutras gained ground. Sutra schools multiplied and secular. According to Dr.S.Radhakrishnan, Brahma sutra interprets the logical conclusions made in the upanishads. It is an aphoristic summary of the upanishads. The Sutras were also known as Vedanga (limbs of the vedas); but the entire vedanga literature has not come down in the sutra style.

Vedangas

Six vedangas, as subsidiary upaveda (supplement) associated with four vedas, are courses of special studies for students of vedic scholarship according to the orthodox method. By their association with vedas, they also acquired a sacred character. Six vedangas are :-

(i)	Siksha - Phonetics	(iv)	Nirukta - Etymology
(ii)	Kalpa - Ritual	(v)	Chhandas - Metrics
(iii)	Vyakarna - Grammar	(vi)	Jyotisha - Astronomy

Among these the most notable are Kalpa sutras, which are classified into three :-

Srautasutras (Performance of mighty sacrifices)

Grihyasutras (Performance of simple ceremonies by the householder)

Dharmasutras (Moral law and the source of Dharamasastras)

Upavedas : Some subsidiary vedas, on the lines of sutras deal with purely secular subjects such as Ayurveda (Medical science), Dhanurveda (Military science), Gandharvaveda (Musical Knowledge) Shilpaveda (science of Architecture) etc. Dharam sastra of Manu Yajnavalkya, Narada, Brihaspati were composed later, after the fall of Maurya empire, but they are based on the vedic Dharamsutras though additions have been made to suit the changed conditions.

Other subjects : It has a (History), Rasi (Mathematics), Sarpa Vidya (Science of serpents), Kshatra Vidya (Military science); works on these subjects are mentioned in references; but many of these works themselves have not come down to us.

Darshanas : The word 'Darshana' means 'Vision' and also the instrument of vision. It stands for the direct, immediate and intuitive vision of Reality, the actual perception of Truth and also includes the means which lead to this realization. Six schools of Indian philosophy expound philosophical speculation regarding the relation of the Infinite to the Infinite presumed in vedic literature as a whole. In all these schools self (Atma) is the keynote. That is why most of the schools are also religious seets. Annihilation of the three kinds of pain: adhyatmik (Physical and Mental suffering produced by natural and intraorganic causes), adhibhautika (Physical and mental suffering by natural and extra organic causes) and adhidaivika (suffering by supernatural and extra organic causes) and Shravana (Hearing the Truth), manana (Intellectual conviction after critical analysis) and nididhyasana (Practical realization) are the means, projected in almost all schools.

NAYE DARSANA

It was written by Gautam rishi. According to this TARKA or logic is basis of all studies. It discusses the problem of doubt and ascribes it to the lapse of memory, or irregularities or aberrations in recognition or perception. Truth reveals to those who have experience. The soul is real and its attributes are desires, aversions, volitions etc. consciousness cannot exist apart from the soul. It believes in GOD, who is full of knowledge and bliss.

VAISESIKA DARSANA

Written by Kanada rishi, it is concerned with Padarthas which include Draveya (substance), Guna (Quality), Karma (action-activity),

Samaneya (generality), Visesha (particularity) and Samaveya (Inference). The substances are earth, water, air light, sky, space, soul, man. Atoms are ultimate constituents of concrete things. This Darsana is not a complete philosophy, since it does not refer to God.

SANKHYA DARSANA

Sankhya Darsana by Kapila; its fundamental principle is dualism of PURUSHA and PRAKRITI. Prakriti is developed by three Gunas (qualities) SATTVA Guna (good and happiness), RAJAS Guna (Activity and pain) and TAMAS Guna (Ignorance, sloth and apathy). World is not real, after sometimes it is destroyed, but Prakriti is eternal. PURUSHA is eternal, JIVAS are bound by the bondage of rebirth. According to this Prakriti and Purusha are independent of the existence of God.

YOGA DARSANA

Yoga Darsana by Patanjali; ' A person can be liberated from the circle of rebirth by the practice of Yoga or the concentration of mind (physical and spiritual development). GOD alone is the object of meditation and HE alone helps us to attain our goal.'

PURVA MIMANSA DARSANA

The author of this philosophy is JAMINI. It is mainly concerned with rituals, authority of the Vedas, plurality of souls, Dharma as the scheme of right living. It is concerned with purely mechanical ethics and the performance of sacrifices.

UTTAR MIMANSA DARSANA

This was authored by BADARAYANA and mainly deals with B'rhma, B'rhma vidya and the future of the soul after death.

PURANAS

Most of the primordial tradition of the Hindus is preserved, perhaps in distorted form, in what we call PURANAS, officially designated ancient writings. There is no regular history of the early phase of Aryan settlements in India. A picture of the life of the then people can, however, be obtained from the Puranas and other literature of the period.

NIRUKTA

Nirukta of Yaksa (500 BC) is intrinsically connected with the vedic language since it tries to explain the origin of some of the vedic words by giving their etymological explanation on the one hand and by interpreting the vedic hymns on the other. Nirukta is an epoch making pioneering and instructive study made at a time when resources were limited. Yaksa in this scripture has analysed the structive of Language and has divided that into four main components viz. noun, verb, preposition and article.

The PURANAS consist of tales which convey the truths of the Vedas and Dharama Sastaras in the form of short stories. Told to children, to the simple villager and illiterate persons, these imaginative stories have formed the religious basic education of ordinary people and help to teach them simple but fundamental truths of religion and morality, of what is wrong and what is wrong in behaviour. For example, to teach that GOD is every where and always comes to the help of the devotees, the story of Prahlada is told; where in Prahlad was challenged by Hiranayakashipu to show if GOD existed in a pillar. Vishnu came out of the pillar and killed Hiranayakashipu. In another story, the power of a chaste and good woman is described; where in SAVITRI gets the life of her husband Sateyavan restored from Yama (the God of death). Another story is about the power of a good woman over Gods. A princess SUKANYA accidently blinded a rishi Chyavana. She married him, as a repentance and to look after him. Aswins (celestial Gods) wished to marry her, she not only refused them, but by her chastity and devotion, restored the eyesight of Rishi Chyavana. DHRUVA, the only star in the universe which stays unmoved, is the name after Prince Dhruva, who by his constancy and meditation won the eternal blessings of Vishnu. Dhruva, the POLE STAR is known to this day in Hindu astronomy. Avoidance of death and gaining of immortality by Markendeya shows the power of devotion to S'iva. Importance of looking after the elders is impressed Sharavana's story in the Puranas. Generosity knows no bounds is illustrated by the great and just king Usinara's offering his body, to save the life of a hawk. Importance of adhering to TRUTH is amplified in the story of Raja Harish Chandra. The story of Sudama impressed on the people that the poorest gift, when given with love, is great enough to please GOD Himself also that the true friendship cuts through barriers of inequalities of position and wealth.

The ten AVTARAS (Incarnations) of Vishnu, described in the PURANAS teach mankind that God has re-established Dharma or righteous justice and destroyed injustice from time to time by appearing on earth in various incarnations.

The Epics

The two great epics, the Mahabharatta and the Ramayana give us plenty of details, sometimes minut details, about the kings and their Brahmin Ministers; the kings who led a spiritual life and of ascetics who played a great role in the affairs of the nations. Difficult situations are pictured whose impact on several human souls is marvelously analysed. Dharama, as the Chief factor in the shaping of human life, is the underlying motive of the Ramayana and Karma, the one of Mahabharatta. These epics contain so much of mythology, parables etc. in their episodes that it is difficult to sift fact from fiction. All is not fiction, the essence of the epics contain facts, spiritual and moral gospels.

Jawahar Lal Nehru speaks about the influence of Indian Mythology and old tradition on him. He says : 'Among the earliest memories of the childhood are the stories from these epics'

(Ramayana and Mahabharatta), in which there was both adventure and the fairy element in them. The stories told and popular open air performance of Ramayana had the effect that 'Indian mythology and old tradition crept into my mind and got mixed up with all manner of other creatures of their imagination', and that, ' if it was so with me, inspite of the diverse influences that worked on my mind, I realized how much more must old mythology and tradition work on the minds of others and, especially, the unread masses of our people'.

The **Mahabharatta** is generally accepted to have evolved during 400 BC - 200 BC. It is neither history, nor chronicle. It is myth (Purana), legend (Itihasa) and Poem (Kavya) and much more. Several branches of knowledge including philosophy, law, ethics, state craft, warfare, history, ethnology are embodied in its structure. Mahabharatta comprising of 100,000 verses is by far the largest poem ever written, by several men of intuition and imagination over a period of several years. The Bhagvad Gita, 'the song of the Lord' is an episode in this great epic, comprising of only 700 verses, but it stands apart and is complete in itself, an important work on Hinduism. It is the culmination of the teachings of the vedas and the upanishads. It is the 'New Testament' of the modern Hinduism, a basic teaching of Dharma and Karma.

Ramayana deals with the devotional and moral movements of Rama (Visnu incarnation) and Mahabharatta, that of K'rsna (Visnu incarnation) where heroes have been transformed into Gods and gathering into the person of their main deity other Gods, persons and events, like flowers strung on a garland of devotion.

Bhagavad Gita (around 5000 BC)

'Song of the Blessed one ', 'Song of the Lord' Divine Song discourse between K'rsna and Arjuna the sacred book of the

Hindu tradition originally comprising the twenty fifth to the forty second chapter of the section on Bhisma in the Mahabharatta. The Gita is a synthesis of several strains, including the three yogas : Jnana, Karma and Bhakti. Indian thinkers such as Sankara, Ramanuja, Aurobindo, Gandhi and Radhakrishnan offer slightly different interpretations of the Gita, but generally agree that its message involves the ideal of selfless action, true knowledge of reality and devotion to the Lord.

Aurobindo on some concepts of the Bhagvad Gita says :-

"The Geeta is nor a weapon for dialectical warfare, it is a gate opening on the whole world of spiritual truth and experience and the view, it gives us, embraces all the provinces of that supreme region. It maps out, but it does not cut up or build walls or hedges to confine our vision[1].

According to Aurobindo, the Geeta is not a book of ethics, it is a book of spiritual life. That, which Geeta teaches, is not a human but a divine action, nor the performance of social duties but the abandonment of all other standards of duty for a selfless performance of the divine will working through our nature.

Dr. S. Radhakrishnan says :- ' The Gita provides the means by which a truly religious life can be attained[2].

The Gospel of K'rsna cult, inserted in the Mahabharatta, has been extended by a supplement 'Harivamsa' (The line of Hari - Visnu) scripture of 4th century ? It is a collection of legends used by the Bhagvata Sect.

Bhagvada Gita is a celebrated literature, where in God (K'rsna) in a fuller manifestation, is a warrior king, made to expound the orthodox doctrine and defend the cause of righteousness. It has

1. Dr. Radhakrishnan S. : The Hindu view of life P 18
2. Bhagvada Gita XIII. 12

been a source of spiritual inspiration to Arjuna (in Mahabharatta) to innumerable Hindus and non - Hindus alike. The Bhagvad Gita saved Hinduism from complete destruction. It united all the living trends in Hinduism into a theism. The identification of Brahma with Visnu distinctly suggests that the Absolute is a personal God and this concept became more pronounced when K'rsna becomes the incarnation of Visnu. While evolving a theism, Bhagvada Gita has taken great care to bring the religion within reach of all. It offered release (Nirvan) not only to all Hindus without any distinction of caste, but was also made available to the layman and his wife, who maintained their household duties and took part in the business of the world. In Bhagvada Gita, the infinite Reality is emphatically distinguished from Sat (Truth) as well as from a Sat (falsehood). 'I will proclaim that which should be known, for, when it is known, immortality is enjoyed. The Beginningless, supreme B'rhma is neither Sat, nor a - Sat'[1].

Annie Besant has summarised Bhagvad Gita, ' It is meant to lift the aspirant from the lower levels of renunciation, where objects are renounced, to the loftier heights where desires are dead, and where the yogi dwells in calm and ceaseless contemplation, while his body and mind are actively employed in discharging the duties that fall to his lot in life.' Tho Gita tries to build up a philosophy of Karma based on Jnana and supported by Bhakti in a convincing manner. ' He who sees the ultimate reality seated equally in all beings and upperishing within the pershing, sees truly'. Gita is a unique synthesis of Action (Karma), Devotion (Dharma) and knowledge (Vidya).

Lokamanya Tilak calls Bhagvad Gita ' a most luminous and priceless ge, which gives peace to afflicted souls and makes us masters of spiritual wisdom.

---

1. Bhagvada Gita XIII. 12

Madan Mohan Malviya sees a unique synthesis of the highest knowledge, the purest love and the most luminous action in Bhagvada Gita.

Mahatma Gandhi describes Bhagvada Gita as 'the universal mother whose door is wide open to anyone who knocks. A true votary of the Gita does not know what disappointment is. He ever dwells in perennial joy and peace that passeth understanding.' It is the 'Gospel of Humanity' that deals with metaphysics, religion and ethics.

Dr. S. Radhakrishnan commenting on the teaching of Gita said, 'The Absolute reveals itself to those seeking for knowledge as the Eternal light, clear and radiant as the sun at noon day, to those struggling for virtue as the eternal Righteousness, steadfast and impartial, and to those emotionally inclined as Eternal love and Beauty of Holiness'. The path to salvation is knowledge, action and devotion. The synthesis of these is 'yoga'.

SEALS AND INSCRIPTIONS

Seals and inscriptions, as a source of religious beliefs, are important, particularly as far as it relates to Hinduism in the initial stages.

Some specimens of magical inscriptions are found in the Indus or Harrappan seals, which were used as amulets and contained magical formulae on them. Deciphering the inscription is yet not full, but they are most likely to contain the names of the deities which are represented by the animals. The animals represented on the amulets are the antelope, buffalo, Brahmi Bull, Composite animal, elephant, goat, hare, monkey, Rhinoceros, short horned bull, tiger and also some human figure. Some of the deities represented on the seals are the Moon, Yama, Siva, Indra, Brahma and Durga.

Magical formulae continued to be written on metals as well as on Birch bar (Bhojapatra) and other materials.

Religious and didactic inscriptions deal with religious and moral matters. Possibly some of the seals and tables of the Indua valley were objects of worship and were not used as amulets. The inscriptions of ASOKA are the best specimens of the religious and didactic inscriptions, called DHAMMA LIPI. Some didactic inscriptions deal with the installation of images and the construction of temples; as MANDASOR inscription of the time of Kumar Gupta II and BANDHUVARMAN and the BHITAR inscription of Skand Gupta and the AIHOLE inscription of the time of Pulakesin II. Donative inscriptions refer to the donations of caves as residence of minks and ascetics, donation of land to temples, monastries and Brahmins. Tamrapata, Tamrapattra, Tamrasasana, Sasanapattra, or Danapatra throw light on religious beliefs and are good sources to discover Hinduism in its early stages.

CHAPTER - 3

HINDUISM : GENERAL

Hinduism is the world's oldest living religious system, which still has a great following, despite its deviations in Buddhism, Jainism and Sikhism. The influence of Hinduism has spread from India, Pakistan and Bangla Desh to several parts of Asia. It is now spreading to Europe and America as well. Its generous, tolerant attitude has great appeal beyond the borders of India. R'gveda (111.38.8) rightly says :-

> Forget not, singer
> This word of thine
> which after ages
> will resound.

Hinduism has no founder like Christ's christianity, Buddha's Buddhism, Mahavira's Jainism, Mohammad's Islam, or of Judaism, Confucianism or Zorastrianism, all of whom acknowledge a holy man as leader, founder or prophet or a legislator. People and communities existed before the founding of these sects. what existed before these sects (that was unnamed Hinduism), which has no founder and has come through the ages ever since mankind is traceable. Since there was no other faith then and none to differentiate with, no was ever given to this religion (now called Hinduism). It has the longest, unbroken span of ritual practice in the world, one that is nearly 4,000 years old. Hinduism is really an anthropological process to which, by a strange ivory of fate, the name of religion has been given. It evolved over a long period, assimilating all kinds of religious and cultural movements in India.

Hinduism; the social institutions and the religion of the vast majority of Indians, date atleast from 2,000 B.C. Unlike Christianity or Islam, it is not a personal religion, the individual being regarded as unimportant and always as a part of a greater whole: Universe, society, caste or village community and as a link between an Infinite number of lives in the past and in the future[1].

Hinduism, as a name to this primordial religious system, had to be given, when other religions came into existence. Then all those living in BHARAT (Sindhu); Persian invaders pronounced Sindhu as HINDU and they termed the inhabitants of India as HINDU and belonging to Hinduism. It is not a name after an originator, but ascribed to the faith of a region called SINGHU, - Hindu. Persians pronounce 'S' as 'HA', so the term Sindhu became Hindu, their existent faith Hinduism and their country HINDOSTAN. All those natives, invaders or immigrants living in Sindhu, Bharat or Hindostan, were classed as belonging to Hinduism. Greeks termed Sindhu as INDES, which later changed to INDIA.

HISTORICAL

The myth that Aryans were the founders of Hinduism, has been exploded for ever by the archaeological discoveries of the Indus valley civilisation, after first world war and by the deciphering of the Proto Indian script. The citadels discovered at HARRAPPA and MOHENJODARO, give us new insights into the ancient history of Hinduism. The religion of the Indus (Sindhu) cities survived long after the cities had been destroyed by the Aryans. The Aryans did not enter a cultural vaccum, but as they expanded, they adopted the religion of the Indus valley region, making it their own, and carrying it into the Gangetic plains and beyond. Thus the religious faith of the people of Indus valley and of Aryans merged in a great and growing synthesis.

The people of the Indus Valley and the Aryans were not the only ones to create Hindu tradition, there was a third source, the

---

1. Crompton Yorke : HINDUISM 1971

Dravidian South Dravidian is a linguistic term, which identifies the group of languages (Tamil, Telegu, Malayalam and Kannad) spoken in the South. This region has a past which goes back to Pre-Aryan times and there is a distinct culture. For a full understanding of Hinduism, the Dravidian culture, cannot be overlooked.

Hinduism is often represented as being immensely complex and confusing. It is complex, but if the historical streams, that flowed together to become Hinduism, are understood and recognised, the complexity need not be confusing. In order to understand Hinduism in its proper perspect and in its bare minimum, one must know of the sources, the Indus valley civilisation. The Aryans, Dravidians and their internal religion cultural faith over the past four thousand years, vis Hindu sacred scriptures, coins and seals.

After Indus valley civilisation, Vedic religion prevailed; when literature: Vedas, Upanishads, Sutras, Brahamanas, The Mahabharatta, The Ramayana and Srimad Bhagvad Gita were produced. Fifth to Second centuries B.C. were the years of intensive encounter with Buddhism and Jainism, and Vedic religion was profoundly modified. Hinduism proper emerged from the encounter.

Hinduism as understood today, is dated back to 200 B.C. when classical religious social codes, religious philosophies and devotional movements came into being. Literature, Laws of Manu, Ramayana, Yoga Sutras, Kama Sutra, Vedanta Sutras and Dharam Sutras, Artha Sastra, Nateya Sastra, Bhakti Sutras and PURANAS, appeared upto 800 A.D. During the period 800 AD - 1750 A.D., there was an encounter with Islam and devotional movements of kabir (1440-1518), Nanak (1470 - 1540 AD) had their hold. GITA GOVIND, songs of Tamil saints, Acts of Rama and more Puranas were produced. After 1750, while the devotional movements continued, there was encounter with the West and their religions. Reforms movements, cultural and religious creativity of great diversity and Hindu renewal followed and continues to the present times, but it still retains the elements of tradition in almost all its sects, but even more, it has borrowed from many local cults which must have been pressed back or altered by the flowing tide of Vedism. Hinduism, or as it is better termed Classical Brahminism, shows itself first of all as an enlargement of the religious horizon. Broader classes of the population have accorded to the cult, though the supremacy of the priest class remains theoretically unchanged. The older ranks have been broken up by sectarianism (Saivism, Visnuism, Shaktism etel), by dispersion into new regions, and by the internal evolution of incessant speculation. It is indeed no longer a religion, it is a complete organisation of society and thought.

HINDUISM OUTSIDE INDIA

That Hinduism (unnamed) was the only religion in the world in ancient times can be proved by a study of 'ANCIENT HISTORY OF THE NEAR EAST' by H.R. Hali. Signing a treaty in 1280 B.C. between Romesus II and Hititess in an Egyptian document, quotes Vedic God MITRA Varuna, as witness to the treaty. Many names of that period had 'Rama' incorporated viz Ramesus I, Ramesus II and III and so forth. 75% of the cities in Madagaskar (South Africa) have names after the heroic names in the Ramayana. Encylopaedia Brittanica volume 23, describes names of the inhabitants of Sahara (North Africa) based on Sanskrit who were related to Kaushal Deva.

Many of the festivals in other countries coincide with the festivals in Hinduism. Navratri, Dussehra are celebrated in India, simultaneously 'RAMA SITA' festival is celebrated in remote Mexico.[1]

1. T.W.F. : The Mayo Indians of Southern Yuketan, North and British Hondutas PP 56.

Many sculptures 'Ganesha' icons have been excavated in Mexico[1] The natives of this country are called Aajtees, resembling 'Aastik', believers in Vedas.

The inhabitants of Peru (South America) are called 'Incas', a term derived from one of the names of SURYA (Sun) Doona. They worshipped the Sun and their main festival fell on Sankranti[2].

Names of many cities in California are based on the Puranic names. California may have been Kapil and Arney of the Puranas and Netherlands (Patal) of the Puranas.

Inscriptions from Java and Borneo testify to the existence of Vedic Hinduism (Yugas and Yageyas) in ancient times. 'The South took the lead in a great enterprise which resulted in establishing Indian colonies all over the islands in the East. These colonising excursions started in the first century A.D. and continued for hundreds of years. All over Malay, Java, Sumatra, Cambodia and Borneo, they established and took Indian culture and Indian Art with them. In Burma, Siam and Indochina, there were large Indian colonies, having faith in Hinduism. Hindu states and empires were established in these Eastern islands and then Buddhist rulers came. There was a tussle for mastery between Hindus and Buddhists for 1400 years, these Hindu and Buddhist states lasted in these islands[3].

INDOCHINA (Kamboja : Cambodia); Upto eighth century A.D., there were three Hindu states in Indochina, later combined into one Jayavarman in Ninth century A.D. for 400-500 years, these settlements remained Hindu states with Hinduism religion, then gradually Buddhism spread all over.

---

1. Sharda H.B. : 'Hindu Superiority' PP 151; remarks of Barren Hembolt
2. Asiatic Researchers Vol. I PP 426
3. Nehru J.L. Glimpses of World History 'PP 101.

Philippines and even Formosa, were both part, for a time, of the Hindu Srivijaya Kingdom of SUMATRA. His empire included Sumatra, Malay Borneo, Philippines, Celebes, half of java, half of Formosa, Ceylon and a part near Canton (S. China). Srivijaya was a Hindu till the 5-6th centuries, when he turned Buddhist. This Hindu state had attained high degree of civilisation. There were 500 temples of finest stone architecture, built between 650-950 A.D. from fifteenth century, muslims obtained control[1].

PHILOSOPHICAL

Hinduism, a religious system of profoundly religious people Hindus, is a religion which will stir the depths of the heart, and give room for the exercise of faith and love. Inspite of the absorbingly religious spirit manifested in Hinduism, a spirit which, for the most part runs in the direction of superstition, the claims of the intellectual and critical faculties of humanity are not overlooked. A code which appeared 500 years later than that of Manu, describes that a Hindu mind clings to its vague notions of pre existence and that ' the success of every action depends on destiny and a man's own effort, but destiny is evidently nothing, but the result of a man's act in a former state of existence: Some expect the whole result from destiny, or from the inherent nature of a thing; some expect it from the lapse of time and some from a man's own effort; other persons of wiser judgement expect it from a combination of all these.'

Hindus believe in all embracing creative spirit B'rhma, within which are included all the properties and processes of life, evil as well as good. From three main Gods:- B'rhma, Siva and Visnu; (the creator, the destroyer and preserver respectively) and their consorts and children; thousands of Gods have been developed, down to village Godlings, who are worshipped with an infinite

1. Nehru J. L. Glimpses of world History

variety of rites and practices, some of these primitive and barbaric. At its best, Hinduism represents a lofty standard of culture and morality stressing the spiritual as against the material values[1].

MAXMULLER, the first European to translate R'gveda :- 'If I were asked, under what sky the human mind has fully developed, I should point to India[2]. This is with reference to Hinduism, wherein there is a transition from the naturalistic and anthropomorphic polytheism through transcendent monotheism to immanent monoism in the Pre upanishadic philosophy. The personified forces of nature first changed into real gods and these later on, became mere forms of one personal and transcendental God, the 'custodian of the cosmic and moral order', who himself, later passed into the immanent.

PURUSA. The upanishads developed this PURUSA into B'rhma of Atman(soul) which is both immanent and transcendent. The mantra portion has been called the religion of Nature, of the poets; the B'rhma ritualism, the religion of law, of the priests; the Upanishadic portion, the religion of spirit of the philosophers.

Hinduism, drawing on its vedic origins, is a religious organisation of life by cases and stages of life and goals.

Hinduism, drawing on the ascetic tradition expressed in Jainism and Buddhism, also provides the option of a religious release from life, through religious knowledge, or ascetism or devotion to a God. Vedism was yajna dominated, Hinduism became Puja dominated. In the beginning, interpretation of Vedic religious ideas were represented. Vedic cult and Puja cult emerged in the middle of first millenium B.C.

Puja cult, construction of temples and adoration to the images of Gods were the important features of the religious culture

1. Sharp E.J. THINKING ABOUT HINDUISM 1971
2. Fuste & Mehta : INDIAN HISTORY AND CULTURE.

of Hinduism. The early medieval age in North India (700 - 1200 A.D.), viewed as the period of decline of the earlier classical tradition, was, in fact, marked by an efflorescence of literary, cultural and artistic achievement. The building of magnificent temples, replete with elaborate sculptural programmes symbolising complex cosmological concepts, was one of the most significant accomplishments of the period.

Citing a Supreme court of India judgement, Mr. Justice Tilhari quoted, 'As against other religions, there is no founder of Hindu religion. It does not worship any one God. It foes not lay stress on any one principle. It does not believe in any one philosophical doctrine. It does not recognise any particular ritual or action. On the other hand, it does not minimise the faith and belief of any other religion, but in fact, it only represents a system of living.'

For a Vedic man, the means for achieving his happiness was the material world. He was frankly materialistic (as is a modern Hindu). The Jainis and Buddhists, directed all their religions energies towards escaping from the world, cultivating dispassion, withdrawing completely and renouncing all joys related to this world. Calssical Hinduism combined it into two different ways. Firstly, a distinction was made between outer action and inner attitude towards the action viz full participation in worldly life, while cultivating inner detachment. Second way was combining two attitudes, but with separate options. Both ways, the worldly and the ascetic, were open to all, to be chosen according to one's Karma (action), one's situation, one's inclination and one's capacity for religious knowledge.

SOCIOLISTIC

The message of BHAGVADGITA and Upanishads, conveys that Hinduism is not a cult, nor a branch of dogmas, but a religion of the highest order that speaks of an immanent and transcendental God. It offers a philosophy of life that cuts across ethnic and geographical barriers between men. The essentials of Hindu religiogeographical teaching are pervaded by the ideal of universalism and love for humanity. Vivekananda, in his speech at Chicago conference on 19.9.83 defined the characteristics of a religion as 'Whose whole scope, whole force, will be centered in aiding humanity to realize its own true nature'. He pronounced that according to Hinduism, a man is a part of a bigger unit. As there are different parts of a human body, whose functions are individualistic, but they are all parts of one body, similarly an individual is a part of the family, the family of the society, the society of the mankind, mankind is a part of the nature and Nature of the Almighty God. When all are one and a part of each other, there is no question of a right. It is only duty (action) entrusted to each part and the others award it protection in the performance of his duties. GITA says:-

'Sway Sway Karmaneye Bhirat - Sansandhuvd Labhte Nar'.; which means 'If all men do their own duty, they will attain salvation and, the whole accumulated, will result in progress of a nation'.

Hinduism aims at the development in totality through individuals. Swami Vivekananda said,'Everyone should not be content with his own progress, but should consider his progress within the progress of all; Thus Hinduism is a Human religion in equality, which is ambitious for the welfare of one and all. The religion of all being one (Human religion: it can have no discrimination against its own individuals. Everyone is equal in this and the cooperation between each other encourages progress in life. On account of its outlook on humanity, many philosophers, saints, priests and national leaders have always held Hinduism in high esteem, and have condemned castecism, untouchability as unscriptured.

Earliest Hindu scriptures, the VEDAS, contain hundreds of hymns, which award inspiration for life for all men in cooperation and equality. The prayers in the incantations are for the welfare of the humanity in totality. There is no discrimination between the high and the low. R'gveda (10.52.6), the dictum is, 'Oh man, Thou living in the struggles of life, should gain knowledge. You should protect the enlightened paths paved by the intellectuals. You should expand the deeds of those who are devoted to knowledge and action. By yourself, become a good man and fill in with Godly qualities those who are devoted to Gods and those who are your kith and kin.'

R'gveda (5.60.5) relates to equality in human beings, wherein it is said that among the human beings, no one is bigger and no one is smaller. All are bretheren in equality. They all should put in a combined effort for secular and transcendental divinity.

Hinduism wishes well for all human beings (irrespective of caste or creed) It prays for the benediction of Mothers, Fathers, Men and the whole universe. (Atharava Veda 1.31.4).

From the thoughts in the Vedas, it is clear that human society is a family, and all men are equal. Time and again, prayer has been made, 'Oh Lord, our mind, intelligence and thoughts of all, should be alike one another and by cooperation of each other, we should progress physically mentally and in spiritualism. We should get rid of reciprocal jealousy and the differentiation between high and low. When we all are children of the same Lord and only one GOD enlightens our mind, then why should there be discrimination.

HINDUISM HAS OPEN DOORS

Indian religion, Hinduism had always a special characteristic, in that its doors were all the time open for mutual development and adaptation of reforms in accordance with the times. In whole of India, there have been popular thoughts (common thinking) and a system of living. The culture of this country differed from that in others. This was because of the thoughts (philosophy) that were acceptable to the public. Religion, religious thoughts, mutual love and equality have always been respected. In this respect, fine arts have played a great role in its development.

Vincent Smith writing on National integeration described, 'As a unit in the history of the sicial, religious and intellectual development of mind.' If there is one palce on the face of the earth where all the dreams of living men have found a home from the very earliest days, when a man began the dreams of existence, it is India'. Amidst all scriptures of Puranas of Hinduism, Vyasa's statement is truly followed in that doing good to others is conducive to merit, and doing harm to them leads to sin.

'SARVASASTRA PURANESHU VYASSEY VACHANAN DHRUNB

PARUPKARSTU PUNNAYEY PAPAPEYEY PARPEEDNAM'.

Mahtma Gandhi, the father of the Nation(India), with reference ot politics and Hinduism said, ' The essence of Hindu religion, as described in MANUSMRITI and GEETA, is that no intelligent person will ever discard Hinduism from Politics or from anyother aspect of life in India. The first and the last aim and duty of politics is to establish Hinduism. For this protection of the saints and destructions of the demons is essential. Without the destruction of demons (evil doers), safety of the saints, is not possible; as K'rsna explained in GEETA, 'Where safety of Sadhus is aimed at, destruction of the demons is automatic, then only religion can be established.

'PARITRANEY SADHUNAN VINASHAYE VA DUSHKRITAMA,

DHARAM SVAPANASHRAY SANBHAMI YUGEY YUGEY.' (GEETA 4.8)

CHAPTER - 4

PRE-VEDIC ANCIENT RELIGION

Hinduism, in its variety, complexity, intricacies of its doctrines and the difficulty of making it intelligible can only be explained in four phases viz Ancient religion, Vedism Brahamanism and Hinduism, which really run into each other.

The present age of the earth has been calculated to be 4 Arab and 50 crore years. The story of mankind can be traced back to 10 Lac years. Brainy people called HOMOSIPIENS appeared about 30,000 - 40,000 years back. Hinduism as a religious belief and faith can be traced since then. Inspite of all the changes, battles and invasions suppression,. the thread of ancient religion has continued to run on in India. The old Indian religion is the basis of Hinduism even today[1]. The vast changes worldwide including India, have affected a great change in the religious thought of the population, but it is interesting and rather wonderful to think of this long range and continuity of Indian religion, right from the dawn of history, through long ages, down to this day. 'In a sense, we in India, are the heirs of these thousands of years. We in direct line, it may be, with the Ancients'.

PRE AND PROTOHISTORIC

During the Prehistoric Paleolithic age, the man had to face climatic changes and had to depend on Nature for production and livelihood. Their belief was that as everything had appeared with creation, it was destined to continue unaltered into the future. So to combat natural calamities (floods, draughts), they had to resort to supernatural and magical forces. People begged or bargained with the supernatural. They believed that by making realistic paintings of their hunted animals, they gained some sort

1. NEHRU J.L. : GLIMPSES OF WORLD HISTORY PP 12-13

of magical power over them. Thus Paleolithic art (cave paintings) shows drawings of Bison, Bear, Horses, Wooly Rhinoceros, Mammoth and wild Boar. Dead bodies were exposed to the sun, a natural disposal.

MESOLITHIC PERIOD

During the Mesolithic period (about 10,000 years BC), the man became food producer with better implements, but there was no change in his religious beliefs. A definite change came during the next Neolithic period, when the belief in spirits and magic was lost and the cultivators felt the need and conceived spirits, who watched over their fields, flocks and hearths. Behind all these spirits, stood a creator, usually vaguely conceived. Most important belief was in the spirit of Earth (PRITHVI), later recognised as GODDESS PRITHVI, as the Goddess of fertility, the mother earth. She was adored as the source of productivity of plants and animals and of the fecundity of women, Life and well being, the cycle of death and rebirth, ultimately depended on her. Many fertility Goddess cults were created and symbolised by numerous clay figurines, unearthed from excavations of ancient sites. These clay figurines show exaggerated female characteristics; pendulous breasts and heavy thighs. The people worshipped phallus (stone worship) and performed sacrifices and animal sacrifices. They buried the dead in tombs and covered them with stones. They believed in life after death and thus sometimes put rice, grain and tools in the tombs alongwith the dead.

INDUS VALLEY CIVILISATION

Indus valley civilisation (4,000 - 3,000 B C) is the first ancient civilisation of India, which gives us an authenticated account of the then religion, beliefs and faith. During this period of Neolithic age, community, political and social organisations, trade and commerce, orthodox religious beliefs, technique of calligraphy, science, mathematics and arts progressed. The faith of the people was in SIVA (RUDRA) and His shakti (Mother Goddess). This period was fundamentally religious and philosophical, as old as atleast the Egyptian and Mesopotanian culture.

Indus valley religion, absence of temples, provides evidence to the fact that there was no public ceremonial type of religion. Stone images of phallus (Linga), some a few inches in size, others 2-3 feet high, have been excavated at Mohenjodaro (Sindh-Pakistan). The workmanship of most of them is of very high quality, indicating the value placed on them. Alongwith these, stone circles have been found called YONI. In later period, Lingam and Yoni were connected with the worship of SIVA. In Mohenjodaro, 5-6 lime-stone figures of men, all in a single pose, have been excavated. They are seated, wearing a robe over the left shoulder that leaves the right shoulder exposed. The left hand is on the slightly raised left knee, and the right hand is on the right knee. The seated pose represents some sort of formalised position, because of its repetition in all these statues. The position is very similar to later YOGA positions of meditation, practised today. From the figures of the women on the seals of that period, it has been concluded that they worshipped a MOTHER GODDESS or BHAKTI. They also worshipped 'SIVA' or 'PASHUPATI', as on several seals, there is the figure of a God, with three faces surrounded by a number of animals. (Pashupati means, lord of animals). TRISUL (Trident), the emblem of SIVA, was also found engraved on several seals. They perhaps, also worshipped stones, trees and animals.

The religion of Harappan people anticipated some features of later Indian religion, Hinduism. Numerous nude female figurines in terracota are believed to represent a Mother Goddess connected with fertility, which cult was popular among the people. The most striking divinity was the HORNED GOD depicted on the seals, nude but for many bangles, necklaces and a peculiar head dress consisting of a pair of horns. On one of these seals, He is shown as surrounded by four wild animals, elephant, a tiger, a Rhinoceros and a buffalo, beneath his stool are two deers. Certainly this God shared many of the traits of the later SIVA. Certain polished stones, mostly small but upto two feet or more in height, have been identified with the Linga and other pierced stones with the Yoni. Phallic worship, therefore, seems to have been in vogue among the Harrappans. The three Harrappan cults: those of the Mother Goddess, Proto Siva and the Linga, later became features of Indian religion. Various tree and animal cults were prevelant, and the subsequent centuries saw their assimilation by the orthodox Brhaminical religion.

Indus valley culture had begun to deteriorate even before the Aryans migrated into the area around 1500 BC, coming down through the North Western mountain passes into the smiling plains of what was to be known as BRAHMAVARTA, ARYAVARTA and BHARATAVARSHA and HINDOSTAN, but the objects found at Mohenjodaro give us clear indications of the religious faiths and beliefs of the people. Many figurines of the mother goddess show the cult of DIVINE MOTHER. This cult may not exactly be the same as the 'Shakti cult' of later days, but the fundamental ideas appear to be the same i.e. belief in Female energy as the source of all creation. 'SIVA', as today, is regarded as a Maha Yogi, also styled PASHUPATI (Lord of beasts), His chief attributes being three eyes and the TRISUL (Trident). In Mohenjodaro, alongwith the women figurines, a male form has also been identified on a particular seal, as a prototype of God 'SIVA'. He is represented in the Yoga posture, seated and surrounded by animals. As referred earlier, as on a seal, the three visible faces give rise to the conception of Three Eyes, and two horns and the tall head dress that of a three pronged trident of today. Discover of stones, looking like SIVA linga, also justify the identification of male figure, as that of SIVA.

In addition to the worship of Siva, primitive religious faith animism was also prevelant. In animism, worship of trees, stones and animals is done, in the belief that they were the abode of spirits, good or evil i.e. worship of Naga and Yaksha spirits.

It is, therefore clear that modern hinduism, which possesses all the features as described here, is indebted to Indus valley culture and religious faith.

Indications of the existence of BHAKTI cult (Devotion) and even of some philosophical doctrines like metempsychosis, have also been found in Mohenjodaro. Therefore an organic relationship exists between the ancient religion of Indus valley people and the Hiduism of today. 'When the Aryans entered India, India was already civilized, indeed, it now appears certain from the remains at Mohenjodaro and Harrappa, that a great civilisation existed there for a long time, before the Aryans came.[1]

Sir John Marshall, first Director of Archaeological Survey of India tells :- 'Equally peculiar to the Indus valley and stamped with an individual character of their own are its art and its religion. Nothing that we know of in other countries at this period bears any resemblance, in point of style, to the faience models of rams, dogs, and other animals or to the intaglio engravings on the seals, the best of which notably the humped and short horn bulls, are distinguished by a breadth of treatment and a feeling for line and plastic form that have rarely been surpassed in glyptic art; nor would it be possible, until the classic age of Greece, to match the Harappa figurines. In the religion of the Indus people, there is much, of course, that might be paralleled in other countries (Egypt and Mesopotemia). This is true of every Prehistoric and most historic religions as well. But, taken as a whole, their religion is so characteristically Indian as hardly to be distinguished from still living Hinduism.'[1]

TREE WORSHIP

As some of the seals of this period contain images of trees,, it will be worthwhile to elaborate briefly on this cult. The seals of painted pottery of the Indus valley show the figures of the PIPAL (popularly called FIG tree and botanically Ficus Religious) and ACACIA (Sami tree) The PIPAL GOD, which was possibly the prototype of the Vedic PRAJAPATI and his seven attendants messengers (sentinals) were also male deities of composite form. The pipal tree was the abode of the supreme deity of the Indus valley. The pipal was the tree of life, of creation and knowledge and was believed to impart highest knowledge to those who doaned its branches on their heads. The tree was heavily guarded by a spirit and also by seven sentinals (all male); because there was always a struggle between the Gods and the demons for the possession of the tree for doaning its branches as crests or pig tails on their heads. The sentinals were a composite animal, human faced and body featuring many animals (Ram, Tiger, Cobra, Some single bodied and three headed animals, unicorn, Bison and an indeterminate quadruped).

Some of the seals and their impressions from Indus valley sites show the ACACIA alone, with or without any inscription. Acacia was regarded as celestial plant and was supposed to be inhabited by Divine spirits with the power of hypnotizing. Acacia (SAMI) is a goddess on her won account and is supposed to contain fire, Tree worship is very old in India and its persistence in historic times clearly shows that the ancient tradition relating to this cult was later on incorporated by the Hindus in their religious system, Hinduism, in a highly modified form.

---

1. Sir John Marshall, quoted by J.L. Nehru in GLIMPSES OF WORLD HISTORY, 1989, PP 187-188.

CHAPTER - 5

INDO ARYAN RELIGION

During the period of 2000 - 500 BC, the religion of the INDO ARYANS developed and expanded. It was, the development of a still earlier belief in man's subjection to the powers of Nature and his need of conciliating them[1]. The efforts of the Aryans, by which the personified forces of Nature were worshipped, on which the material welfare of the Vedic people depended, were the influence of Sky, Air, Light and Sun i.e. VARUNA(Air), AGNI (Fire), SURYA (Sun) and USHA(Dawn). To these, people turned with awe and veneration. Earlier relationship between spirit, mind and matter was imperfectly apprehended, the phenomenon of Nature as of mysterious forces. This conception changed to the homage of luminous ones (DEVAS). The Vedic people conceived of the universe as three layered. The Gods lived in the upper regions (Swarga; Heaven), men on the earth below (Prithvi) and the demons lived in the underworld (Patal). They believed that Man's miserable condition in this world (due to death, disease, famine and other calamities) came from the actions of the Gods in response to their own failure to offer prayers and sacrifices.

Like men submitting to an early leader, Gods assigned superemacy to one celestial being called the 'Light Father' (Dyu Pitar, Jupiter). A kind of pre eminence was someitmes accorded to all investing Sky or atmosphere (VARUNA), the representative of an eternal celestial power presentingly watching earthly actions, and listening to their words by night as well as by day. SURYA (sun), by whose influence lands were fertilised, pasteurs were enriched and crops fructified, was another principal object of veneration alongwith MITRA (Orb of the sun), AGNI (Fire), USHA

(Dawn) and IRIS (Ida-Ira) were by degrees regarded with varying degrees of veneration. These names still exist and are worshipful. Aryans, in the early vedic period worshipped natural triad Viz Sky, atmosphere and Sun in its three forms Aryaman, Varuna and Mitra. A hymn to Varuna is :-

'Sing forth a hymn sublime and solemn, grateful to glorious VARUNA imperial ruler.

Who hath struck out, like one who slays the victim, Earth as a skin to spread in front of Surya.

In the tree tops the air he hath extended, put milk in Kine and vigorous speed in horses.

Set intellect in hearts, fire in the waters, Surya in heaven and Soma on the mountain.

Varuna lets the big cask, opening downwards, flow through the heaven and earth and air's mid region.

Therewith the universe's sovran waters earth as the shower of rain bedews the barley.

When Varuna is fain for milk, He moistens the sky, the land and earth to her foundation.

Then straight the mountains clothe them in the rain cloud: the heroes, putting forth their vogour, loose them.

I will declare this mighty deed of magic, of glorious varuna, the lord immortal.

Who standing in the firmament hath meted the earth out with the sun as the measure.

None, verily, hath ever let or hindered this the most wide God's mighty deed of magic.

Whereby with all their flood, the lucid rivers fill not one sea wherein they pour their waters.

If we yave sinned against the man who loves us, have ever wronged a brother, friend, comrade.

The neighbour ever with us, or a stranger, O VARUNA, remove from us the trespass.

If we, as gàmesters cheat at play, have cheated, done wrong unwillingly or sinned of purpose,

Cast all these sins away like loosened fetters, and, Varuna, let us be time own beloved[1].

R'g Vedic people believed in a life after death, but were not much concerned about it. They did not put emphasis on the sadder aspects of life, and showed optimism. The Aryans were men of vigour and activity and they viewed life with hope and ambition. Their great concern was with success, happiness and prosperity. Their pre eminent veneration was to VARUNA (sky god), the custodian God of men and Gods; who rewarded the good and punished the wicked. The religion presented in the R'gveda is a simple one, but it contains the core of Hinduism. It is the seed from which procent day Hinduism fructified.

Homage to Nature, natural Gods was made singly, in groups or collectively. The worship process was simple, natural consisting of praise, flattery, hymns and invocations with the offerings of such presents of food and drink, respectable of the power. Rice, Ghrit (Ghee) and Soma juice were usually included in the offering. There were no rituals (hard and fast rules) for worship and people were at liberty to worship as they wished. R'gveda Aryans adored and worshipped the natural force which were out of their

1. Quoted from Mahajan V.D. : ANCIENT INDIA 1990

control and which were considered beneficial. They also respected men with extraodinary qualities of leadership. They feared mysterious animals, such as snakes and worshipped them. They had no idea of any God, as He is understood in present day Hinduism, wherein He is considered as an entity separate and superior.

Vedic DHARMA, which means more than religion and derived from the root meaning 'to hold together', signified all those philosophies, moral teaching, worship and practices, which were supposed to have derived from the Vedas (To knoe-knowledge), are the repository of religious faith of majority of the Indians and the core of Hinduism..

In short, the religion of the Indo aryans was simple and plain, though it has many Gods (Natural powers). Most of the objects of devotion are the personification of Natural phenomenon. They are:

Terrestrial Gods (Prithvi, Soma, Agni, Rudra)

Atmospheric Gods (Indra, Vayu, Maruti, Parjanya)

Neavenly Gods (Varuna, Dyaus, Aswins, Surya, Savitri, Mitra, Pushan and Visnu)

Though there is a reference to a large number of Gods in the R'gveda, the unity of God was not ignored, It was not polytheism, as understood in the Greece and Roman conception, it was monotheism, the unity of God as is evident from the following hymn:-

'They call Him Indra, Mitra, Varuna,
And Agni; he is the heavenly bird Garutman;

To what is one, the poets give many a name,
They call it Agni, Yama, Matarisvan'.[1]

The religion of the Aryans was 'ARYA DHARMA'. Dharma is an ethical conception which includes the moral code, righteousness and the whole range of man's duties and responsibilities. It is an inmost institution of the law of inner being. Arya Dharma would include all the faiths (Vedic and Non Vedic of ancient Indians), that originated in India. With its definite philosophy that all religions are one, it was later used by Buddhists, Sikhs and Jainis and by all those who accepted the Vedas. Hinduism of Indo Vedic origin is infinitely absorbent like the ocean. This vitality and rejuvenation of Hinduism has retained itself, then and now.

1. Quoted from Mahajan V.D. ANCIENT INDIÃ 1990

CHAPTER - 6

EARLY VEDISM (2500 B.C. - 2000 B.C.)

Ancient Indus Valley religious beliefs were iconic with emphasis on the worship of Mother Goddess and a male deity (Protosiva). Phallic cult (Lingam) was prevalent, but there were no sacrificial fires (Yageya or Havans). Higher up than the Indus valley region, there lived many tribes, who were more advanced, had the military advantage of iron weapons, horse drawn chariots and Ox drawn carts. These tribes called ARYANS, immigrated into Indus Valley region around 1500 BC.C in groups, invaded inhabitants of Indus valley, and there was a cultural synthesis and fusion between the two.

There, came up a new classical civilization with new religious, social and philosophical systems. The region was named ARYA VRATA or the land of the Aryans. The religion of the Aryans was aniconic, where images had no place, female element was subordinated to the male and the place of honour, worship was given to natural forces INDRA (Thunder), VARUNA (Cosmic order : Rita), SURYA (Sun), SAVITRI (God to whom Gyatri mantra is addressed), PUSHAN (Guardian of roads, herds, men and stray cattle), Miter and Nasatyas, (Solar deities).

R'gveda hymn (3:62.10), which is atleast 1,000 years earlier than Christianity, addressed to SUN(Surya) is :-

Let us meditate upon the adorable

Glory of the Divine vivifier

And may He direct our thoughts.

The Aryans believed in ONE GOD, as is clear from the following hymn :-

Who is our father, our creator, Maker,

Who every place doth know and every creature,

By whom alone to Gods their names were given,

To HIM all other creatures go, to ask HIM.

But He bore many names, according to the following Hymn:-

'They call him Indra, Mitra, Varuna,

And Agni. HE is the heavenly bird Garutmat,

To what is ONE, the poets give many a name,

They call it Agni, Yama, Matrisvan.'

God was all powerful and had numerous manifestations and HE was worshipped in various forms called Gods and Goddesses, such as 'VARUNA', 'USHA, 'AGNI' and 'INDRA'. The Aryans sang hymns in praise of these gods to invoke their blessings. They also performed sacrifices and made offerings of milk, ghee and grain, to gods, who in their turn blessed them with happiness, success and prosperity. Such was their belief. There were no temples and no idol worship.

With the Aryans, came the VEDAS, R'gveda being the oldest and the first to be brought in. R'gveda, compiled about 2,000-1,000 B.C., is the most important, possibly the earliest work of Sanskrit translated in many Indo European language.

'VEDA' means 'knowledge' (from the root 'VID' : to know) and is used principally for the Divine knowledge. It is eternal, antecedent to any oral or written teaching or book. Basically 'VEDA' means 'Uncreated Knowledge' similar to that of the the word 'Wisdom' in OLD TESTAMENT. It is only secondarily referred to, the words in which the knowledge is couched; the scriptures.

In modern usage, VEDAS are always classified as SACRED SCRIPTURES of the Hidus. Modern system of varied religious beliefs and practices, began with the Vedas long ago[1]. In the vedas, GOD or the Divine is universally accepted as ONE which human speech could never adequately express nor the imagination of the human mind conceive. It is said to breathe by its own power without breath; the one principle, beyond words, to which sages have given different names. In some prominent hymns of the Vedas, the supreme power is said to be neither 'Being' nor 'NON BEING'. These words are not applicable to God.

What appears to be the supreme god is addressed in some outstanding texts as our heavenly father (DYAUS PITAR); the first cause of all and the LORD of all. He is said to encompass the universe with HIS eternal law. Nothing can escape HIS vigilant gaze; He is the 'HIRANYAGARBHA', 'The effulgent first born'; the ONE by whom all things were made, and the word (VAC), exalted as the queen of all creation; who makes the 'Father' known to all men. The Primordial BEING, not only transcends the universe, but also is immanent in it. At creation, he offered himself as a divine model for man in an allegorical immolation of complete self sacrifice to set the norm, by which all sacrifices may thereafter be ordained and regulated. This is the first of the Divine knowledge, the orthodox Hindu hears and accepts.

Aryan victories were celebrated, hymns in praise of the ruler, called Indra, were sung by court bards at sacrificial fires and feasts. The official priest, called 'HOTRI' chanted sacred verses (Mantras). These mantras and hymns sung by bards have been preserved in the form of Samhitas (collections) and are R'gveda Samhita, 'Samveda Samhita', 'Yajurveda Samhita' and 'Atharvaveda Samhita'; the four VEDAS.

---

1. Williams M: RELIGIONS IN ANCIENT INDIA pp 29

VEDIC GODS

The R'gvedic gods were predominantly male, as was natural in a patriarchal society. Their favours could be won through sacrifices. A number of domestic and public sacrifices have been mentioned in R'gveda. A passage from this book tells us that the creation grew out of first cosmic sacrifice. PRAJAPATI (later known as B'rhma) is thought of as a primeval man. He is said to have been sacrificed to himself by the Gods, who were apparently his children, and it was from the body of the Divine victim, that the universe was produced. Real development fo the sacrificial cult gained importance in Later Vedic era.

Among the VEDIC GODS, the most popular was INDRA, who shared some of the characteristics of the Greek God ZEUS. Always ready to smite dragons and demons, he is credited with the sacking of many cities.

INDRA: VEDIC GOD

Rowdy and amoral, Indra, is described as fond of feasting and drinking Soma (a heady dring of Vedic gods and aryans). The largest number of hymns in the R'gveda are addressed to Indra. e.g.

'Thou art our guardian, advocate, and friend,
a brother, fathre, mother, all combined.
Most fatherly of fathers, we are thine,
and thou art ours. Oh let thy pitying soul
Turn to us in compassion when we praise thee,
And slay us not for one sin or for many.
Deliver us today, tomorrow, every day.'[1]

Indra is the chief of ancient vedic trinity and, at the beginning

1. Williams Monier : HINDUISM p 29

of time, he secured an elephant, on which he always rides, a beautiful dancing girl called Tambha, Uchaisrava; a snow white horse, an the Parijata tree, which grants wish to its owner. Indra is represented with a thunderbolt in his right hand and a bow in his left.

The AITERAYA BRAHAMANAS[1] says : 'The gods headed by Prajapati said to one another,' This one (Indra) is among the gods the most vigorous, the most valiant, the most perfect who carries out best any work to be done. Let us install him as a king'. While it shows the importance of Indra, it also shows that kingship, then was elective (individual possessing the qualifications needed in a king). Elective theory is comparable to that of Locke.

Indra is not worshipped because of his escaped with the wife of Gautam Rishi (Ahaliya). On repentance, Indra was cursed with NOT to be worshipped, Ahaliya was turned into stone (later redeemed by Rama) and Moon, who was an accomplice in elopement, was cursed with a black scar, which is seen in everyday moon.

INDRA(Thunder God) has three minor gods viz VAYU, MARUTS AND RUDRA, who come into prominence later.

SURYA GOD

Surya is also SAVITRI, PUSHAN and has minors VARUNA, MITRA, Vishnu, USHA and ASWINS, as solar deities.

The worship of the SUN(Surya) was prevalent among almost all the nations of the world, for the celestial luminary appealed greatly to their religious instincts. HE was held by the Indians of the VEDIC age in the highest esteem alongwith other NATURE GODS. The SUN God his various aspects were worshipped

---

1. AITREYE BRAHAMANAS VIII.4.12

throughout the age of the Brahamanas, Upanishads and Sutras. The R'gveda verse (1.115.1) says that the sun is the soul of movable and immovable things. Literary, as well as archaeological data clearly prove that it was the sun cult prevalent among the ancient Iranians, which was mainly instrumental in remodelling the worship of SURYA in Northern India. The GYATRI Mantra, also known as SAVITRI uttered in daily rites is derived from a R'gvedic verse in which Savitris prayed to inspire the thoughts of those who contemplate on the excellent brilliance of the SUN GOD.[1]

AGNI : VEDIC GOD

AGNI (the earth born fire), was one of the three Gods, who was a special object of worship of the early vedic Indians. AGNI may be regarded as the next god to INDRA in the estimation of Vedic worshippers and certainly he takes precedence over every other God in connection with sacrificial rites. Even SURYA, who is generally first in all Pagan systems, is held to be a form of heavenly fire. Fire has always been an object of veneration among all nations. Agni was sometimes held to possess a kind of trinity or triple essence in himself, consisting of terrestrial fire, celestial lightning and Solar heat. Sometimes he represented a simple creative energy, which evolved all things out of its own eternal essence. AGNI, literally fire, dwelt in the domestic hearth and acted as intermediary between Gods and men. AGNI is man's domestic friend, the father of the sacrifice, the mediator between men and Gods, the bearer of the hymns and prayers from every family altar upwards towards heaven.

An early hymn to AGNI, the God of fire is:-

Knower of all that lives, O Agni, may we, both singers of praise and chiefs, continue in your keeping.

---

3. R'gveda 3.62.10

Lead us to glorious wealth, abundant, excellent. And make us rich in hero sons and their descendents[1].

Both Indra and Agni were, like Varuna, often addressed as if each deity were supreme. This aspect can be conjectured in three letters A.U,M.[2] 'These three letters combine to form the sacred syllable OM-afterwards typical of the Brahamanical trinity were originally the initial letters of the trinity of gods, fire, Wind and Sun (Agni, Vayu or Varuna for Indra and Mitra).

R'gveda (I.34.11; I.45.2) mentions thirty three Gods or three groups of Gods, their names are given variously, but they are little more than manifestations of the three leading divine personifications. YAMA, God of death stands alone, as the God of departed spirits (Pitris), who have departed and have occupied Swarga (upper sky), Middle intermediate air and lowest the atmosphere near the earth. They are presided over by YAMA, who along with his twin sister YAMI were the first born and the first to die. In the Vedas, he has no office, but in later theology he is the God of death.

The older Gods may be traced back to the period when Aryans had not branched off from the Indo European community. Amongst them DYAUS(The heavens personified) was the father God, but lost his position of prominence in the Vedic pantheon. NON ARYAN influence on religion must have been felt very early, for some of the R'gvedic Gods had a distinctly nonaryan origin. The deity RUDRA (Prototype SIVA), whose arrows brought disaster, evolved from a HARRAPPAN cult; so did TVASHTRI (the vedic vulcan) in the previous life. from this evolved the theory of KARMA(action) which preached that the deeds of one life affected the next. This doctrine sought to provide an explanation of human

1. R'gveda II 2.9.12
2. Williams M : RELIGIOUS LIFE IN ANCIENT INDIA, 1883.

suffering and became fundamental to most, later in Indian thought.

What today is seen, as a complete system of varied religious beliefs and practices, began with the VEDAS long ago. Dr S Radhakrishnan[1] has tried to establish the view that 'all religions are the same, which was the view held by HINDUISM from times immemorial.' The basis of his arguments are the excavations of HARRAPPA, MOHANJODARO, The VEDAS, the narratives of BUDDHA, the RAMAYANA, the MAHABHARATTA and the PURANAS.

1. Radhakrishnan S : EASTERN RELIGIONS AND WESTERN THOUGHTS PP 306-310

CHAPTER - 7

LATER VEDIC RELIGION

Early vedic religion was simple. there was no rites, rituals or temples, in the later vedic period, it became complicated. Later when the Aryans (Indo Aryans) began to think of the mystery of natural forces, they imagined some deities who controlled those natural forces. Nature worship gave place to sacrifice, which became a imortant feature of worship. The lustre of the older natural Gods gradually diminished, though in Atharvaveda, magnificient hymns celebrating the omniscience of Varuna[1] or the beneficience of the Earth Goddess Prithvi were still found, sacred rites and ceremonies were performed everyday since their performance required technical knowledge, the presence of Brahmin at all such function became essential. Monotheistic and Monostic tendencies, that attained prominence towards the close of R'gvedic period, became more marked with the efflux of time. Thus the Brahmins established superiority over others. They became the chief beneficiaries of sacrifies and consequently gained power.

While the priests and theologians were absored in elaborate sacrificial rites and muttered litanies in honour of Prajapati, the Lord of created beings, the first sacrificer and the embodiment of sacrifice, philosophers doubted the efficacy of the ritual, speculated about the underlying unity of the universe and strove for union with the supreme Brhma or Paramatman, the Universal soul or the Absolute that dwelt in everything that guides all beings within, the inward guide 'Immortal'.

The vedic religion thought, which continues in Hinduism, was

1. Atharva Veda IV. 16.

that external world is Maya (illusion). Behind this appearance, there is a unique principal, which is transcedent and deliberately remains impersonal on the plane of B'rhma, the idea of supreme personal God has no support. Attainment of deliverance (emergence from the cycle of rebirth, escape from Karman) was the aim and the means were knowledge, a deepening of reflection, reinforced by certain rites. They believed that the body consisting of gross matter, is connected to the soul by the pneumatic principal which governs breathing, speech, vision, hearing and understanding. Parallel to it, there is a subtle body which is a link between pure matter and pure spirituality, which functions correspondingly to those of the gross body. At death, the subtle body carries the predispositions and accompanies the soul to it's new destination. The soul is affected by it's associations with matter, not endowed with 'personal' immorality. The soul of those, who have attained deliverance, alone are finally free from association with matter.

The common people did not understand philosophical speculation and began to show predilection for the known R'gvedic deities, who were not so prominent as Varuna, Indra or Agni. These older vedic Gods were by the worship of Rudra (Siva), Visnu or K'rsna. Rudra, was a known deity in thc R'gvoda, but not so prominent, who already bore in the early litatanies the epithet of Siva (Propitious) and soon came to be regarded as the Great god (Maha Deva) and the Lord of the animated being (Pashupati). His popularity may have begun due to his identification with the Chief male deity of the prehistoric people of the Indus.

Visnu, a solar deity famed in the R'gveda for his three strides; was regarded as the source of cosmic and moral order, as the deliverer of mankind of distress and as the saviour of Gods. Visnu soon gained importance and occupied the place of the Varuna.

Visnu as the most sublime among the celestial and his highest step (Parmapadam) became the goal of the Sages and Seers. Before the close of the vedic era, he came to be identified with Vasudeva, an incarnation known to the epic, Kadini as K'rsna Devkiputra (Son of Devki) in Mahabharatha.

Priests, Brahmins, Sheers and Sages gained dominance on account of their essential presence at elaborate sacrificial rites. Cattle were slaughtered at sacrifices, often in large numbers. Excavation at Atranji Khera have revealed animal bones with cut marks, as of cattle. Cattle wealth, so important for agriculture, agricultural economy, diminished because of public rituals.

At the end of the vedic period, or the beginning of Brahmanic era, Brahmanical dominance and the extremely ritualistic reflects of the Aryans, could be seen in the upanishads, which reflects a wider spirit of inquiry (philosophy) in the vedas. The upanishidic thought centres round the idea of soul (Atman) and not sacrifice (Yajna). In these creation is said to have grown out of the Primeval desire of the world soul. In unpanishads, we find the first clear exposition of belief in the passage of human soul from life to life (rebirth). Souls were thought of as being born to happiness and sorrow according to there conduct (Karman). People then believed in transmigration of the soul or rebirth and Karman (Deeds). In one upanishad, K'rsna is described as associated with the school of thoughts which rejected the purely ritualistic interpretation of sacrifice and considered the practice of Viztue (True deeds) to be as effective as gifts to priests. According to this school, at death bed one should take refuge in three thoughts viz 'you are the imperishable; the never failing and the very essence of life. Accordingly the spiritual endeavour was the realm of light higher than heaven where dwelt the Supreme God among the Gods, Bhagvata creed was based on this doctrine.

The prevalent faith was the idea of a Supreme God, who was the master of all, the whole world and all existence. He is the creator, master and ruler of all. He treated all existence, Sun, Moon, stars, earth, water, fire, air, life, animal, men and women and all of them, who lived worked according to the will of the Supreme God. (Supreme B'rhma, Parmatmam, the universal soul or the absolute); who ordained all Gods, Goddesses, humans and all in their actions and deeds (individual souls).

CHAPTER - 8

THE EPICS

The EPIC period comes after Vedic period and before the Buddhist. This period was the same as of the SUTRAS. The Epics RAMAYANA and the MAHABHARATTA, are the vedas of the masses, who 'turn in sorrow, in joy and in daily toil to these noble poems for solace and inspiration'. The characters mentioned in them have become legendary heroes and some of them are actually worshipped as the various incarnations (Avataras) of GOD himself.

THE RAMAYANA

The Ramayana is the oldest, idealistics, most popular epic of the Hindus compiled in 300 B.C. It consists of seven books and 24,000 couplets. The Ramayana furnishes pictures of kings, who led a spiritual life and of ascetics, who played a great part in the affairs of the nations. Difficult situations are pictured, whose impact on several human souls is marvellously analysed. DHARMA, as the chief factor in the shaping of human life, is the underlying motive of the Ramayana and of its many episodes.

In brief, the salient points of Ramayana story are :-

1. Fulfilment of a boon given by Dasrath to his youngest queen KEKKIYE, when she had earlier saved his life.
2. Obedience to the father by RAMA, in order to enable has father to fulfill the boon.
3. Self exile of Lakshmana, out of love for his elder brother.
4. SITA, as an ideal Hindu wife, undertook self exile with Rama.

5. Rama's help to Rishis in different ashramas, during his exile, in the cause of righteousness.
6. Ill treatment of Ravana's sister Swaroopnakha by Lakshmana.
7. Sita's abduction by Ravana.
8. Role of GARUDA (Visnu's conveyance) in combating Ravana on his way back to Sri Lanka.
9. Assistance of Hanuman and his comrades in the onward march of Rama.
10. Restoring life to AHALIYA, the stone turned wife of Rishi Gautam.
11. Restoration of the wife of Sugriva and his kingdom, from treacherous Bali.
12. Exhibition of chastity by Sita in Ravana's captivity.
13. Ravana's high character, in not forcing Sita for marriage.
14. Rama's devotee Bhabhikshana's help to Rama.
15. Kumbhkarna's opposition to Ravana in abducting Sita; but ultimately agreeing in obedience and allegiance to his elder brother Ravana's fighting against Rama.
16. Ravana's defeat and the end of evil.
17. Rama's advice to Lakshmana at Ravana's death bed, to learn the administration of the kingdom.
18. Bharata's sacrifice not to sit on the throne, but rule in the name of his elder brother Rama.
19. Sita exiled in response to the popular demand of the ruled public, doubting her chastity.
20. Sita's submersion in the cracked earth (Prithvi) in order to save her husband Rama, from any further harrasment.
21. After crowning his son KUSA, with his headquarters at Kusathali, and his other son LAVA, with his capital of

Saravasti, Rama (incarnation of Visnu) departs to heaven (Swarga), alongwith Bharata and Shatrugana and the citizens of Ayodhya; Lakshmana having died earlier.

LESSONS LEARNT FROM THE RAMAYANA

(i) Ideal behaviour of the ruler and ruled, of men and women, were shown by the action of characters in this epic, there by teaching subtlety, yet effectively, what ideal behaviour should be.

(ii) Qualities of ideal queens, Kaushalaya and Sumitra, soft spoken but strong, who placed the prestige of the king and the kingdom above their love of their sons.

(iii) The high value and importance of a boon.

(iv) Obedience to parents.

(v) Qualities of a high principled man, Bharata.

(vi) Qualities of an ideal man, prince and king Rama.

(vii) Ideal woman and wife, but gentle, sweet and devoted character embodied in SITA.

(viii) Qualities of ideal brothers from the behaviour of Lakshmana, Bharata and Shatrugana.

(ix) Ideal qualities of loyalty, unstinted devotion and love are depicted in the character of HANUMANA.

(x) Destruction of evil by Good either by oneself or by Divine intervention is a constant theme (of Hinduism), exhibited in the Ramayana.

(xi) The great virtue of loyalty, even for a lost cause, shown by Kumbhkarna.

(xii) Forgetting the enemity, Ravana's imparting tips on king-ship to Lakshmana.

THE MAHABHARATTA

Vaisampayyan, disciple of Ved Vyasa, while describing the importance of the Mahabharatta said, 'Mahabharatta is as piety and great as the VEDAS or the PURANAS. This historic work narrates the ways for prosperity and action, in accordance with religious beliefs. This also leads to wisdom about liberation. This narrates the origin of BHARATA dynasties, therefore called MAHABHARATTA (great Bharatas). Just as the ocean and Sumeroo mountain, are the mines of diamonds, similarly this work is the principle origin of the legends. Whatever is there about Dharma, wealth (Arth), activity (Kaam) and salvation (Moksha) in it, that is the greatest, the highest; whatever is not there in it, is in no where else[1]. The MAHABHARATTA is usually ascribed to be between fourth century B.C. and fourth century A.D., although Pargiter dates it as 950 B.C. and Patanjali Mahabhashya as a well known epic in second century B.C.; latest studies at B.M. Birla science centre, on the basis of astronomical and literary references, supported by Dr. B.G.Siddartha's archaeological evidence, date Mahabharatta war as to have been fought in 1350 B.C., which was recorded as an epic between fourth and second century B.C. The Mahabharatta consists of 18 books and about one lac couplets and is more realistic rather than idealistic Ramayana.

In the modern sense of the term, it is neither history, nor a chronicle. It is all the three; the myth (Puranas), legend (history) and poem (Kavya). It is averitable encyclopaedia covering several branches of knowledge (Philosophy, ethics, law, state-craft, warfare, history, ethnology etc.). Tradition claims that what is found in it, may be found scattered in other books too, but what is not found in it, will not be found anywhere else.

---

1. THE MAHABHARATTA : ADI PARVA

In the Mahabharatta, seeds of tragedy are sown, when Shantanu, king of the KURUS, desired to marry Satyavati, daughter of a fisherman, whose parents wished to marry her to Shantanu's son DEV VRATA.

Dev Vrata, in order to fulfill his father's desire, renounced both the kingdom and the matrimony and became BHISHMA.

PANDU , the younger brother renounced kingship to become a religious hermit. DHRITRASHTRA, the blind Kaurava, assumed kingship.

Pandu's sons (Yudhishtra, Bhima, Arjuna, Nakula and Sehdeva) received training alongwith DARYODHANA (Kaurava) and his many other brothers. Jealousy and hatred developed between ruling Kauravas and dependant Pandavas, right from childhood.

Pandavas left the kingdom and in exile married DARAUPADI, and met their cousin K'rsna (Visnu's incarnation in disguise). Yudhishtra lost all in a game of dice with Daryodhana. Panadavas went into exile.

The feud ultimately culminated in the great war of Kurukshetra, described in the Mahabharatta, a book which Mughal AKBAR called as THE BOOK OF WARS.

The most important part of the Mahabharatta, from our point of view, is the sermon of BHAGVAD GITA, given by K'rsna to Arjuna, when the latter was reluctant to fight against his Guru and relatives. From this, evolved the theory of KARMA (action) and duty (function) as adopted by the Aryans, in the classification of persons.

The Mahabharatta depicts the story of human beings, caught up in live situation of attachment, jealousy, commitment, dilemma and confrontations. In this epic composer Vyasa's characters are intensively alive and markedly distinguishable from one another, as those found in real life.

Swami Vivekananda compares the Kurukshetra battlefield to the world, we live in. The five pandavas represent righteousness and the hundred Kauravas, the myriad wordly attachments, we have to fight against. Arjuna the soul awakened by the teachings of K'rsna, is the general, who leads in this battle.

LESSONS FROM THE MAHABHARATTA

(i) Importance of one's DHARMA or duty.

(ii) War to fight for righteousness.

(iii) Emphasis on NISHKARMA viz action without desire or passion and without any worry about the fruits or results of one's actions.

(iv) Duties of the ideal man; as a yogi, one unattached to wordly desires, as far as his heart and mind are concerned; but also as a man of action setting right the wrongs of society.

(v) People learnt the rules and the codes of ideal conduct laid down for man and woman, king and commoners.

(vi) In Bhishma, we meet the stern regard for TRUTH, combined with sense of duty, heroism and filial love.

(vii) Pandava brothers typify the sweet brotherly relations.

(viii) Yudhishtra is a model of moral virtues.

(ix) Subhadra is a model of selfless devoted wife and matron.

RELIGION DURING EPIC PERIOD

The religion had an important change during the epic period.

The Vedic Gods (Indra, Surya, Varuna) were relegated to the background. The TRINITY (B'rhma, Visnu and Siva) in particular Visnu's incarnations of RAMA and K'rsna, came to be worshipped. The BHAGVAD GITA, became an important popular religious book of the Hindus. Santinists, Vedantists, Arya Sajists and Brahamanas, all classes of Sanyasis and Sudhus, read it, rever it and quota it in support of their dogmas and contradictory doctrines and with equal confidence.

CHAPTER - 9

POST VEDIC RELIGION : BRAHMANISM

After vedism, the second phase (Dharmasastras - Caste system) in the history of Hinduism was Brahmanism. As Brahmanism were based on vedism, no hard line of demarcation can be drawn between the two. It may be called Aryadharma, Vaidikadharma or according to Patanjali[1] Rishi Sampradaya' viz a religion established by an association of Rishis (Saints and Priests). It's development extended from Eighth Century B.C. to the 12th century A.D.

In the vedic period, the man carving for the perception of the infinite, personified the Sky, Sun, Fire, Air, Water and Earth. This concept now changed and the spirit vivifying their own bodies with the breath of life, enshrined in their thoughts and their own consciences. This mysterious, all pervading, vague spiritual power and presence, thrilling through the imagination of Hymn composers, which was wholly unbounded by limitation of personality and individuality, was now identified as Atman (the breath of life). Atman or B'rahma was thought to be a pure essence, which expanded through all space, diffused itself everywhere. Men and Gods were merely manifestations of that spirit. Brahmanism in it's earliest origin had this fundamental doctrine.

This complex system doctrine had four phases viz ritualistic, philosophical, mythological and nomistic. Ritualistic phase constituted in the compilation of sacred treatises called Brahmanes, which were in prose composition, an integral portion of the vedas and contained divine knowledge and directions. The procedure to be adopted by the Brahmins in the performance of sacrificial ceremonies. Sacrificial acts (Karman) invigorating offerings of food, to secure the favour of Gods became ingrained in the whole Brahmanical system. Aitareye, Satapatha, Tandya and Gopatha Brahmanas were composed in conformity with the Mantras (Hymns) in R'gveda, Yajur, Sama and Atharva Veda respectively. These were composed in the 7th and 8th centuries B.C. Everyman thought by continuous oblations, offering of food to God through sacrifice, he could be happy, Hymns, praise, prayer, teaching and repititions of the sacred words of scriphires were subsidiary to the ear of sacrificial offerings. The last offering made by man was by fire, burning his body.

First it was only thanks giving, next was to strengthen God by offering food, to invigorate and gratify deities with offering of food and so to accomplish some earthly object and most ambitious idea was to attain superoushuman powers and even exaltation to the heavens. The elaborate system of complicated rituals with proper repetition and intonation of numerable hymns required the presence of priests. Thus sixteen classes of priests came into being. The magnanimity of the sacrificial rites can be gauged by knowing some names viz Asvamedha, Jyotishtoma, Agnishtoma, Aptoryama and vajapeya. Sacrificial rites, properly performed were considered to effect anything in the world, a great preservative from all evil, the great maintainer of the energies of the universe and a great source of all benefits. It could procure a whole line of sons and grandsons of secure the attainment of the highest heaven. Sacrifice (Yajna) was sometimes, even personified as a God. Blood sacrifice (killing innocent for riddance of sin of the guilty) was sometimes undertaken. It was called BALI, but this existed in few region under a few sects of brahmins.

People became wearied with sacrifices and sacrificers. External rites and sacredotalism were disgusted. The thought prevailed that if every man was a part of God, what necessity was there that God should propitiate himself. This was a philosophical thought and the result was the philosophy of Veda scriptures; the UPANISHADS, revealing hidden spiritual doctrines of the Vedas.

UPANISHADS, the philosophical brahaminism scriptures, are a combination of Mantra and BRAHMANA portion of Vedas with the addition of treatise such as ISA, CHANDOGYA, KATHA,. MUNDAKA and BRIHAD aranyaka. These also include sutras with their branches NYAYA with Vaiseshika, SANKHYA with yoga and VEDANTA with MIMANSA. Philosophical brahminism, thus scriptured in Upnishads is a form of mystical religious speculation, an inquiry into the best method of escape from the troubles of life, deliverance from the necessity of transmigration, liberating the spirit of man from the bondage of repeated bodily existence and reuniting it with the supreme spirit (B'rhma).

The Upanishads tell us that the Vedas - the store house of knowledge have been breathed forth from HIM(B'rhma), but they regard the KARMAKanda (actions) as secondary, being only a help to purify the mind, by which purified one is made fit to receive the real teaching about B'rhma. Ritualism and Ceremonialism of the BRAHAMANAS was arrested and lofty philosophical conceptions found in the Mantras, were faithfully acknowledged and developed.

Indian philosophy, in particular Philosophy of Hinduism, is a very vast complex and is outside the scope of this book, which is only a short account of Hinduism.

The doctrines in philosophical Brahaminism viz disbelief in rituals, uselessness of sacrificial ceremonies and austerities for the attainment of true knowledge, were such doctrines as were also practised in Buddhism. Gautam Buddha (the enlightened) self practised doctrines of universal charity, liberty, equality and fraternity; which were irristably attractive and resulted in expansion of Buddhism. The only hope of arresting the progress of Buddhist movement lay in inventing human gods and a system of mythology equally attractive, equally suited to the needs and capacities of the people enmass. Unfortunately Buddha died and brahmins availed the opportunity in introducing mythological Brahamanism, by supplying the people with personal and human formed gods, out of their epics RAMAYANA and the MAHABHARRATA. Popular songs were modified to show that the great warrior dynasties in the epics, the brahmins traced back to Divine origin, Sun God and MOON God. A kind of anthropornorphic mythology, appealing to the popular mind, was devised. The mythology greatly changed, largely shedding off its naturalistic basis, though the fertility myths retained a certain vitality. New systems came into being, in the form of stories of the geneology of Gods. Divine attributes were raised to the level of autonomous figures; TRIAD of B'rhma, Visnu and Mahesh (Siva), while minor gods were also drawn into the wake of great Gods. B'rhma, the one sole, self existing supreme self, the only real existing eternal essence, who exercises itself in infinite expansion, in infinite manifestations of itself, in infinite creation, dissolution, recreation, through infinite varieties and diversities of operation; the old supreme principle (Neuter) of the Vedas, was developed into the outer God in this secondary 'Hindu Trinity B'rhma still remains devoid of cult and schematic representation. The brahmins attributed all visible forms on earth, stones, mountains, rivers, plants, trees, animals, man and his emanation, to be emanations from this one entity B'rhma. The highest human manifestation of the eternal B'rhma were called Brahmins, whose condition could not be changed and who sink or rise according to their actions in this life to their next birth. Between human beings and B'rhma stood Demigods, supernatural beings, inferior gods and superior gods.

VISNU

The act of creation involved two other acts preservation and dissolution. Hence B'rhma was associated with Visnu, the preserver of the universe presiding over human destinies and representing mystical love. His posture is often passive, reclining on the cosmic serpent, or mounted on the eagle Garuda (hereditary enemy of the serpents), His four emblems; the conch, the disc, the club and the lotus are the subject of symbolical explanations. His twenty four attitudes and indeed every aspect of His being, as a focus of mystical powers. His ten incarnations (Avtaras) to save the world from evil and destruction were :- Matsya, Kurma, Varaha, K'rsna, Narasimha, Vamana, Parsurama, Rama and Buddha and the tenth, still to come KALKI. Avoiding the details of the different incarnations, suffice it to say that the first and second assisted by Gods deal with natural forces and demons, Varaha and Narasimha and also Vamana fight against particular demons, Parsurama destroys the whole fighting caste of the human kingdom, Rama fights against demon Ravana and is the cause of righteousness, an example of perfect living. K'rsna fights against warriors, against deceitfulness and evil, and inculcates the doctrine of KARMA (action) alongwith knowledge; The ninth BUDDHA teaches a way of life to the common people and complete absence of fighting. The tenth Kalki is still to come and yet to be experienced, but the speculation is that HE will conquer for all time the evil in the world, his white horse being the indication.

RUDRA SIVA

The third in the trinity, Rudra Siva (Mahesh) is above all the destroyer, who seeps away all things, who kills enemies and is identified with TIME(Kaal) and death[1]. He is 'King of the dance', originator of Music, creator of VYAKARNA(grammar) and a perfect

1. Singh C.L. : Paintings of Siva in Indian Art (1990)

householder as well as an ascetic, inventor of Yoga. His destructive activities are compensated by his attitude of favours to his devotees. His ascetic, most ancient aspect, is in the posture of a yogi, with an eye in the middle of his forehead and dressed in skulls and snakes. His mount is the white bull 'NANDI'. His essential symbol LINGA (a stylised Phallic emblem), which is the object of an independent cult.

In Brahaminism, these three Gods were all equal, none first and none third; as Kalidasa out it:-

In those three persons; the one God was shown-

Each first in place, Each last-not one alone;

Of B'rhma, Visnu, Siva each may be

First, second, third among the blessed three.

Triune coequality of the Trinity has been beautifully sculpted in a TRIMURTI in Elephanta Caves (Bombay), where out of one body, three majestic heads spring out. A cardinal feature of the Brahaminical system was that the universal spirit can never itself be, directly or spiritually worshipped, except by turning the thoughts inwards; internal knowledge (Yajna), because that spirit is enshrined in every man's heart and that internal meditation was regarded as the highest religious act leading to perfect spiritual knowledge.

In religious worship, paying homage to the supreme spirit is through his spirit as manifested in persons and objects. Supreme being may be worshipped through the worship of these three or of any one of the three, none being superior or inferior. Homage may be paid to the universal spirit by and through the worship of inferior gods (other than the Trinity), Goddesses, departed ancestors, living Brahmins, heroes, animals, plants and even stones and images, who may represent Divine presence and so become media through which great eternal spirit may become an object of adoration. The thought was worship of the supreme being, medium may be any. Belief was in one (Monotheism), as R'gveda (1.164.46; viii.58.2) quoted by M. Williams[1] states, 'That the Gods are one BEING under different names'.

The fourth phase in Brahamanism was the NOMISTIC BRAHAMANISM, in which Brahmins composed codes of law (SMRITI SASTRA, DHARAM SASTRA) and laid down precise rules for the constitution of Hindu social fabric, for the due coordination of its different orders and for the regulation of everyday domestic life. Codes of MANU, that of YAJNAVALKYA and that of PARASARA were produced. Code of Manu (MANU SMRITI) was most remarkable literary work. Originally there could have been different authors of fifth century B.C., but it was, as at present, attributed to MANU; who is supposed to have composed upto 1.60 and later ones by saint Bhrigu. The date of compilation is doubtful, but can be assumed as in fourth century A.D.

The codes of Yajnavalkaya and that of Parasara are later ones, laying additional rules. Brahamanas of ritualistic period are concerned with public Vedic rituals and sacrifice (SRUTI KARMAN) but these three codes deal with domestic ceremonies (Smriti Karman).

These three codes, still in practice, after a lapse of two thousand years, illustrate very strikingly the close inter wining of law, politics and social life with religion and religious ordinances.

MANU says; 'The root of all law is the VEDA and the tradition of those, who know the Veda.' The superiority of the brahmins is the hinge on which the whole social organisation turns, other castes revolve like satellites around it. The doctrine of Manu was that the deity created distinct kinds of men like different varieties

---

1. Williams M : RELIGIOUS LIFE IN ANCIENT INDIA

of plants and animals, and that Brahmins, Kshatriyas (soldiers) Vaishayas (Merchants) and Sudras (servants) were born and not made; as elephants, lions, oxen and dogs; wheat, barley, rice and beans; different from the very creation. Perfection is attained by him alone, who is a strict observer of his duties of his caste, as explained by K'rsna to Arjuna in the MAHABHARATTA, when Arjuna was reluctant to fight against his teacher, elders and relations. This was ARYA DHARMA, the system of law and religion prevelant among the Aryas and the creed of BRAHAMANISM. Thus HINDUISM as Brahamanism, quite apart from religious teachings lays down social codes and rules about marriage, inheritance, civil and criminal law, political organisation, and indeed almost everything else. In other words, it lays down a complete structure for society and try to perpetuate this by giving it religious sanction and authority. It is a system of living. It has gone farthest in this respect by its rigid system of caste. This religious perpetuation of a social structure makes change difficult.

CHAPTER - 10

ROYAL PATRONAGE OF HINDUISM

(6th Century B.C.- 12th Cent : A.D.)

Many kingdoms and republics have been mentioned during the period (6th - 4th centuries B.C.), but their history and religious beliefs are obscure, except for Maghada. Kingdoms mentioned with their modern cities were :- ANGA (Monghyr and Bhagalpur), KASI (Varanasi), VATSA (Allahabad), KURU (Indraprastha, Delhi), PANCHALA (Foothill of Himalayas in Uttar Pradesh), MALLA (Gorakhpur), MATSYA and CHEDI (Jaipur, Alwar, Bharatpur), SURASENA(Yamuna valley), AVANTI (western Malwa), ASMAKA (Indus valley), GANDHARA(Peshawar, Rawalpindi, Taxilla), KAMBOJA (Rajori, Hazara, N.W.F.P.), VRIJI (North Bihar, Mithila, Videha), KOSALA (Oudh, Ayodhya), and MAGHADA (Rajgir, Gaya, Patna).

Hinduism, during the early days of the Maghada ascendancy had eventful change within the fold of Brahmanism. Old ideas changed, new ones sprang up into vigorous life. Popular cults and beliefs were recognised, by upper classes. Humanitarian and theistic movements gathered force and momentum as popular faith in animal sacrifice and barren ritual tended to diminish with the growth of free speculation according to Upanishads. Spiritual leadership passed from the hands of priestly theologians and sacrificers to ascetics and wanderers, who laid the utmost stress on NON INJURY to living beings and the cessation of craving for the things of the world (materialistic).

Vedic rain God INDRA and PRAJANYA were still revered, as mentioned in the ritual of GRIHEY SUTRA and PRAJANYA in Buddhist Suttonias. Brahamanical texts refer to the growing popularity of Vaisravana, Kumara (Karttikeye) and the Goddess UMA Himavati (Parvati) and VASINI: different aspects of mother Goddess Durga, the consort of Siva. Spirits dwelling in waters, herbs, trees were also recognised side by side of the Divinities Vaisravana points to the influence of YAKSHA CULT, attested by epic and Buddhist evidence.

The cult of trees and water deities like the GANGES is noted by Curtius and Strabo and the boon giving KALPA VRIKSHA, occurs prominently in literature including that of the Jainas. Most of the deities, by now, had thoroughly anthropomorphised and become quite human in dress. talk and action. With it came the increased use of the images and the construction of temples for prayers and daily service. Icons were known and vedic texts mention some images. A passage from QUINTUS Curtius mentions the first historical reference to image worship; image of Herakles; an image carried in front of the PURUVA army, as it advanced against Alexander. Patanjali refers to the exhibition and sale of images of Siva, Skanda and Vaisakha by the Maurayas. Temples of a primitive kind have been mentioned in SATPATHA BRAHAMANA. Epics clearly refer to temples sacred to deities. Brahmins did not east flesh of animals and growing feeling of reverence for the cow took hold. The Doctrine of AHIMSA or non injury was specially inculcated by the ascetics and wanderers, who had great influence. Onesikritos, accompanying Alexander in 326 B.C. on invasion on Taxilla has given an account : a glimpse of the ascetics. Doctrine of SAMSARA (belief in repeated transmigration) and doctrine of KARMA (law of the deed-action) were two most important religious. concepts of the period. This doctrine of KARMA is preached, among others, by Vasud vakas, later Bhagvatas. They teach Bhakti in Vasudeva(K'rsna Devkiputra), who is identified in an ARANYAKA with VISNU (Narayana). They preach doctrines of NISHKAMA

KARMA (deed done without seeking any reward) and loving faith (Bhakti) in a God of GRACE (Prasada). Bhaktas of Vasudeva, followers of Bhagvad Gita in Mahabharatta, can be identified with the worshippers of Indian Herakles, whose cult was popular with the Surasenas of Mathura, in the fourth century B.C. Rival sects, most notable being Siva sects called Saivites (Siva Bhaktas), Maheshwaras and Pashupats appeared. Svetasvatara Upanishad mentions Siva as the Lord (Isa or Isna) of the universe, the BHAGVAT or the Blessed One, the object of devotion to the faithful. By devoting oneself to HIM, ignorance is depleted, the nooses of death are snapped and eternal peace is attained.

The new theistic sects, Bhagvatas and Siva Bhagvatas and others preserved their separate entity, yet they did not break away altogether from Brahamanism, and attempts were made for a synthesis in the epic period. Gods of Bhagvatas and Pasupatas (Siva sect) were recognised as emanations of the supreme divinity of Brahamanism.

Buddhism and Jainism, though believing in the doctrine of transmigràtion and Karma, rejected the authority of the Vedas and Vedic priests, denounced blood sacrifices, brahamanical rituals and even denied the existence of God. Right conduct was the way of getting out of the meshes of Karma and Samsara and according to them, the practice of AHIMSA or noninjury to living things was one of the essential constituents of right conduct. Surprisingly these two sects were founded by two scions of Kshatriya clans; Vardhamana Mahavira of Jnatrika clan of Kundapura (Kundagram) near Vaisali in North Bihar and by GATAM BUDDHA, prince of the Sakya clan of Kapilavastu near Rummindei in Nepal Terai. During the Mauryan period (324 BC - 184 BC), there was growing influence of Buddhism and Jainism, and Brahamanism was on the decline. Sacrifices were no longer common. Cults of Siva and Visnu replaced the worship of the old Vedic Gods; Indra, Varuna, Agni and others. Buddhism and Jainism were popular, but there was no persecution of forced conversion. There was perfect freedom of worship to followers of all religions, irrespective of the religious faith of the ruler. Even the great exponent of Buddhism; ASOKA, the great, a great innovator, took pride in calling himself devanampiya (beloved of the Gods). The vedas did not completely loose their hold on the people. Kautilya extolled the Vedic way of life. He prescribed the Vedic sacraments (Samskaras) of CHAULA KARMA, UPANAYANA, GODANA etc. Magesthenese as Dionysus mentions Siva and Sam Karashna and Herakles (may be K'rsna) at Mathura. ARTHASASTRA mentions SHRI, who could be identified as SHRI LAKSHMI (consort of Visnu). According to Kautilya, the worship of these deities consisted of prostration (Prampala), offering of gifts (Upahara) to the deity. Flowers and incense were essential constituents of the offering. Popular belief in malevolent spirits, magical practices and superstitions of all kinds have been mentioned in KAUTILYA ARTHSASTRA. Whereas Buddhism flourished, a great brahamanical revival followed the rise of the houses of Pushyamitra, Simuka Satavahana and Varman Pallava. Rites like Asvamedha and Vajapeya came to be celebrated by the princes on a grand scale. Bhagvatism or Vaisnuism showed great missionary activity. Heliodoros, the ambassador of Antiolkidas, king of Taxilla set up a Garuda column at Besnagar in honour of Vasudeva the God of Gods. The in honour of Vasudeva, the God of Gods. The cult of Vasudeva and Sankarshana (K'rsna and his brother) prevailed specially in Central India and the Deccan. Rival cult of Siva enjoyed the patronage of KADPHISES II and Vasudeva Kushan.

In the POST MAURYAN period (184 B.C. - 300 A.D.). heretical attack on Vedic institutions and sacrifices seriously undermined the prestige and authority of the brahmins. Therefore Brahmanical religion underwent some important changes. Most of the Vedic Gods passed into oblivion and their place was taken by Trinity of Gods; B'rhma, Visnu and Siva. In course of time, Visnu and Siva emerged as the most important Gods of the Brahmanical pantheon. Two main sects Bhagvatas and Pasupatas prevailed. Visnu, the supreme God, awoke from his bed on thousand headed snake Shesha and made Vaikunth, his abode. He observes the world, when evil is rampant, he appears in various incarnations to save the mankind. SIVA, evolved from R'gvedic God RUDRA and Tamil God MURUGAN. Non aryan fertility cults : phallic emblem LINGAM and the bull Nandi emerged with the worship of Siva.

Phallic cult, traceable since Harrappan period, was incorporated in Brahamanism around the beginning of christian era. Siva in Linga has been worshipped, the earliest representation of Siva in his human form in the village of GUDIMALLAM, near Madras, where a five feet high and extremely realistic phallic emblem bears upon it the malformed dwarf, on whose shoulder stands a two armed figure of the God, holding a ram in his right hand and a water vessel and a battle axe in the left one, with his sex mark prominently shown below the diaphanous loin cloth.

Simultaneously with those Gods in symbolic and human form, a variety of popular cults animals, trees, mountain and rivers were associated with Divinity. The cow became an object of worship, the snake (centre of primitive fertility rites), Baikunth mountain of Visnu, Kailasa mountain of Siva, were also identified.

Tree cults from primitive levels were also absorbed into Brahmanical faith viz the PIPPAL or ASHVATTHA, Vata (Banyan), TULSI (Basil herb)became sacred. Waters of the Ganges were held sacred as spring from the feet of Visnu through the matted hair locks of Siva, The Brahamanical religion, which evolved through a process of syncretism with popular cults, which had primitive roots, was now based on the doctirne of BHAKRI, later clearly ostensibly expounded by K'rsna in BHAGVADGITA.

The religious importance, previously enjoyed by Vedic texts, now came to be attached to the epics; the RAMAYANA and the MAHABHARATTA and the PURANAS, Brahmins revised the epics to give them a religious character. GITA dated around second century B.C. contained seven hundred tightly woven stanzas, became the first basic text of the Vaisnuites. MANU SMRITI and MAHABHARATTA have hundreds of verses in common. BHARATA, during this period, compiled NATYASASTRA, the first important work on dramaturgy.

Gupta period (300 AD - 500 AD) is described as the Golden age in Hindu kingship. Shanti Parava of MAHABHARATTA contain nine verses which stress the need of combination by brahmins with Kshatriyas. Brahmins had established themselves as religious priests and with the advent of Buddhism and Jainism, Kshatriyas also trespassed into the realm of religion and may be, on account of this, need for a combination of the two was realised. This combination was opposed by Vaishyas and Shudras. Shudras were particularly hostile. Anushasana Parva of Mahabharatta represents them as destroyers of the king. Another document describes them as hostile, violent, boastful, short tempered, untruthful, extremely greedy, ungrateful, heterodox, lazy and impure. Conflicts between them and higher castes existed, but there is no record of a revolt.

Theory of KARMA (deed - action) emphasised that the character, fortune, social status, happiness or sorrow of a person depended on his actions in his previous birth. This doctrine appealed to all castes (Varnas), for even a Shudra could hope to be reborn as a king in his next birth, if his Karmic sheet (table of actions) in present birth was favourable. DOCTRINE OF BHAKTI, enunciated in Gita and a vital force in Vaisnuism and Saivism became socially more relevant during Gupta period. It preached that one could attain salvation through devotion and faith in God, and not just by performing sacrifices. Special features of Bhakti cult were : Belief in personal God; faith in Avataras of God; belief in Ahimsa; denunciation of sacrifices and construction of temples.

THEORY OF INCARNATION (Avataras) also became more meaningful during this period. VAYU PURANA, compiled during this period mentions Narayana, Nara Simha and Vamana as divine incarnations and others as human ones. Out of the ten incarnations of Visnu, mentioned earlier, KALKI is still to come. Visnu, as Kalki is supposed to appear at the end of KALIYUGA, on a white horse to uproot the malechhas (wicked, evil doers) and restore Dharma. Saivites have also adopted this doctrine as twenty eight manifestations of Siva, more or less imitations of Visnu incarnations.

MOTHER GODDESSES; female divinities attained a high position of importance during this period. Although they were always worshipped in Hinduism, but now they emerged from obscurity and came to be associated with important brahmanical Gods; Shri or Lakshmi, the Goddess of wealth and plenty, consort of Visnu, became popular among vaishyas and Shudras; in the times of SKANDA GUPTA. PARVATI, consort of Siva was first artistically presented in the epigraph of KUMARA GUPTAI.

SAKTI CULT, which preached that the male could be activated only through union with a female, was assimilated into the brahmanical pantheon. Later this Sakti cult developed the TANTRIC sect in early medieval period. Visnuism became popular with all varnas because there was adoption of various deities, beliefs and superstitions, assimilation of different popular cults and substitution of faith for logic.

SAIVISM was equally revered. It also received Royal support, Two Siva temples at NACHNAKUTTARA (Ruhelkhand) and NAGOD(Madhya Pradesh) of GUPTA royalty have still survived. SANCHI, LADH KHAN, Deogarh, Bhaitargaon, Tigawa and Bhumara temples date back to Gupta period. BAGH caves, AJANTA caves and BADAMI cave paintings supply the norm for all contemporary painting.

Six schools of PHILOSOPHICAL thought (Shaddarshana) came up during this golden age. The six systems are NYANA (analysis), VAISHESHIKA(individual characteristics), SANKHYA (enumeration), YOGA (application), MIMANSA (inquiry) and VEDANTA (end of the Vedas).

VEDANTA (uttaramimansa), originated from the Vedas, rejected theories of Non brahamanical schools. BADRAYANA and GAUDAPADA (6th Cent : AD) formulated its main tenets but most forceful exposition is by SANKARA OCHARAYA (8th - 9th Cent AD), when Vedanta became an immortal theme of Indian philosophy.

Before discussing Vedanta and Sankaraacharaya in greater details, a glimpse of Hinduism as patronised by South India Rulers is necessary, because it was in the South that development of Hinduism continued uninfluenced.

CHALUKYAS of Vatapi or Badami (550-746 A.D.) were Hindu rulers, who built several temples, decorated them with exquisite sculpted images. Badami cave paintings are a rich treasure of ART.

PALLAVAS of Kanchi (3rd CAD - 655 A.D.) were responsible for building some beautiful temples. Famous rock cut RATHS or the seven pagodas were built by NARSIMHA VARMAN I and his successor built magnificent temple of KAILASHNATH at Kanchi, and the shore temple at Mamallapuram. Kanchi, the capital of Pallavas, was a great seat of learning in South India, where Sanskrit was the medium of instruction.

RASHTRAKUTTAS (753-953 AD) : KRISHNA I (754 - 773 AD) was a great lover of art and built the famous rock cut temple Kailash at ELLORA. Numerous temples were built by Rashtrakuta rulers. AMOGHA VARSHA I (815 - 877 AD) was a noted writer, who adopted jainism.

CHOLAS of Tanjore (I cent AD - 1054 AD):- RAJA RAJA Temple of Siva at Tanjore was constructed by RAJA RAJA I (985 - 1016 AD). Its walls were inscribed with his achievements. RAJENDRA CHOLA (1016 - 1044 AD) also built many temples. These massive temples were beautifully decorated with fine workmanship in sculpture. Two largest and most interesting temples to Lord SIVA were built by KULOTTUNGA I; a chola chalukya line emperor 1070 as AIRAVATESWARA and KAMPAHARESWARA in Tanjore district.

Hinduism, Buddhism and Jainism, all three thrived in South India also. Large temples, far more famous and artistic than the temples of North, were built in South. The subjects enjoyed perfect freedom of worship and under royal patronage, literature, art and architecture made remarkable progress.

Hinduism produced some outstanding reformers known as Acharayas. They travelled from place to place singing hymns in praise of SIVA and VISNU. They reformed the Hindu system and initiated a new movement called the Bhakti cult. Sankara acharaya, by his forceful logic, shook the faith of the people in Buddhism and once again Hinduism was revived in full force.

CHAPTER - 11

VISNU - VISNUVITES — AND VISNUISM

Visnu, the pervader from the root VISH (to pervade), the God of protection in the Hindu Trinity the embodiment of Satavaguna. He is associated with the watery element and is called NARAYANA, 'moving in the waters', and is represented as slumbering in SESHA, king of serpents floating on the waters. His avtaras (incarnations) are ten in number. He has a thousand names. His wife is LAKSMI or Sri, Goddess of fortune. His abode is Vaikunth and his vehicle Garuda. Aittareya Brahamana of the R'gveda states, Fire (Agni) has the lowest place among the Gods; VISNU the highest; between them stand all the other deities. Narayana is the supreme spirit Visnu, as moving in the waters, according to MANU SMRITI (1.10). Visnu is thus represented reposing on the thousand headed serpent Ananta, and floating on the ocean. ANANTA denotes cosmic energy and the ocean symbolises Ananda or endless bliss and grace of B'rhma.

Visnu, irrespective of his incarnations, has a material character and an individuality of his own. He is described as living in Vaikunth (heaven); a locality on the slope of world mountain MOUNT MIRU (80,000 miles in circumference, made of gold and precious jewels. This spot is more inaccessible and less easy to identify with any definite spot on earth. Ganges flows through it, said to be originating from Visnu's feet. His wife is Lakshmi or Sri, the Goddess of fortune and beauty, who sprung out of the churning of the ocean. Visnu, with Lakshmi, in non avtara condition, live a life, which has fewer features in common with humanity, unlike

Siva and Parvati. The blue colour given to Visnu symbolises INFINITY. His chakras (discus) denotes DHARMA (righteousness) and order in the universe. The SANKHA (Conch) is for the removal of ignorance and is also symbolic of music of the COSMOS (NADA B'rhma). The GADA or mace is for removing the evil in the world; and the LOTUS is the symbol of beauty and purity of the cosmic universe. His vehicle is GARUDA, the man eagle, a figure of great strength, power and piety. More human sides of Visnu and Lakshmi, as God and Goddess, is reserved in their incarnations of Visnu as RAMA and K'rsna and of Lakshmi as SITA and RADHA. BHOODEVI or mother earth, is depicted as second consort of Visnu.

Visnu's separate personality, as distinct from his avtaras, has been described in the PURANAS. Accordingly, he has a peculiar auspicious mark (Sri Vatsa) on his breast (peculiar twist or curl of the hair). He has four arms, and holds a symbol in each of his four hands; viz a wheel or circular weapon (chakra) called SUDARSHANA, a conch shell called PANCHAJANYA, a Gada called KAUMODAKI, and a lotus PADMA, described earlier. Bearing in mind Visnu's connection with the sun, the wheel (discus) may be regarded as emblametical of the Sun's circular course in the heavens. In the later mythology, it is supposed to represent a missile weapon hurled by Visnu like a quoit, at the demons who are ever plotting against Gods and men, and with whom He is always at war. Chief demons destroyed by Visnu or K'rsna were Madhu, Kanca, Bana, Bali, Mura etc. The conch shell is blown by him like a trumpet in his battles; its miraculous sound filling his enemies with terror and helping him to secure victory. The mace, also used in battles, but he is also armed with a wonderful bow called SARANGA and a sword NANDAKA. He has a jewel on his wrist named SYAMANTAKA, and another on his breast called KAUSTUBHA. Garuda, semihuman, may be a personification of the sky or ethereal element which supports Visnu, (identified with the Sun) one of whose names is VAYU VAHANA (Air borne vehicle). Details of the characteristics of Garuda have been given in a subsequent chapter 'Fauna in Hinduism'.

In R'gveda (I.22.16.17), Visnu is a form of the evermoving Solar orb. He is striding through the seven worlds, consisting of seven lower regions (Atala, Vitala, Sutala, Rasatala, Talatala, Mahatala and Patala), seven lokas or worlds (Bhur: Earth, Bhuvar, Svar, Mahab, Janab, Tapab and B'rhma or Sateye). Bhur (earth), Bhuvr (atmosphere) and Svar (heaven) are supposed to comprehend all the worlds; in three steps and enveloping the universe with the dust of his beams.

Though Visnu existed as a God in vedic times, his role as preserver is essentially a late development. It can be assumed under two heads; First the theory of Samsara, which teaches that every human is born many times over and that each life represents a punishment or a reward for his previous life, according to how well he had performed his Dharma (path of duty assigned). If in each life, he has faithfully performed his duty, he may hope to progress steadily upwards, until he becomes a saint, or even a deity. On the other hand, if he does not perform his duty, he progresses as steadily, towards life as a demon. The second assumption is that Gods and demons represent the two poles of existence. Both are active in the world, a constant struggle being carried between the two forces. Normally good and evil are evenly matched in the world; at times, however the balance is destroyed and evil is deemed unfair to humans, when it takes the upper hand. At such times, Visnu, as preserver, intervenes by descending to earth in human incarnation (Avtara).

Visnu is a God, who is equated with Prajapati, the creator and supreme God. As Prajapati, he encompasses B'rhma, Visnu as preserver and Siva as destroyer. Visnu is a God, who could satisfy the yearnings of the heart for a religion of faith, love and prayer. As the preserver, he is the embodiment of the quality of mercy and goodness, the self existent, all pervading power, which preserves and maintains the universe and the cosmic order and Dharma. Visnu is the cosmic ocean, NARA, which spread everywhere before the creation of the universe. B'rhma is sometimes said to have arisen from a lotus growing from Visnu' naval, as he slept thus. After each destruction of the universe, Visnu resumes this posture. His mildness combined with his power, proves him to be the greatest of Gods. Visnu, as preserver, is the object of the devotion rather than that of fear (as in Siva) and this affection is similarly extended to his consort Laksmi, Goddess of fortune.

Visnu, the God who evinced his sympathy with mundane suffering, his interest in human affairs, and his activity in the welfare of all created things, by frequent descents (avtaras) on earth, not only in the form of men, but also of animals and even of plants and stones. Avtaras are not chance events, but during each incarnation, Visnu has a specific task to perform.

AVTARAS (INCARNATIONS)

In the light of etymology, AVATARA is the Godhead's crossing over from the celestial regions down to the earth. The doctrine of AVATARA in Hinduism is that the ONE who is presented in a carnation is at the same time the transcendent Deity, the changeless and Supreme, and also the fulfilment of all human aspirations.

VISNU, the God, assumes concrete form and shape, intervenes in history, delivers the pious when they are in distress and also restores morality, piety, virtue etc., when they are on the decline.

The idea of incarnation, which was unknown to the Aryans, and is never mentioned in the VEDAS, appeared about the year 700 B.C. and was developed to the point where any Deity, hero, spirit or human being might be an incarnation of any other. By applying the principle to the old and new Gods, it became possible to claim that the priests were really worshipping the same deity as the common people under another name and in another incarnation or Avtara. Alternatively the brahmins might contrive that resurgent old traditions or new practices be justified on the basis of their supposed proclamation in the past, preferably by one of the Major Gods. Thus the Pre-Aryan worship of cobras is incorporated into the Siva cult, because Siva is said to have told the people to worship cobras in order to make them safe.

Although VISNU has 1,000 names, given in Anusasna Parva of the MAHABHARATTA (1144-1266, 6950-7056), some of them common with Siva, but his addicts and characteristics can be fully understood in his appearance in incarnations (Avataras), described in brief in this book.

It is sometimes thought that Visnu is called upon to descend to earth, once in each cycle of the universal time, as an avatara. There are ten avaratas in the present Mahayuga (cycle), the first four of the following having been in Kretayuga. Later texts say that there are twentyfour, and some say innumerable.

MATSYAAVATARA (FISH INCARNATION)

The legend is that a RAJA MANU, having withdrawn himself from all wordly concerns, in the Dravida country, in the city of Bhadravati, during the Satye yuga, lived in great austerities. On the banks of river Kritamla, he, on request caught a small fish and put it into the cup. The cup could hold that no longer and increased day by day, so much so that that had to be put in the ocean through the Ganges. Rajamanu realised the Divine grace in the fish and requested for a revelation. He heard, 'I am the supreme Being. I have assumed the form of this creature for thy salvation and that of a few of the elect. After seven days, the world will be destroyed and a flood shall cover the earth. Get thou into a certain ark with a few of the righteous together with the divine books and choice medicinal herbs a fasten the ark to this horn which cometh out of me.' This story is told in the MAHABHARATTA with reference to the Matsya Purana.

KURMAAVATARA (TORTOISE INCARNATION)

In the sateya Yuga, in the light half of the month of Kartikeye, on the twelth day (lunar day), Visnu infused a portion of his essence into the body of an immense tortoise to aid in producing or recovering certain valuable articles, lost in the sea. For this purpose, he (tortoise avtara) stationed himself at the bottom of the sea of milk (one of the seven concentric circular seaso surrounding the seven concentric circular continents of the earth, that his back might serve as a pivot, for churning of the sea, from which among 14 articles recovered by Gods, one was the Nectar conferring immortality called AMRITA.

VARAHAAVATARA (BOAR INCARNATION)

IN The SATEYA YUGA (KRITA YUGA), On The Day of THE FULL MOON, in the month of Kattikeye, in the city of Brahmavarta near Nimishara and Ayodhya, this avatara took place. Vishnu infused a portion of his essence into the body of a huge boar, symbolical of strength who was to deliver the world from the power of the demon Hiranyaksha who had seized the earth and had carried it down into the ocean.. Boar avatara upheaced it from the watery grave and made it fit to be reinhabited.

NARA SINHA AVATARA (MAN LION INCARNATION)

The fourth avatara to have incarnated in the Krita (Sateye)

yuga, was a form, which from head to the waist was like a lion and the lower parts resembling a man. This is said to have been manifested on the fourteenth of the light half of the month of Vaisakha, in the city of Hiranyapura (Hindaun). Hiranyakasipu, a demon , had by extreme austerities obtained aboon that his death would not occur by day or by night, and further that his death should not be caused by any animal (which he named) and that he would gain sovereignity over all realms above and below. With this boon and the power, Hiranyakasipu appropriated the sacrifices intended for Gods and filled the world with unrighteousness. When his son Prahalad praised Visnu, the tyrant wished to kill Prahalad. At that very time Visnu as Narasinha Avatara, appeared out of the centre of a pillar and tore the demon.

VAMANA (DWARF INCARNATION)

In the TRETA Yuga, on the twelfth day of the light half of the month of Bhadrapada (Aug - Sep), in the city of Sonbhadra, on the banks of river Narbada, this new avtara form was born of Aditi in the house of Kashyapa, the son of Marichi, the son of B'rhma. The avtara was incarnated to wrest from the tyrant demon Bali, who by severe austerities had obtained the sovereignity of the three worlds. Bali, divided the kingdom under personalities and himself undertook sacrifices to Gods. The Gods, having lost their kingdom Heaven, were anxious to restore it. So they requested Visnu. The moon orb, displayed its radiance, when the child grew in wisdom, he was placed under training of sage Bhardwaja. With his preceptor, the dwarf avatara attended the sacrifice of Bali. When Bali, as per custom, asked the dwarf to seek a boon, he asked, (I ask of thee as much ground as I can cover in three steps. The request was granted and the dwarf was asked to take the steps. The first step was so great that

---

NOTE : TIME OF APPEARANCE OF DIFFERENT AVATARAS (ABUL FAẒL = A-in-z̄-Akbarz̄)

it covered the whole earth including the lower regions. The subsequent two steps covered the celestial world in the second, but the third was left to the king in compassion. The universal sovereignity of the king was lost and became those of the Gods.

PARASURAMA AVATARA (INCARNATION OF RAMA WITH THE AXE)

PARASU means Axe, so the name of the Avatara. Visnu came into the world as Parsurama, the youngest son a strict brahmin hermit Jamadagini. One day Jamdagini's wife happened to see a young couple frolicking in the pool, and was filled with impure thoughts. When Jamadagini learnt, he asked his sons to strike off their mother's head, but none agreed. It was only the youngest Parasurama, who obeyed the order. The brahmin was pleased with Parasurama and asked him for a boon. Parasurama asked the restoration of life to his mother. So granted, the family lived happily.

One day, king Kshatriye Kartavitya came to the ashram, when Jamadagini's was alone. The king saw their cow KAMDHENU and asked her to give that away. Not agreeing, the king forcibly drove away the cow, When Parsurama, heard of this, he was enraged and killed Kartavira and brought back the cow. The king's sons invaded the ashram and killed Jamadagini. Pursurama could not tolerate this and other atrocities of the Kshatriyas. So he was determined to take vengeance, and to destroy the whole caste.

In the RAMAYANA, Parasurama was annoyed with RAMA for having broken the Bow given to Parsurama by Lord Siva. He challenged Rama to a dual, but was defeated. Parsurama, having achieved his goal of killing Kshatriyas and disgraced by a defeat from Rama, retired to the mountains. Because of a fight with RAMA Avatara, Parsurama was not given a seat in celestial world. He is still believed to be living and his habitation is pointed out in the mountain Mahendra of the Konkan[1].

Parsurama, is said to have been born in the house of Jamadagini, at Renukatta, near Agra, on the third day of the light half of the month of Vaisakha, in the Treta Yuga.

RAMA AVATARA (RAMCHANDRA)

The story of Visnu's seventh Avtara Rama, is well known and the Epic The RAMAYANA describes it in all details. It is a story of ideal behaviour in all walks of life, obedience, and actions and deeds in the cause of righteousness. The literature of the RAMAYANA is sufficiently well known, to be described anymore in this book.

KRISHNA AVATARA (K'rsna)

More than 4,000 years ago, Daityas Jarasandha, Sisupala, and other princes of the Daityas and rebellious son Kansa (son of Yadu race Ugarasen) of Mathura, exercised unbounded tyranny over the earth, which was unable to stand cruelty anymore. On PRITHVI (EARTH) request supported by a B'rhma and other Gods, Visnu agreed to incarnate and relieve the terrorism. Visnu, therefore appeared as KRISHNA (K'rsna), whose life right from childhood his playful actions with cowherds, His dallies with cow girls devotion to Radha, killing of the serpent KALIYA and later killing Kansa and other daitya demons are deeds of his childhood and younger age. Later his role in the MAHABHARATTA and his gospel of SRIMAD BHAGWADGITA, the sermon of KARMA and Jnana, are well known to every person. Therefore details are not given in this book.

---

1. ABUL-FAZL : The A 1 N-1 AKBARĪ; Vol. 2

In the beginning of KALI Yuga, on the eighth lunar day of the month of BHADRAPADA (Aug-Sep), in the city of Mathura, Krsna is said to have born, who lived one hundred and twenty five years and died as a king in Dwarika, which is said to have submerged in the ocean with him. The present Dwarika, near OKHA in Kathiawad is different.

BUDDHA AVATARA

Buddha, ninth Avatara of Visnu, appearing at the start of the Kaliyuga, was born of Maya in the house of Raja Sudhodhana of the race of Ramachandra in the city of Magadh.

It is said that as many sacrifices were performed at that period and the number of animals sacrificed was very large, Visnu willed to appear in human form to condemn the Vedic institutions and their sacrificial rites. For this reason, He became incarnate and lived to the age of a hundred years. The Brahmins appropriated Buddha much as some of them are now appropriating Christ, as an incarnate of Visnu.

KALKI AVATARA

This avatara of Visnu is yet to come, and will come when the life on earth would have degenerated to the lowest point, that is the end of the Kaliyuga. At this point of degeneration, Visnu will appear in person on earth, riding a white horse, Kalki Avatar. Riding through the earth, slaughtering the wicked still left with his sword blazing like a comet. He will accomplish the final destruction of the wicked and prepare for the renewal of creation and the resurgence of virtue in the next mahayuga.

All the four Yugas, (Satye (Kreat), Dwapar, Treta and Kali) will end. SURYA SIDDHANTA STATES THE DURATION OF KALIYUGA as 432,000 years, having commenced in 3102 B.C. or 1177 B.C. two different opinions. The duration of the previous

Yugas is stated as KRETA-Satye (1,728,0000, Treta 1,296,000) and Dwapar (864,000) years.

VISNUISM, VAISHNAVISM, VISHNUISM

Visnuism, unlike Sivaism, depends more on personal leadership and influence, is one of perpetual decay and revival, collapse and recovery. Its fluctuations resemble those of a vast ocean having this way and that in continual flux and reflux.

Intense faith in a personal God is the chief characteristic of Visnuism. Irrespective of brahmins and their motivated preachings, the mass of the people exalt Divine kings, Government and heroic leaders as forms of power and worship every great righteous leader as an incarnation of the deity, such as RAMA, K'rsna.

Visnuism is , like Buddhism, the most tolerant of Hinduism systems. it is always ready to accommodate itself to other creeds, and delights in appropriating to itself the religions ideas of all the nations of the world. It admits of every form of internal development. It has an organised hierarchy under ONE supreme head, but it may have any number separate associations under separate leaders, who are ever banding themselves together for the extension of spiritual supremacy over ever increasing masses of population. It has no formal confession of faith, but it has an elastic creed capable of adapting to all varieties of opinion and practice, It has no one Bible or Quran, no one collection of writings in one compact volume. It has a series of sacred books, called PURANAS, each of which professes to be as direct revelation from the SUPREME BEING, and each of which may be used as an authority for the establishment of almost any kind of doctrine. It can, like Brahamanism, be pantheistic, monotheistic, dualistic or polytheistic, It can like Sivaism, enjoin asceticism, self mortification and austerity. It can like Saktism, give the reigns to self indulgence, licentiousness and carnality, It can, like Buddhism, preach liberty, quality, fraternity, or inculcate universal benevolence, brotherhood and avoidance of injury to others. It can proclaim Buddha or any other teacher or remarkable man to be an incarnation of Visnu. it can even set face against Image worship, as in the case of kabir. it can look with sympathising condescension on any other religion. It is owing to this all comprehensiveness of the Visnava system that any new doctrine or any new view of old doctrines may be promulgated by any man of originality and ability, with an almost certain prospect of success.

VAISNUITES

Vaisnuites are believers in one personal God VISNU, not only as the preserver, but also as above every other God, including Siva. Their one God, in fact exists in an external body, which is antecedent to his earthly incarnations and survives all such incarnations. It is a form of monotheism, The primary idea of a good Vaisnu is permeating and infusing His essence into material objects was originally connected with the personification of the infinite heavenly space.

Among the Vaisnavas, there are four main sects:-

(1) SRI SAMPRADAYA (Vasistadvaita) of Ramanuja :

The followers are called Shri vaisnavas or Panchratras or Bhagvatas and Satvatas. Their sacred literature is Vaisnava agamas; PANCHRATRA and Vaikhanasa; generally divided like Siva Agamas viz. into Jnana, Yoga, Kriya and Charaya.

(2) BRAHMA SAMPRADAYA (Dvaita) of Madhava achaya; also called Anand Tirtha and a branch Chaitanya Sampradaya.

(3) RUDRA SAMPRADAYA (Shuddh advaita) of Visnuswami of Vallabha.

(4) SANKA SAMPRADAYA (Dvaita advaita) of Nimbarka.

The ALWAR saints are the most ancient Vaisnavas, the sect

founded by a Tamil saint poet of South India. Their hymns are full of intense devotional love for Visnu. ALWAR means one, who has a mystic intutive knowledge of God and who has merged himself in the Divine contemplation. The alwars were succeeded by the theologian philosophers called Acharaya who provided philosophical basis for the personal theism of Alwars and tried to combine their doctrines of BHAKTI with KARMA and JNANA.

NATHUMANI was the first acharaya of vaisnuism. He was the disciple of the last Alwar: Madhura Kavi Alwar. He compiled Nayatattava, the first work of Visistadvaita.

YAMUNAACHARAYA was the grandson of Nathumani, who expounded the doctrines of Visistadvaita in his SIDDHI TREYA, Ramanuja became deeply attracted towards him, after hearing his hymns.

RAMANUJA wrote SRI BHASHAYA, a commentary on the Brahamsutra and also Geeta Bhashaya, Vedanta Sarani, Vedanta Dipa, Gadya traya, and Vedanta Sangreheya. One day he was in great distress and he seems to have heard the voice of God saying, 'I am the Supreme reality, the illustrious possessor of SRI, the Divine power; Identity is in and through difference complete surrender to ME is the way to liberation; individual effort is not so necessary (as the Divine Grace); liberation is bound to follow after death; MAHAPURANA is the best of the teachers.'

Two centuries after Ramanuja (1017 - 1137), two schools were formed viz VADAGALAI or the Northern school and TENGALAI or the Southern school, among the followers of Ramanuja.

VADAGALAIS, founded by Venkatanatha, follow Sanskrit literature, believe that one has to purify in order to receive Divine Grace; one has to renounce everything else and has to make individual effort to cling to God in order to receive his grace.

TENGALAIS or LOKACHARAYA (Southern school)

Tengalais follow Tamil PRABANDHAM as authoritative and is indifferent to Sanskrit canon. They believe that GOD enjoys sin and that no individual effort is necessary for the attainment of Divine Grace. GOD bestows his GRACE on the sinner and lifts him above.

The philosophy, faith and beliefs of the followers of the Acharyas have been discussed in the next chapter, ' ADVAITA VEDANTA PERIOD'.

An ACHARYA, for vaisnuites, is regarded as little inferior to K'rsna himself, and may even be identified with him. He receives homage as a visible and tangible mediator between earth and heaven, a mediator between themselves and GOD.

All the Vaisnava sects are more or less opposed to the pure NON DUALITY (Advaita) of Sankaracharaya, which makes the spirit of man identical with one spirit of the universe (Atman - soul) B'rhma.

VAISNU SCRIPTURES

The Purusa - Sukta of R'GVEDA is the foundation of the Vaisanava philosophy. The SHATPATA BRAHAMANA tells us that NARAYANA (Visnu), by performing the Panchratra sacrifice became the GREAT BEING, the transcendent as well as the immanent.

In the MAHABHARATTA, NARA and NARAYANA worship the changeless B'rhma. Vaisanava Upanishads are like Avyakta, K'rsna, Narayana and Gopalatapini. Puranas : Visnu, Bhagvata, Garuda, Padma, Varaha favour Panchrataras.

Kurma, Vayu, Agni and Linga PURANAS strongly condemn Panchratras, as non vedic low caste sinners.

PANCHRATRA

Panchratra was so named because it deals with five philosophical topics or because it incorporates the essence of the four vedas and the Sankhya Yoga or because it was taught by Narayana to his five disciples during five nights. This Agma is recognised as an authority by all Vaisnava schools, but considered most sacred by Sri Samparadaya. This AGMA is more popular as against the other VAIKHANASA, both of which glorify Visnu. Panchratra is believed to have been revealed by great GOD himself, in the form of Visnu. These agamas guide the faithful, who are moved by their devotion to the supreme God, to worship one of his manifestations (Avatara).

The BIBLE of all worshippers of visnu are two chief books BHAGVATA PURANA and the BHAGVAD GITA. Followers of RAMA also acknowledge two special books in Valmiki's RAMAYANA and Tulsidasa's RAMCHARIT MANAS. All these four form 'Sacred books of the Hindus'.

The attempt to combine personal THEISM with ABSOLUTISM took three main lines viz (i) Sivaism (ii) Visnuism and (iii) Saktism, according as the personal divinity was identified with SIVA, VISNU or SAKTI. Having described the first two, the next chapter deals with the Acharayas of Visnuism and the next one is on Saktism.

CHAPTER - 12

SIVA - SAIVISM - SAIVITES

According to Sankara school of Hindu philosophy, the Supreme Being (PARA B'RHMA, PARMESWARAO in the ultimate analysis is NIRGUNBRAHAMA, an absolute entity with no form or attributes; but the ordinary man, with his limitations, cannot fix his mindor contemplate on such an abstract entity, therefore Hinduism has postulated also the SARGUNBRAHAMA, that is God with form and attributes called ISWARA or Narayana, who is given the three names of B'rhma, Visnu and Siva., when he is perceived as performing respectively the functions of creation, protection and dissolution. For the purposes of individual worship, PURANAS have presented several names and forms of divinity such as RAMA, K'rsna Durga, Lakshmi, Saraswati etc., so that the individual may choose anyone of these various forms or names for his worship. The forms may be distinct and the names may also differ, but in truth all these deities are manifestations of the same SUPREME GOD.

B'RHMA

B'rhma is the formless supreme deity itself, who has designed the wonderful organisation for effecting the welfare of the souls, and had interposed three corporeal emanations viz TRIMURTI between them and itself.

The supreme deity called PARASIVAM is the most high BEING; in whom irresistible power (PARA SAKTI) resides, and from whom all rays or radiations of peace, enlightenment, activity, joyfulness, order of righteousness and beauty, have gone forth to fulfill its beneficient purposes. It is formless and being almighty, it can assume any form at will and can control everything, living or lifeless.

With the ever changing matter, the souls in disregard to God and their own high spiritual status, came to associate with the deceptive, misleading matter, the wicked condition of fallen souls arose, characterised by excitement, doubt, care and sorrow. In order to uplift them and to lead them back to purity and peace, the supreme deity (Parameshwara - Parasiva) caused its spiritual power to enter matter (cells, bodies, worlds) and act according to certain righteous principles known as SANATAN DHARMA (eternal laws for the uplift of the fallen souls). It is in accordance with Sanatan Dharma that all things are evolved and involved.

One of the first three Isvaras or deities possessed of almighty powers, all three having been created by MAHAISVARAN (Mahaisvara - Prameshwara) in the order, at great intervals of time viz (i) RUDRA (ii) VISNU and (iii) B'RHMA. These almighty personalities are known as TRIMURTI or three embodied deities. Their souls were vested with subtle and gross bodies (Sukshma and Sthula sharafas) and each has his own place of abode. The usual abode of B'rhma is SATYALOKAM, of visnu BAIKUNTHAM and that of Siva, the KAILASAM.

In RAMAYANA, B'rhma counselled the Devas to pray to Visnu for RAMA's victory and Ravana's destruction ; endowed the Yakshini TARAKA with extraordinary beauty and strength; granted a boon to Bhagiratha to bring down Ganges and advised him to beseach Siva for help; made Human invulnerable; appeared to Rama when Sita entered fire test (Agni Preeksha); announced to Rama that he was an incarnation of Visnu; gifted a beautiful crown to the first king of Ayodhya; which Vashista placed on the head of Rama.

In mythological Brahamanis, of which MAHABHARATTA is the chief exponent; out of the trinity Gods (B'rhma, Visnu and Siva), the act of creator B'rhma was a single act (creation and organisation); so once completed, it was liable to receive scant recognition and as a matter of fact, the worship of B'rhma fell into desuetude. There is one solitary temple devoted to B'rhma at Pushkar (Ajmer-Rajasthan); although he has been sculpted in the Trimurti at Elephanta (Bombay) alongwith Siva and Visnu, in about the sixth century A.D.

SIVA (RUDRA)

SIVA is partly a development from the Vedic RUDRA, he is equally reminiscent of the Praryna yogic Lord of the beasts, while his consort resembles the sacrifice exacting Mother Goddesses of the same period. Rudra or Siva is early identified with Fire, from its role as God of red lightning and can take the place of AGNI. Siva, as Prearyan LORD of the BEASTS, and at the same time the idea of violence present in Rudra is underlined. Siva Bhairava, the destroyer, is thus by extension Siva, the bringer of fertility, the creator, the auspicious; thus B'rhma becomes inferior to Siva. So Siva is called MAHADEVA or ISWARA. His supreme creative power is celebrated in worship of LINGAM or phallus.

In the R'gveda, Siva is addressed as SIVA RUDRA, SIVA meaning 'kindly, gracious'. He was in fact a cruel destructive God, associated with storms and lightning. He is addressed as 'kindly' in an effort by the worshippers to induce him to be 'kindly', to turn aside his weapons and to spare the worshippers from the unpredictable and great 'wrath of the impetuous ONE'(R'gveda II.33.14). In the same hymn Rudra is also implored to grant the worshipper fertility and the healing and good health that will promote long life. This request for fertility and long life, has also been made to other Gods, but none was so much feared.as Rudra. Thus from the earliest times, Siva Rudra was associated with fertility and death, he was adored and feared as the creator-destroyer.

Vedic Rudra is Brahamanical 'SIVA'. Siva is the name of the supreme God, from whom the trimurti (B'rhma, visnu and Rudra) derive their respective powers of creation, protection and destruction. His boons to Ravana, his destroying Kamadeva with a mere look, his austerities in the Sita ashrama rendered thus sacred to his devotees, his keeping Ganga in his matted hair to avoid devastation, his grant to Vishwamitra of power over all weapons, his stay on the Somagiri mount in the form of Rudra, his appearance before RAMA (at the time of Sita's entering the flames test, after Rama's conquest over Ravana), his words of counsel to Rama, 'O righteous one, thou hast done well. It is good that Ravana hath been removed by thee. Go to AYUDHYA, console Bharata and Kaushalya, cheer thy friends, establish the dignity of thy family, perform horse sacrifice, confer wealth upon brahmins and having finished all, ascend to heaven. Behold now thy father, King Dasratha, who has attained the region of Indra, and together with Lakshmana do obeisance to him'.

Not going into the details about God Siva (a subject for a separate book 'HINDU GODS'). suffice it to say, that in the later Indian scriptures, Siva has 1008 recognised names (all enumerated in SIVA PURANA Lxix, Anusasna parva xvii), besides countless local applications and a corporeal existence almost as anthropomorphic as that of Visnu. These names are in accordance with his attributes, functions, nature and acts, all comprehensive. He has no incarnations.

As a distinct personality of his own, Siva has his abode on mountain Kailasa, where he lives with his family, attendants and the place, where his worshippers hope to be transferred. In his corporeal aspect, he has sometimes five faces (Pancanana). These five faces may be representing five schools of vedas (Rig, Yajur, Sama Taittiriya and Vajasaneyin) or five Pathas (Samhita, Pada, Karma, Jata, and Ghana) or five Gyatris or five headed serpent forming his canopy. Sometimes he has one face with three eyes, thought to denote his insight into the past, present and the future. Other items of his adoration have been explained in a subsequent chapter on Symbols in Hinduism. His dress costume and things which he carries, Siva assumes a very bewildering and confusing variety of personalities at different times.

Siva is impersonation of the dissolving and disintegrating powers and processes of nature. He is the impersonation of the eternal reproductive power of nature, perpetually reintegrating after disintegration (BHUTA, BHAVANA, SADASIVA, SANKARA, SAMBHU). In this character, he is most generally worshipped under the well known symbol of LINGA (described later). In the third place, Siva is the great ascetic and self mortifier (Yogi, Tapasvi) and as such called Mahayogi - Mahatapah. Be smeared with ashes and a matted hair, he sits in meditation under a PIPAL tree (Flora in Hinduism chapter) and often like contemplative BUDDHA, under a canopy formed by a five headed cobra (Fauna in Hinduism chapter). In the fourth place, Siva is contemplative philosopher and learned sage, the revealer of GRAMMAR to the great PANINI. Pandits say, 'No one, not as skilled as Siva, can repeat the Krama'. As such at least one form of Siva (saivism) is as much the peculiar system of brahmins, learned men viz SANKARA etel. MANU says, ' Siva is the god of brahmins, K'rsna (Visnu) of the Kshatriyas, B'rhma of the Vaisyas and Ganesha of the Sudras'. In the fifth place, Siva is exactly the opposite of an ascetic or philosopher. He is wild and jovial mountaineer KIRATA, addicted to hunting, drinking, fond of dancing (NATESVARA). His followers in this character are called SAKTAS, whose religious books are TANTRAS, having faith in SAKTI.

Another more remarkable aspect of Siva is as a being half male and half female (ARDHNARISVARA)[1]. It is a secondary character. It symbolises both the duality and unity of the generative act and the production of the universe from the union of the two eternal principles (Prakriti and Purusha; Maya and Atman).

SAIVISM

In keeping with so great a variety of characteristics of God SIVA and his different aspects, there should have been corresponding sects, addicted to his worship, but Saivism, like Vaisnuism, has not resolved itself into many separate organised societies under great religious leaders. There is no celebrated Saivism teacher.

As dissolver and regenerator, Siva is worshipped by even Vaisnuites. In SANKARA VIJAYA by Sankaraacharaya, six sects are named:-

(1) SAIVAS, who had the Linga branded on both arms.

(2) RUDRAS, who had the trident branded on the forehead.

(3) UGRAS, who had the Damru branded on the two arms.

(4) BHATTAS, who had the linga on the forehead.

(5) JANGAMAS, who bore the trident on the head and carried a Linga made of stone on their person, and

(6) PASUPATTAS, who had the Pasus (animals) branded on the forehead, arms breast and naval.

Of these only two sects, Jangamas and Pasupattas survive to the present day.

SAIVITES, followers of Siva, with their religion called Saivism, are hostile to the doctrine of Nonduality. They mostly worship Siva, as an ascetic. They profess to practice, like their God, severe austerities and bodily mortifications. Saiva ascetics DANDINS sect, said to carry ten different kinds of Staff, was founded by Sankaracharaya.

---

1. SINGH Dr. Chitralekha : Paintings of Siva in Indian Art, (1990)

AGHORA PANTHIS, who propitiate Siva by their revolting diet, are now getting reduced day by day. URDHA BAHUS, who extend one or both arms over the head and hold them in position for years, are no longer common. The AKASA MUKHINS, who keep their necks bent back, looking up at the sky and the KAPALIKAS, who use a dead man's skull for a drinking cup, have become rare. LINGAVATS, popularly LINGAITS wear the Linga in a silver or mettalic casket; suspended round their neck with a cord like a necklace, are usually identified with the Jangamas. They are extremely unorthodox and despicable.

Like Vaisnava sects, Saivites deviate more or less from orthodox Vedanta doctrine of the identity of the supreme and human spirit, the amount of deviation depends, of course, on the intensity of the personality attributed to Siva.

Monastic brotherhoods have found an important place in Saivism and have taken aggressive action in the spread of Saivism. On the positive side, Goddess Kali represents for Saivites, the most powerful form of the female forces in the universe and she is sometimes depicted as overwhelming Siva himself.

Saivism sect LINGAYATS, observe no caste differences, highly respect women and honour them. TANTRIC SAIVITES recognise primal active force in the universe as female Sakti and not male. Tantricism is a complicated and vast topic, which is outside the scope of this book.

WORSHIP

On ordinary occasions, the form of worship consists in simply pouring water over the Linga and offering BILVA(Bel)[1]. On great festivals like Sivaratri, complicated ceremonies are performed; putting Bilva leaves on the head of the Bull (NANDI; Siva's carrier

1. BILVA LEAVES : See chapter on FLORA IN HINDUISM

bodyguard); besprinkling of saffrom power, piling more Bilva leaves on the lingam, ringing of bells, chanting of hymns, making three streaks on the forehead and on shoulders by brahmins, counting of beads of the rosary, sitting in meditation and prayers. Saiva services have the merit of being exceedingly simple, as compared to Vaisnuism.

Sacred literature of the Saivites are the SAIVA AGAMAS, divided into four parts; knowledge (Jnana), concentration (Yoga), Kriya (founding of temples and installation of images) and charya (worship).

LINGAM

The most important with regard to God Siva, in literature, history, mythology, worship and in popularity, is the LINGAM. The Saivites or Saivas, adore the Linga-Yoni symbol; the Lignites worship the Linga, the Saktites or Saktas, the Yoni, and the Ganapathas follow Ganesha. In these sects Phallic worship gives prominence to the male and female generative principles in nature.

There is a special significance in the Siva Linga, that is, the image of God Siva in the form of a Linga. The word LINGA means a symbol or manifestation which points to an inference. The Siva linga does not have any specific form like the image of other Gods (Visnu, K'rsna, Rama etc.). At the same time, the linga does have a cylindrical shape and for. Accordingly, the Siva linga represents both Nirguna B'rhma and Saguna B'rhma, that is formless as well as with form. Among Siva lingas, there is a special significance attached to SPATIKA linga, made of pure quartz. The linga is hardly visible as it colourless, but when any abhisekha is performed such as with sandal paste or milk, it acquires the colours of the substances, showing that Nirgun B'rhma becomes a Saguna B'rhma, when worshipped.

In the R'gveda, Siva was never associated with lingam. In

INDUS valley excavations, the most important of objects were many stone images of the Phallus, the male generative organ. Lingam was the name given later. Some of them are only a few inches in size, others are two to three feet high. A six feet high lingam with five faces was seen by them in a small village, on the bank of a stream, between MHOW and Neemuch in Madhya Pradesh. The legend about this is that this linga was lying horizontally on the bank of the stream, on which a washerman used to beat the clothes everyday. One day he saw a dream and was told, 'How long will you beat me'. The washerman asked the meaning from the headman of the village, who ignored it. Then, again after few days the washerman got the dream and was asked, 'Now let me be relieved.' The washerman again approached the Headman, who after discussions, got the stone dug out. It appeared to be a Sivalinga. The six feet Linga has since been installed, high up on the stream bank and temple erected. the workmanship, on most of the Indus valley lingas is of very high quality, indicating the value placed on them. Along with these have been found stone circles of the type called YONI, symbol of the female generative organ. In later historical times, the Lingam and Yoni are connected with the worship of God Siva, in whose temples, the central image worshipped is the Lingam of Siva. It is often set in a Yoni, thus providing two symbols of the generative power in the universe. Sankara acharya, who lived in about 788-829 A.D., himself was an aggressive Saivite. He established an order of monks and a monastery at BODH GAYA, where he took over the Buddhist temple that commemorated the event of Buddha's enlightenment, walled in the statue of the Buddha, and installed a Lingam of Siva for worship. Rameswaram (the tip of the land from which Rama launched his attack on Ravana) was a place of Vaisanava pilgrimage; but since Rama/ Sita worshipped Siva on this spot, now the main shrine is Siva Linga temple.

Unlike most vaisnavas, the Saivites, in many places exclude Non Saivites, from the inner sanctum of their temples. One exception is the temple on the campus of Varanasi Hindu University, where anyone may enter, but few do. It is not a living centre for devotion. In UJJAIN is located but one of the seven holiest Siva Linga temples. It is known as the temple of MAHA KAAL (Siva Mahadeva). The lingam here is about three feet in height and ten inches in diameter, set in a Yoni. Men and women, both murmur formulae of adoration and request. The lingam is worshipped by bathing it in water or milk, by touching it, by placing fragrant ointment on it, by decorating it with flowers and by giving money offering to the priests. Above the lingam, hangs a golden vessel, from which water dripped continuously onto the lingam, keeping it moist. The water is collected as it runs off, is collected as holy water and distributed to the devotees, as a boon for fertility.

SIVA (Rudra) worship has come through the ages, since the Vedic era, and has progressed day by day. At present, there are more worshippers of Siva, than they were during the British rule in India.

1. Dancing Siva in Madwa Temple

2. Kali - Tempera on Paper, Courtesy Indian Museum, Calcutta.

3. Goddess Saraswati. Lakshmi, Parvati with their consorts, Courtesy Pahari, (Guler), Bharat Kala Bhawan, Varanasi.

4. Kali - the black earth mother, most blood thirsty aspect of the fierce Devi. She wears her necklace of skulls, hold's a giant's head in one hand, and her protruding tongue drips blood. Like Siva, she has a third eye. Courtesy Victoria and Albert Museum. London.

5. Siva and his consort Uma Chola Style 1000 A.D., Courtesy Victoria Albert Museum.

6. Mahisasura Badha, Courtesy Indian Museum, Calcutta.

7. Bansi Gopal *(Jaipur, Rajasthan)*

8. Ganesh-Parvati and Kartikay *(Amber, Rajasthan)*

9. Dancing Ganesha and his Consort on the eastern terrace of Harshad Mata-ka-Mandir *(Abaneri, Jaipur*

10. Durga worship by Gods - Pahari Style, Courtesy Bharat Kala, Bhawan, Varanasi.

11. Chaturambha lings *(Ajmer, Rajasthan)*

12. Radha-Krishna *(Jaipur, Rajasthan)*

13. Surya in Sun Temple *(Nahargarh Fort)*

14. Siva-Parvati *(Jaipur, Rajasthan)*

15. Krishna — eighth incarnation of Vishnu.

16. Narasimha — fifth incarnation of Vishnu

17. Parasurama — sixth incarnation of Vishnu

18. Rama — seventh incarnation of Vishnu

19. Mysore side view of Colissal Nandi from Chamunda hill

20. Devi Riding on a tiger slightly coloured

21. Hampi Linga in Linga Temple

22. VEESHNU repofing during a CALPA an aftronomical period of a thousand ages upon the serpent ANATA, copied from a feulptured rock in the ganges.

CHAPTER - 13

SAKTISM : GODDESS WORSHIP

It is a rooted idea with all Hindu theologans, of whatever denomination, that the highest condition of the self existent BEING is a condition of quiescence and inactivity, as well as of complete oneness, solitariness and impersonality. The theory of Brahmanism admits that the one self existent being is ABSOLUTE spirit and that spirit is life without anything to live for, joy without any pleasure. But the moment this one self existent pure spirit begins to conscious of existence, to exercise thought and free joy, it assumes personality and material organisation, a kind of duality, a double nature, partly male and partly female. In Hinduism, as against other religions, the male side of the God was believed to relegate all his more onerous and troublesome executive functions to his female counterpart. Hence it has come to pass that the female side of the personal God is often more honoured and propitiated than the male. The worshipper is thus more inclined to turn with greater devotion to the Goddess than the God, when he supplicates any powerful Intervention, on hic own behalf, in circumstances of unusual exigency or peril. The role of DURGA or KALI, bear testimony to this thought.

R'gveda (X.129) gives a dim outline of the later philosophical theories of Brahamanical saktism. A remarkable hymn in the R'gveda, translated by M. Williams in his INDIAN WISDOM, reproduced below, we find that in the beginning, when there was neither entity nor nonentity, when the universe was about to be developed, there arose in the ONE BEING desire, which produced mind and all existing things. The union of male and female idea developed in later Vedic texts.

'In the beginning, there was neither nought nor aught;
Then there was neither sky nor atmosphere above.
What then enshrouded all this universe?
In the receptacle of what was it contained?
Was it enveloped in the gulf profound of water?
Then was there neither death nor immortality;
Then was there neither day, nor night nor light, nor darkness,.
Only the existent one breathed calmly, self contained.
Nought else but he was there, nought else above, beyond.
Then first came darkness hid indarkness, gloom in gloom;
Next all was water, a chaos, all indiscrete,
in which the ONE lay void, shrouded in nothingness.
Then turning inwards, He by self developed force
Of inner fervour and intense abstraction, grew,
First in his mind was formed DESIRE, the primal germ
Productive, which the wise profoundly searching, say
Is the first subtle bond, connecting ENTITY
And Nullity.'

This idea developed in later texts into male and female. Indrani, Agneye, Lakshmi, Saraswati, though mentioned in the VEDAS, were not exalted to equal rank of their husbands, in matters of worship. It is only in SATPATHA BRAHAMANA (XIV.4.2.1), BRIHAD ARANAYAKA UPANISHAD (III.1) that the ONE BEING, divided into two and husband and wife were produced. MANU(1.5 etel) describes the self existent as dividing his own substance and becoming half male and half female. ARDHNARISVARA manifestation of SIVA is represented as half male and half female[1], right side male, left female; Linga and Yoni. Vedanta and Sankhya philosophical systems teach the separate existence of the two as SELF (male) and PRAKRITI(Maya-female).

1. Dr. Singh C.L. : Paintings of Siva in Indian Art (1990)

THE PURANAS make a special laudation of the active power of the Goddess, and even place the name of the goddess first as SITA RAMA, RADHA K'RSNA, LAXMI NARAYANA etc., but do not inculcate exclusive worship of the Goddess. Later sacred writings, especially TANTRAS, however, identified all forces with the female principle in nature, which consists of Siva, Visnu and others, came to be worshipped as Goddesses and their powers (SAKTI) exalted.

SAKTISM, of today, is a mere offshoot of Saivism and worshipped in the form of Devi, Durga, Kali and also in Vaisnuism as Radha K'rsna, Sita with Rama or Laxmi, alone or with Narayana (Visnu).

Just as the PURANAS are the Bible of Saivism or Visnuism; TANTRAS are the Bible of Saktism, Tantricism, though a part of Hinduism, have their own peculiar AGAMAS, as against Vedas; the detail of which are outside the scope of this book.

SAKTISM : SAKTI

By SAKTI, it does not only mean Matri Sakti (Power of mother), or that of consort, or of anyother human being or Divinity, but it also means and includes Mantra Sakti.

SAKTI is in many manifestations; Bhagwati of Devi Bhagwati, Visnu of Visnu Purana, Siva of Siva Purana, Sri K'rsna of Srimadhbhagwat and Sri Rama of Ramayana. Because of the characteristics of Vedic B'rhma, present in all these, they are all B'rhma.

Rajrajeswari or Shodhashi or Mahashodhashi, or Jagdhamba or Mahatri pur Sundari Bhagwati, is the one who causes creation, preservation and destruction.

Sakti is also given the names of asceticism, devotion, knowledge, illusion, leadership, nature, power, energy, consid-eration and ignorance (Devi Bhagwat). Whenever there is a combination of Bhagwati, then only NIRGUN B'rhma becoming SAGUN B'rhma, can cause creation. In VINAY PATRIKA (41), an incident is described; 'Once Goswami Maharaj went to RAMA and requested him for liberation. Rama replied that his number had not then come. Distressed, Goswami went to SITA (Rama's Sakti) and sought advice. He was then contented. Without Bhagwati (mother sakti) no good can be done to the world.

In SKANDA PURANA, JAGDAMBHA is an epithet of the spiritual power. In that Bhagwati, the creative power of the universe, is exalted.

BRAHAMAND PURANA also supports Bhagwati as a manifestation of B'rhma, in soot Samhita. DEVI BHAGWAT has also accepted Bhagwati in NIRGUN and Sagun forms.

When Hanuman went in search of Sita in Sri Lanka, he saw that Sita was surrounded by horrifying demon women. Hanuman sought permission from Sita to destroy them. Sita refused the permission and said that they were all her comrades. She said that in the meetings of men, one has to seek shelter, lay prostrate and so on, but in the meeting of women, mere salutation is enough; one has not to bow low. The meeting of women is meeting of mothers. Mother worship is easier and simple. In Hinduism, there is a vast mythological personnel of female Goddesses (Sakti), spreading out as it does into countless ramifications, has its root in the wife of Siva; Parvati (DEVI), Mahadevi. In Saktism the consort is not one God's counterpart, but a representation of all his attributes intensified. She is simply, in all respects, a duplicate of her husband, but a duplicate painted in deeper and more vivid colours. Just as Siva is sometimes white (Sveta, Sukla) or black (Kala); so is Devi, white (Gauri or black(Kali). White complexioned Saktis are Uma, Gauri, Laksmi or Saraswati and black Kali[1].

---

1. Singh Dr. Chitralekha : Paintings of Siva in Indian Art (1990)

SAKTI is female active energy principle. In some sects, she is regarded as destructive and dangerous as well as beautiful and seductive (cosmic energy in its dynamic form is symbolised for us, ordinary mortals, in the form of Sakti, the world mother, who is the power and energy by which the great God creates, preserves and destroys the world. She is represented in many forms, as described earlier.

Saktism, is the worship of the power of force personified as a Goddess, with a view to the acquisition of magical and supernatural faculties through her help, or to the destruction of enemies through her cooperation.

The devotional movements, and primarily Saivism, integrated into Hinduism the indigenous religious worship of powerful Goddesses. They are addressed as DEVI (Goddess) or SAKTI (Power), Like Saivism, it traces back to philosophical Brahaminism and through Brahaminism to the earliest conception of the Vedas.

DURGA is said to represent the female power (Sakti) of Siva, to avenge wrong, but she is unpredictable, and 'wrong is whoever is against Durga'. KALI is a great and powerful goddess capable of terrible destruction. For Saivites, she represents the most powerful form of the female forces in the universe, sometimes overwhelming SIVA. A man worships Tantric Sakti, in order to master her and thus eliminates her threat.

DEVI SAKTI

The great mother (DEVI, Kamakshi, Rajrajeswari) is represented as holding a noose in one hand (signifying wordly attachments from which one should free himself), a hook in another hand symbolising her imploring people on the path of righteousness. The carrying of a sugarcane plant is a symbol of the sweetness of the mind. The arrow in the hand shows our five sense perceptions, which should be conquered. In Durga Sakti, her riding a tiger shows that Ego and annoyance in man should be subdued. With the weapons in her hands, she fights the eight evils of hate, greed, passion, vanity, contempt, envy, jealousy and the illusion, with which man binds himself.

MAHAVIDYAS

Chief incarnations of Visnu are ten, and so are the ten Mahavidyas[1] (sakti), sources of Goddess's highest knowledge, which confers preternatural powers. These are Kali, Tara, Shodasi, Bhuvaneswari, Bhairavi. Chhinamastaka, Dhumavati, Vagala, Matangi and Kamalatmika. More important than the Mahavidyas are the eight MATRIS or MATRIKAS, Mahamatrikas or Divine Mothers viz Vaisnavi, B'rhmi (Brahamani), Karttikeye (Mayuri), Indrani, Yami, Varahi, DEVI (Isani) and Laksmi.

Saktism is more or less a monopolised doctrine in Tantricism, which is a complicated system, practised by few in India, much exploited by Mantra Sastris (Tantric pandits); which version of saktism is gradually dying. The Saktis worshipped and revered in Hinduism, are the eight Divine mothers, whose worship is as simple as of their lords.

RADHA SAKTI

From a short description of Sakti of Radha, the reader can well imagine the importance of Saktism in Hinduism.

In ATHARVAVEDA (19.7.3.3), Radha has been venerated as a power and a benevolence, as, 'O' Radha, O'merciful, May May RADHA be comfort bestower to us.' In GARG SAMHITA (12.32); Radha has been adored as the natural manifestation of K'rsna and it is said by K'rsna, 'Those who do not differentiate

---

2. Singh C.L. & Nath P : Hindu Goddesses

between ME and Radha, are the ones who attain salvation.' In BRAHAM VEYVARAT PURANA, K'rsna Janm Part (chapter 125), K'rsna described Radha as a part of himself and addressed, 'O' Radha, like the mother of cow land, you are also the mother of Gokul. You are the Mahalaksmi of Vaikunth (Visnu's abod) and Mahasaraswati. You are the emerged Lakshmi of the ocean of milk. As the consort of DHARAM(Righteousness), you are the saviour of life. As BHARATI, the consort of Kapil Rishi, you have been established. In Dwarika, in the form of RUKMINI, as consort of K'rsna; You are the one. You are Sita, the wife of Rama.' From this it is clear that Radha is the Sakti (Power Cosmic energy) of K'rsna. This power always remains with K'rsna in whatever form or wherever He may appear. Thus K'rsna and Radha are indivisible, inseparable and the devotees worship both together.

Without going into the details of Tantricism, viz Mantras, Tantras, Bijas Yantras and magic diagrams, we pass on next to Bhakti movements.

CHAPTER - 14

MINOR DEITIES

Primitive man, just emerging from the depths of a merely animal existence, finds face to face with mighty mysterial natural forces. So he worships them, out of fear or for their benevolence. Natural forces are then recognised as mysterious Vediç gods. Then they are personified in the Brahmanical age. When the trinity were adored with them came their righteous consorts (Sakti), who were followed by their bountiful offsprings. More new Gods were also introduced in Brahamanical era. Tutelary functions were no doubt ultimately associated with both Siva and Visnu, but in the case of Visnu, they were delegated to his incarnations, (main being ten, but said to be twentyfour) on earth, and in the case of Siva to his sons Ganesha and Karttikeye and to his consort, the great Goddess Devi, regarded as the mother of the world and worshipped under great variety of different names in different localities. Whether the worship of these new or minor deities, is a mere offshoot or ramification of the religion of Siva and Visnu is very doubtful, for instance Ganapati (Ganesha) has been mentioned in R'gveda (2.23.1 and 10.112.9). Therefore it is much more probable that these deities represent far earlier and more primitive objects of worship.

GANESHA

GANESHA, also known as Ganapati, Vinayaka or Puliyar in Southern India, is the most popular of all Gods, as he is the God of goodluck. His figure is placed over the entrance doors of houses. His figure appears of the first page of account books of merchants. He is the son of Siva and Parvati and is also the leader of Siva's hosts, As Siva was always surrounded by countless hosts (Ganas, servants and officers, saints) ready to traverse earth and air for execution of Siva's orders, Ganesha was entrusted with the function of looking after them.

As the remover of obstacles, Ganesha is propitiated at the beginning of every undertaking, whether it be a journey, the building of a house, the writing of a book or even of a letter. He is also the God of wisdom and prudence, a good scribe and learned in the scriptures. It was he, who at the dictation of sage Vyasa, wrote the Mahabharatta (MAHABHARATTA : AdiParva). It is said that this harmonious epic could be written because Ganesha, prior to undertaking writing, laid a condition that the dictation should never falter and that he should, at all times, be able to understand its meaning.

Ganesha is regarded as the patron God of all great enterprises, and not only the merchants, but the authors also invoke his help. In Hinduism, writing of a book is a very serious and solemn undertaking, peculiarly liable to obstruction from spiteful and jealous spirits of evil, and the favour of Ganesha is invoked to counteract their malignity. It never occurs to any Hindu writer to suppose, even for a moment, that the failure of his literary effort is ever likely to be due to his own incapacity. Proper precautions against demoniacal jealousy and obstruction are taken by invoking Ganesha.

Because of Ganesha's wisdom, it is he, who was selected by Paravti, to go with Narada to Gautam Rishi's ashram and pave way for the release of Ganges from the matted hair of Siva[1].

Ganesha is also called the God of Sudras, by Manu:-

1. Singh Dr. C.L. & P.N. : HINDU GODDESSES (1995) PP 94-95

VIPRANAM DEVIATAM SAMBHUH
KSHATRIYANAM TU MADHAVAH
VAISYANAM TU B'RHMA SUDANAM
GANA-NAYAKAH.

It is quite reasonable to suppose that the R'gvedic deity 'GANAPATI - BRAHAMANASPATI), also called Brahspati or Vachaspati, got metamorphosed into the deity GAJAVADANA GANESA - VIGHNESVARA. In the subsequent centuries, this concept has passed through the mills of the epics and the PURANAS to produce the GANAPATI (Ganesha), as we know him and worship today.

As Siva is ever engaged in two opposite duties as RUDRA and Kala (dissolution and deaths) and as SIVA and Sambhu (reintegration and new life); so these functions and execution of his wishes, were entrusted to his two sons Ganesha (for good) and Karttikeye (for protection against evil and demons).

ORIGIN

There are different descriptions about the birth/origin of Ganesha. As the son of Siva and Paravati, when he was born, he was the most beautiful baby ever seen. His mother was very proud of him and showed him to all gods and planets. Among them SANI(saturn) also came, who according to the ancient, possessed the evil quality of destroying everything. He looked at the head of the baby Ganesha and the head vanished instantly, simultaneously burnt up the terrible blaze of the destructive planet. Ganesha became headless; in despair Parvati consulted B'rhma, who said that HE, unfortunately, could not restore the head, but he told her the best thing, she could do, would be to take the head of some man or beast, whichever came in sight first, ans, twisting it off, stick it on to the boy's shoulders. The unhappy mother found an elephant, removed its head and placed it on her son's shoulders. It took root and ever since Ganesha has gone about with an elephant's head.

Another explanation of his parentage and the origin is that Siva was in the habit of surprising Parvati in her bath. Parvati did not like it. So one day, she scraped the scurf from her body, mixed it with oils and ointments, formed it into a man's figure, and gave it life by sprinkling it with water from the Ganges. She then, set this figure; Ganesha, outside the bath house door to guard it against anyone's entry. When Siva came back from his frolicking in the jungles, he wished to enter the house, but Ganesha would not permit it, being his mother's orders. As Siva had never seen Ganesha before, he was enraged at this obstruction, so outraged Siva cut off Ganesha's head and entered. When Parvati learnt about this, she requested Siva to put life in her dead son anyhow. Siva sent out messengers to seek another head for him. The first creature, they found was an elephant, so they brought his head back, and thus Siva planted the elephant head on Ganesha's shoulders, and he moved about with elephant head.

Yet another version of Ganesha's birth is that Parvati, during one of the twilight periods between the ages, a number of unworthy people had obtained access to heaven by visiting the shrine of Somnath, with the result that heaven was full to bursting, while the hell was empty. With Indra, as their spokesman, the Gods asked Siva for his help in remedying this situation. On his advice, they approached Parvati, who by rubbing her body, produced a BEING, with four arms and an elephant's head, who would induce in people a desire for riches, so strong that they would never think of spending their time in pilgrimage

Another version of the origin is that Gods and sages, once approached Siva and said that they had been reflecting on the fact that there was no obstacle to the performance of good or bad deeds. They requested Siva to create for them a being who would suppose the commission of sins Siva pondered for sometime on how he could help Gods and then he turned out his radiant look on Parvati. As he looked, a radiant youth of great beauty and endowed with the qualities of Siva sprang forth from his dazzling countenance. All the heavenly hosts were amazed and captivated by his beauty. But Parvati was angered and jealous of her husband's son. She cursed him to be ugly, to have a pot belly and to have an elephant's head. But Siva countered this curse by declaring that the being whom he had thus created should be called Ganesha, son of Siva and leader of Siva's hosts, that success and failure should derive from him; that he should be great among the Gods and in all spiritual and wordly affairs; and that he should be invoked first on all occasions, those that did not do so being doomed to failure.

In this version, a deviation has beed described that Ganesha's deformity was not due to Parvati's curse, but on account of Siva's previous offence of killing the son; though he had restored the son to life, but by then sage Kashyap had pronounced a curse by which Siva's son should lose his head.

GANESH'S BODY

Ganesha is represented as a short, pot bellied man with yellow skin and four arms and with an elephant's head. In his hands, he holds a conch, a noose (Pasa)and the other two hands are in Abhay (fearless), Varada (blessing) pose, the fourth holds a ankush (goad). Clad in beautiful robes and ornaments, his belly is decorated with a snake belt. There is also a yajnopavita (sacred thread) of thread or of serpent. He wears a lovely carved crown. He is normally seen himself helping to liberal quantities of sweets.

A mouse, of small proportions, is seen near him nibbling at

the sweets. Ganesha is shown with only one tusk, he lost his other one in a curious way. Visnu, in one of his incarnations (PARSURAMA), came to see Siva, who was sleeping at that time. Visnu desired to awake his brother God, but Ganesha objected to him being disturbed. There was exchange of words and Ganesha caught Visnu in his trunk and glung him away. Visnu felt slighted at this sort of treatment by a minor deity and out of rage flung his axe at Ganesha. It happened that axe had been given to Visnu by Siva; so Ganesha could not disrespect it. So he took the hit on one of his tusks, which was cut off. So Ganesha is always with one tusk. Just at that time, Parvati appeared and wanted to curse Parsurama, but other Gods intervened; B'rhma promised her that to make up for the lost tusk, Ganesha should be worshipped by the other Gods.

GANESHA'S MARRIAGE

Ganesha is generally represented as unmarried, but in fact he had two wives ; BUDDHI and SIDDHI (Prosperity and success). Both the sons of Parvati wished to marry these two and the parents were at a loss to favour anyone. So they planned a challenge bet, that one who goes round the world and comes back first, shall be married to Buddhi and Siddhi. Immediately Karttikeye with his peacock ran off, but Ganesha slowly got, circumambulated his parents for seven times and reported that he had gone round the earth and come back. The parents were happy and married the two to Ganesha.

Ganesha was already married to the two girls, when Karttikeye came back Another version of the challenge race is that Ganesha circumambulated the cow (Prithvi) seven times and won the race. Yet another version of this episode is, as Ganesha said; I have made the whole tour of the world in the course of my deep studies of the scriptures. ' He was so gifted for learning and logic that he had completed his tour of the world long before his brother.

This was not to Karttikeye's liking, so he left his parents and settled in Southern regions, where he is worshipped as SUBRAMANYAM.

FESTIVALS

Ganesha charturthi - the birthday of Ganesha, is observed on the fourth of the light half of the month of Bhadron (Aug-Sep). Clay figures of the deity are made, and after being worshipped for a few days, are immersed in water.

The cult of Ganesha is a mere offshoot of Saivism. The usual offering is of sweets.

PRESENT DAY GANESHA, really represents is a complex personification of sagacity, shrewdness, patience and self reliance, all qualities which overcome hindrances and difficulties; whether in performing religious acts or another. He is primarily the embodiment of success in life; with its accompaniments of good living, plenteousness, prosperity and peace. Ganesha is a curious combination of Divine and demoniacal, benevolent and malevolent, intellectual and animal propensities, all of which are typified by somewhat grotesque symbols noticeable in his image. As 'Vighnesa' and 'Vighna raja' (Lord of obstacles), he may also, if not propitiated, allow malicious imps to harm men, cattle and harvests.

WORSHIP

Ganesha is claimed by all sects, so his images appear in most of the shrines alongwith or at the entrance of all temples. He is worshipped in images, Lingas, Salagrams, Yantras and Kalsas (pots of water), The Swastika is also accepted as a graphic symbol of Ganesha. Ganesha (Ganapati) is sometimes depicted as a Sakti (female deity) under the names of Ganesani, Vinayaki, Surpakarni, Lambamekhala and so on.

KARTTIKEYE

Karttikeye, has several names, in confirmity with his different characteristics. His well known names are Kumara, Subramanya, Saravanabhava, Sanmatura, Tarakari, Sanatkumara, Skanda, Krauncabhetta, Sadanana, Sanmukha, Devasenapati, Saktidhara, Muruga, Brahmasasta, Guha, Gangeya, and Svaminatha.

KARTTIKEYE, because he is the Deity of war, guarding right and destroying evil; because of his foster mothers, the six Krittikas.

SHANMUKHA, because he is six headed and teaches that One has five senses and one mind and that when all six are in harmony, there is spiritual growth.

SUBRAMANYA, 'Very devotional', because he likes holy people brahmins and is always good to them. It means 'One who tends the spiritual growth of aspirants'. He represents the perfected state of spiritual consciousness or psychic energy of consciousness in the human body (Chakras). The chakras are Muldhara (at the anus), Svadhistahana (at the root of the sex organs, Manipura (at the naval), Anahata (at the region of the heart, Visuddha (at the throat), Ajna (between the eye brows) and Sahasrara (at the top of head) is the destination for this energy. When the yogi successfully raises his psychic energy to this topmost centre, he has a vision of Siva Sakti.

SARAVANABHAVA, because he was born in a forest of arrowlike grass.

SANMUTRA, because he was reared by the six divine mothers of the constellation.

SADANANA or SANMUKHA, because he assumed six faces to suckle the milk of the six mothers.

DEVASENAPATI, because he was appointed as the commander in chief of the Gods.

SAKTIDHARA and TARAKARI, because with his matchless weapons, he easily destroyed Taraksura.

KUMARA or SANATKUMARA, because being very young and virile.

SKANDA, means one who has accumulated the power of chastity. He is Skanda because he is a forceful attacker in war.

KRAUNCABHETTA, because he once broke down the Kraunca Parvata (a mountain).

BRAHMA SASTA, because at another time, he exposed B'rhma's ignorance of the VEDAS.

GUHA, because he is the secret one.

GANGEYE, because he is the son of Ganga, born on its banks.

SVAMINATHA, because he is the preceptor of his own father.

MURUGA; a name by which he is known in Tamil Nadu.

IMPORTANCE AND POWER

Karttikeye controls demons, evil and malignant spirits by the exercise of bravery and physical energy. He is a great yogi and also a great worker as represented by his six heads and twelve hands.

Taraka was a demon, protected by a boon. Under this protection, he set off extending his domain. He subdued creatures on the earth and also caused humiliation to Gods. Indra was forced to give him his white horse. The rishis were made to give away the famous cow, Kamadhenu, which granted all desires Kubera had to yield him his thousand sea horses. Vayu had to obey Taraka's commands. In terror, the sun gave no heat, the moon remained full at all times. The Gods were frightened. They gathered together to find out the ways how to put down the tyrant. Siva at that time was undergoing severe austerities, after the self immolation of his wife Sati. They knew that it was only Siva, who could produce a strong deity, who could destroy Taraka. So they wanted that Siva should marry again and produce such one, but Siva would not agree. B'rhma ordered Kama to create a feeling of passion in Siva's mind, but Siva burnt him to ashes[1] . B'rhma created UMA, in form of Parvati, daughter of Himvan, extremely beautiful and very virtuous. Somehow Siva married Parvati[2]. The Gods were very happy, but their pleasure was premature, because no children were produced for a very long time. Gods gathered together again and this time they decided to send AGNI to Siva, to urge him to beget a son. Agni reached Mount Kailasa at such a time, when Siva had just left, after meeting Parvati. So Agni took the form of a dove, managed to pick up a seed of Siva and flew back to Indra. But Indra, being a lesser God could not hold it, meanwhile the burden became heavier and as Agni was passing over Ganga, the seed dropped. There on the bank of the Ganges, arose a child as beautiful as the moon and as brilliant as the sun. As he appeared on the bank of the Ganges, the six pleiades, daughters of six kings came to that spot to bathe. Each of them claimed the boy and all became his foster mothers. Everyone gave him a head and two hands, thus the boy got six heads and twelve hands. This was Karttikeye.

Later when he grew up, he became the commander in chief of the forces of the Gods, and according to the boon killed Taraka. At the time, when Karttikeye set out meet Taraksur, with a big force, all Gods and deities encouraged him, said prayers and

1. Skanda Puran
2. Ibid

venerated him, on his success. A terrible, horrifying fight took place between the two. The fight frightened all Gods. Both the braves received lot of injuries, but still they were attacking each other. The weapons used were blessed with Mantras and both were using them. Both of them were attacking all parts of the body of each other and were keen to massacre the other. Assembled Gods and deities were uncertain as to who will be victorious. At that time, there was a heavenly voice, which said that the God and deities should not apprehend any doubt because it is Siva fighting in the form of his son. Hearing this Kumar was instigated to determine to kill Tarak, the attendants (Ganas) were also assured. Kumar, then with full force and Sakti attacked on Tarak's chest, but Tarak skidded it off, and attacked in reverse, by which Kumar became unconscious. All rishis chanted prayers and Kumar got up soon. Immediately with full force, Kumar attacked Traka. Both were trained in man to man fight on ground in all traditional methods. Because of the terrible fighting, even the air stopped blowing. At that time, all deities headed by HIMVAN, father of Parvati, went to Kumar, but Kumar assured them that should not be worried. Then Kumar attacked, after saying prayers to Jagdamba Siva and all Gods, The attack with mantra enforced spear, was so severe that Tarak could not stand it and fell down on the ground and chief of the Demons Tarak died. Kumar, as per tradition, did not attack anymore. Followers of Tarak took to heels. All Gods and deities became very happy, applauded the laurels of Kumar. B'rhma himself, along with others came and praised Kumar. Parvati was so pleased that she put Kumar in her lap. Among chanting of hymns, worship of Kumar was done[1].

Although Karttikeye is younger to Ganesha and is not much worshipped, yet he holds a more ambitious office, as the

---

1. SIVA PURANA : RUDRA SAMHITA KUMAR KHAND

Commander in chief of the good demon armies, and is adored as 'God of War'. He leads the force against the hosts of their enemies the evil demons, notably against those rebellious and arrogant arch-friends who seek to overcome and enslave the Gods, as in the case of TARAK, described earlier.

ORIGIN / BIRTH

In addition to Karttikeye's birth on the bank of Ganges, by siva's seed, carried over by Agni and dropped in Ganges and his rearing up by six foster mothers, there is another version of his origin.

The simplest legend is that Karttikeye was born of Agni's seed, thrown into a sacrificial fire. He was afterwards received by Ganges and the six foster mothers.

MARRIAGE AND CONSORTS

It is generally described that after departure from Kailasa to the south and having lost interest in Buddhi and Siddhi, he no longer took any interest. It so happened that one day.Indra was in the forest when he heard cries for help from a nearby glade. Running to the spot, he saw that a demon KESIN had tried to ravish a young girl. The girl appealed to Indra to find a good husband for her. She told Indra that her name was DEVASENA, which means army of the Gods .Indra decided that a military husband would be suitable for her. Indra thought that with the strengthened army with this girls auspicious name, he would be able to lead the celestial army to victory. B'rhma was approached, who advised Indra to go to Agni and the sacred Ganges. B'rhma arranged that Agni should come out of sacrificial fire, fell in love with one of Rishis wives and produce a husband for Devasena.But the wives of the rishis avoided Agni. Agni saw SWAHA, daughter of Daksheye in the forest, but he was not allured by her, as his interest was in Rishi wives, but swaha,fell in love with

Agni. So Swaha, in disguise as Rishi wife, approached Agni five times each time as a different Rishi wife, so she had six unions with Agni, ultimately a six headed, twelve armed and twelve legged beautiful Karttikeye, appeared, who when he grew up married DEVASENA and drove the Asuras out the Kingdom of Indra.

Karttikeye has two consorts; Devasena,also called Devayani and the other Valliamma; both of them embody Jnana Sakti, the power of knowledge and Kriya Sakti (the power of action). They are believed to grant childern, to prevent the attackes and thwart the malice of devils and to cast off evil spirits. Although Valliamma is the daughter of a chieftain of an agricultural race, yet Karttikeye loves equally both.

A LANCE, called Vel, which means a sharp spear, of dazzling brightness is the weapon of Skanda ,with which this davasenapati vanquished many an enemy. The lance actually stands for knowledge and wisdom, with which all the ugly demons of ignorance can be destroyed. The sharpness symbolises developed sharp intellect and with it he guards the progress of the world.

A peacock called PARAVANI, is the vahan (conveyance) of Karttikeye. In icons, it is shown as belabouring a snake with one of its legs. The peacock is opposite of the snake which stands for Time The peacock signifies the power of celibacy; Skanda is the personification of chastity. The peacock with its beautiful plumage represents creation in all its glory. Hence Karttikeye, who rides it, is the supreme lord, the master of creation. Karttikeye rides the peacock, reminding one not to let pride and egotism get the better of one.

WORSHIP

KARTTIKEYE is considered as a syivan deity connected with

serpent and tree worship, but generally as a younger brother of Ganesha. The worship of this deity is confined to Southern India, although Ganesha is worshipped in many parts of the world, other than India. In the south, Karttikeye is recognised and venerated as SUBRAMANYAM. In Tanjore and some other places, temples have been erected in his honour. Other temples devoted specifically are at Tiruchendur, Muruga temple at Tirrupparankunram, Murugan temple at Palamuthircholai, Subramanya temple at Tirupathi, Worship cult is SIVA CULT.

AT VAITHEESWARANCOIL, Six kilometers south of Sirkali, there is a temple with presiding deity as Sri Vaidyanathan. Here Subramanyam goes by the name of MUTHUKUMARAR and the image of the deity is very attractive. Every month, during the Krithigai day, a great abhishekam is performed to Him. It is said that Lord Muruga got his divine Vel here.

Among many other deities, recognised and worshipped in all parts of India the popular worship and recognition in Hinduism is that of HANUMAN.

HANUMAN

The ideal qualities of loyalty, unstinted devotion and love are depicted in the character of Hanuman, the monkey God, who helped Rama, the Avatara of Visnu, in crossing over to Lanka and defeating Ravana. He was the one, who could bring herbal medicines for Lakshmana, when he became unconscious. The RAMAYANA pictures him as a highly erudite, cultured and refined person. He is as strong as he is wise, and as devoted as he is strong and wise, a rare combination indeed.

In the Ramayana (Kishkanda and Sundar Kands), the heroism, faithful and devotional service of Hanuman, has been

---

THE RAMAYANA : KISHKANDA KAND AND SUNDAR KAND.

described. When Sugriva, raised his army of bears and monkeys, for the assistance of Rama, Hanuman was made its General. Hanuman, the celestial, son of Vayu, the wind, who could fly, went ahead in the invasion of Lanka. While the army marched south towards Lanka, Hanuman flew across, met Sita, sitting alone in the garden, he told all the plans made for her deliverance. At that time, he also gave Rama's signet ring to her, as a mark of identification. Then, he uprooted trees and plants, when he was caught by Ravana's rakshasas and produced before Ravana. Ravana wanted to kill him, but when reminded about the immunity granted to ambassadors, Ravana set fire to Hanuman's ling tail. After burning a good part of Lanka, Hanuman flew back to the mainland and rejoined Rama, giving him valuable information about Ravana's defence.

Lanka, was a mighty fortress, originally built by Visvakarma for the God of wealth KUBERA. It was originally on the summit of Mount Meru, which was broken by Vayu and hurled into the sea, and so it had become an island. The vast city, mostly made of gold, in the fortress, was surrounded by seven broad moats and seven great walls of stone and metal. Therefore, as desired by Rama, a bridge across the strait to Lanka was built. Its chief architect was a monkey leader NALA, who was a son of Visvakarma and knew the expertise. This bridge is called NALASETU (Nala's bridge). After crossing, a mighty battle was fought between Rama and Ravana. By an arrow from Indrajit, Ravana's son, Lakshmana became unconscious. Medicinal herbs were required to cure the mortal wound. Hanuman had proved himself as a vailant soldier and warrior, but his greatest service was to fly to the Himalayas to bring the specific herbs. The rakshasas naturally set obstacles to his flight and many difficulties arose. KALANEMI, was a giant, to whom Ravana offered his half kingdom, if would kill Hanuman. Kalanemi flew ahead of Hanuman and invited Hanuman to a dinner.

Hanuman, however had been warned earlier, so Hanuman killed Kalanemi, and hurled him down to Lanka. Hanuman, on reaching the mountain, began the search for the herb, but Indra, who bore him ill will, confused him. Ultimately exasperated, HAnuman lifted the whole mountain and flew back with it to Rama. On his wayback, when he flew over Ayodhya, Bharata thinking it to be some evil shot an arrow. Hanuman fell down, then Bharata realised his mistake and sent him to Lanka. When Hanuman was about to reach battle field, the moon was about to rise when the action of herbs would fail. So Hanuman swallowed the moon and safely delivered the magic medicine to his master in time.

ORIGIN AND BIRTH

Hanuman, the monkey deity, renowned for his learning, agility and speed, found complete fulfilment in selflessness and service to master Rama. He was born of a monkey queen, ANJANA, as one of the creatures fathered by the Gods so that He could be of assistance to VISNU, in his incarnation of Rama. He has the ability to fly because of his father VAYU, the wind God.

A common account of Hanuman's birth is more complex and it is said that Dasratha performed ceremony for the award of sons. After the ceremony was over, he distributed the offering among his queens. The youngest Kokkei was offered the cake last, which she resented. Meanwhile a kite came and flew away with the piece, to the forest, where Anjana was drying her wet hair. Anjana, who by curse had become a monkey from being an Apsara, was praying for a son. Vayu, the wind God came forward and handed over the fallen cake into Anjana's hands. Siva appeared on the site and guided Anjana to consume the cake, by eating which she conceived HANUMAN. Soon after birth, Hanuman felt very hungry and Anjana was unable to satisfy his hunger. In the meanwhile, he saw the SUN, thinking it as a fruit, he tried to catch it, but could not. In its pursuit, he entered Indra's domain, heaven. There Indra was annoyed and he injured his jaw with his thunderbolt. Hanuman fell down on earth, but his father Vayu was quick enough and caused colic in the bodies of all Gods. Indra realised his mistake, apologised to Vayu and agreed that Hanuman should be immortal.

Hanuman's immortality is often considered to be a reward for his services to Rama. His physical strength and agility made him an invaluable ally of Sugriva, then Rama. He could not only fly at the speed of wind, but also had the strength to uproot trees and mountains. He could alter his size at will and make himself invisible. In battles, he was a terrifying figure, as vast as a mountain and as tall as a tower. His skin was yellow, like molten gold, the face red like a ruby and his tail was of enormous length. His fierce roar, itself shattered the enemies.

When the war was over and Rama went back to Ayodhya and enthroned, Rama asked Hanuman to ask for a boon. Hanuman asked that he should live as long as the deeds of Rama were on the lips of the people. These deeds were, are and will be ever described by men and so Hanuman lives for all times. The wise Hanuman, in fact, attained immortality.

WORSHIP AND TEMPLES

Hanuman is worshipped as the type and model of a faithful servant to God. Usually large size images of Hanuman are installed, generally made of strong stone and covered with red vermillion from head to foot. A very common site of his images are the wrestling grounds, where the wrestlers and others, keen for body building undergo exercise.

A temple dedicated to Hanuman outside the town of Kaira, is well endowed, where the offering is huge. The images of Rama and K'rsna occupy subordinate positions. Whereas worship of HAnuman is worship of Visnu, but in this temple, a LINGA shrine also exists in the enclosure. Hanuman image also has been installed in Sri Stanumalaya Temple at Suchindrum, also in Rameswaram temple.

At Ayodhya, there is a temple to Rama, and the image of the God contains a huge gleaming jewel, which is said to be a diamond (probably a light coloured sapphire). This temple is surrounded by massive high walls, which convert it into a sort of fortress. It is called Hanuman Fortress (Hanuman Gadhi), and the neighbouring trees swarm with sacred grey monkeys, who represent the troops of the monkey God.

There are many Gods and deities, who are worshipped in different corners by the Hindus. In addition to the Vedic Gods, many deitied came to be recognised under the Brahamanical age, such as KUBERA (God of wealth), DHARMA (God of duty, just as Soma and Agni in Vedic times), KAMA (God of love,Dharma's son, creative power of B'rhma to arouse desire in Siva's mind), VISVAKARMA (Divine artificer, Functionary and mythology of Vedic Tvashatri : Indra or Surya) and others, who were identified as separate deities in Hinduism, although their antecedents were from Vedic Gods. As the worship of these deities, minor Gods, is not popular, we are not going into details about them in this small book, to avoid complexity and to retain simplicity, which is the aim of this book.

CHAPTER - 15

ADVAITA VEDANTA PERIOD (HINDU RENAISSANCE)

A period of 1500 years separates the upanishadic dialogues of Yajnavalkya and Uddalaka Aruni from the period of Sankaracharya (788 AD). This long stretch of time included those formative centuries when the vedic and non-vedic streams were fused into Hinduism. The vedanta philosophy came to dominate all other religious philosophies of India, and the great teacher Sankara exerted the most far reaching influence of all vedantic philosophers, right into the present day. During this period a vast religious and cultural resurgence was seen in the country, where Puranas were the gospels. Beliefs and practices of most of the cults accepted vedanta, as a final source. Religion was reflected in architecture (Kailasa temples at Ellora, Chandella Dhanga's Siva temples at Khajuraho). This period was an age of catholicity, different creeds joined hands to respect each other. The gods of different cults were all worshipped ; Siva with his whole family. Trimurtis, Panchayatana and Matrikas. This period of Puranic Renaissance gave added sanctity to the Dharmasastras. Medhatithi, the author of a commentary on Manu Smriti said, 'Satisfaction of the learned and the virtuous is a vital test, it may find what appears to be Dharma as adharma and what appears adharma as dharma. When those learned in the vedas feel that a thing is pure, it is to be deemed as pure.'

The great movement which provided Hinduism with a catholic philosophy and a conception of God, which were acceptable to the highest thought of every sect, had its origin in South India. Both philosophical and devotional schools following Siva and Visnu existed there from very early times. Though devotional, its philosophic forms have close affinity with the orthodox doctrines of Hindu philosophy.

This period of Hindu Renaissance was a great era of constructive thought and creative inspiration, without which the re-emergence of the people of Independent India among the free nations of the world, would not have been possible. Ramananda, Kabir, Mira, Nanak and Vallabhacharya in the North, Caitanya, Ramakrishna Parmahans and Vivekananda in Bengal, Madhava, Ramanuja and Nimbarka in the South, and Swami Narayana in the West and others gave to the religious life a vitality which Hinduism never seems to have enjoyed before.

During this Renaissance period, Hinduism had just then begun to revive[1] and to do its modern garments. The force of Buddhism, Jainism and Atheistic systems having weakned, the strongholds of orthodox beliefs, this reactionary age set about to place the old dogmas and observances on a rationalistic basis. The coat armour of ancient Hinduism, battered as it appeared to be by the repeated onslaughts of opposing creeds, was then slowly patched up and tried to be rendered impervious to the darts of reason or sentiment. An age of construction, of readjustment and rearrangement of ancient beliefs, had now succeeded a destructive age of scepticism. As against this the superstition, taste for the marvellous and the extraordinary, exaggeration in the puranas were beginning to distort facts into fabulous legends.

SHANKARACHARYA, Chief representative or the very incarnation of street Brahmanism, a personality around which Brahmanical doctrines may be gathered was (788-820) Born at Kalady, on the banks of Periyar in Kerala. He seems to have

1. Dr. R.G. Bhandarkar's article on the Social History of India in Chintomani's Indian School Reform P 2

been a person of amazing genius. He set about reviving Hinduism or rather special intellectual kind of Hinduism viz Saivism, the worship of Siva. By his forceful logic, he convinced the people that Buddhism and Jainism were not new religions, but were only branches of Hinduism. Hinduism contained the basic principles of both of them. Govindapada was the teacher of Shankara and Gaudapada was the teacher of Govindapada. Shankara fought against Buddhism, fought with his intellectual arguments and established an order of Sanyasins, open to all castes, like the Buddha Sanga. He travelled all over India, established four centres in four corners of India. He came to Varanasi, as a conqueror, but a conqueror of the mind and in arguments. Ultimately he went to Kedarnath in the Himalayas, where the eternal show begins, and he died there, at the age of 32 years.

ADVAITA VEDANTA

Shankara acharya built a system of philosophy called Advaita Vedanta or nondualistic Vedanta, to which modern Hinduism belongs. This system is based on pure monoism, the only, ultimate REALITY in the metaphysical sense being 'PARMATMAN' the Absolute soul. That is the subject and all else is objective. Absolute soul is indivisible and pervades everything, now the one appears an many, and yet remains whole. ISAVASYA Upanished describes Parmatman; That is whole, this (too) is whole: from whole comethwhole: subtract whole from whole (yet) whole remains'.

Shankara built a subtle and intricate theory of knowledge and proceeding from certain assumptions, step by step, by logical argument, developed the complete system of Advaita philosophy. The individual soul is not a separate entity, but that Absolute soul itself, though limited in some ways. It is compared to the space enclosed in a jar, the PARMATMA being universal space. Distinction between two is unreal. Freedom consists in realising this unity and establishing contact or communion or oneness of the individual with the Absolute soul.

The phenomenal world around us, thus becomes a mere reflection of that Reality or a shadow cast by it on the empirical plane. It is called MAYA (Illusion), but it is not nonexistent. It is a relative existence. Accepting the Brahmanical caste system of social life, Shankara held that any person belonging to any caste, could attain the higher knowledge. According to Shankara, ultimate REALITY is Atman or B'rhma (soul), which is pure consciousness (Jnana Svarupa) or consciousness of the pureself (Svarupa Jnana), which is devoid of all attributes (NIRGUNA) and all categories of the intellect (Nirvishesa). B'rhma associated with His Potency (SAKTI), Maya or Mulavidya appears as the qualified B'rhma (SAGUNA or SAVISHESA or APARA B'rhma) or the LORD (ISVARA), who is the creator, preserver and destroyer of this world, which is HIS appearance.

Shankara emphasises that from the phenomenal point of view, the world is quite real. It is not an illusion. It is a practical reality. He distinguishes the dream state from the awake state. Things seen in a dream are quite true as long as the dream lasts, they are sublated only when we are awake. Similarly the world is quite real so long as true knowledge does not dawn. But dreams are private. They are creations of the Jiva (Jivasrsta). The world is public. It is the creation of Isvara (Isvarasrsta). Jiva is ignorant of the essential unity and takes only diversity as true and wrongly regards himself as agent and enjoyer. Avidya conceals the unity (avarna) and projects names and forms (viksepa). Isvara never misses the unity. Maya has only its viksepa aspect over him. The highest Brahman (Para Brahman) is both the locus (Ashraya) and the object (Visaya) of Maya. When the jiva realises through knowledge and knowledge alone, Karma being subsidiary, this essential unity, liberation is attained here and now (Jivan Mukti) and final release (Videha Mukti) is obtained after the death of the body. Shankara's is considerably influenced by Buddism and he preserves the best that was in Mahayana in his own philosophy.

Sankara Advaita reconciles popular Hinduism with the philosophy of upanishads. By offering worship of Siva, Visnu and other members of the pantheon without any difference he condemned the narrow sectarianism of his contemporaries and reaffirmed the vedic truth. 'Ekam Sat Vipra Bahudha Vadanthi', the reality is one, the sages call it variously. He abolished liquor and bloodshed in worship. Both Sawas and Vaishnavas differ in the mode of branding their breasts, arms and other parts of their bodies with distinctive marks of their sect. This practice was severely denounced by Sankara, but apparently with little effect.

In his introduction to the second chapter of the Geeta, Sankara has clearly said that knowledge (Gyan) and action (Karam) are two separate paths and one person cannot follow these simultaneously. They are meant for two different classes of people. While all the Karmas are prescribed for an ignorant man, the path of knowledge is followed by the men of knowledge and these two are not to be combined. There is not the slightest hope of attaining Moksha through combined Knowledge and deed nor it is taught by the Geeta. No Karma is prescribed for the Sanyasins. For a knowledgeable, no action is compulsory except that which is necessary for the maintenance of his physical body. The performance of Karma results in self purity.

Both Sawas and Vaishnavas differ in the mode of branding their breasts, arms and other parts of their bodies with the distinctive marks of their sect. This practice was severely denounced by Sankara, but apparently with little effect.

The importance of his 'Manaspuja' or mental worship, still

remains to be appreciated. It enables every man of faith to worship his 'Ishtdevta' or favourite deity, without any material apparatus, ancillaries or rituals.

The main organisational work that Sankara undertook was the establishment of the four great maths or monasteries in four corners of India, at Jyotirmath Badari in the north, Govardhanamath at Puri in the east, Sharadamath at Dwarka (Dvaravati) on the west coast and at Sringeri (Mysore) in the South. These pontifical seats were to be occupied by Sankaracharyas, who were to maintain unpolluted teaching of Advaita and to maintain the ascendency of the upanishedic thought. These maths maintain the orthodoxy of Sankara's teachings and hold the Hinduism on the people. The most noted successor of Sankara at Sringeri math was sayana Madhava, (14th CAD) the well known author of the commentary on R'gveda.

The most noted successor of Sankara at Sringeri math was Sayana Madhava, the well known author of the R'gveda commentary, who lived in the 14th century the vedic truth. 'Ekam Sat Vipra Badudha Vadynthi, the reality is one, the sages call it variously. He abolished liquor and bloodshed in worship.

To quote Dr. S. Radhakrishnan 'It is impossible to read sankara's writings, packed as they are with serious and subtle thinking, without being conscious that one is in contact with a mind of very fine penetration and profound spirituality - His philosophy stands forth complete, needing neither a before nor an after - whether we agree or differ the penetrating light of his mind never leaves us where we were. (Indian Philosophy Vol. II PP 446 - 447).

Sankara, the Advaithin, the believer in nonduality or identification of all beings with the highest Brahman, views sub specie aeternitatis all beings, be it Gods, Men animals and plants, as essentially of the same value. From the transcendental point of view, the small difference in value and capacity do not matter much. His main concern is to establish the dependency of all of them on Brahman, the root principle, which is Immanent; and yet beyond, all of them. all of them are but secondary and transitory evolutions from B'rhma. They are among themselves, and with regard to the highest principle, SA Atmaka, identical.

RAMANUJA ACHARYA (1017 - 1137)

Ramanuja was born at (Sri) Param Bettur, 26 miles west of Madras. He studied and taught at Kanchipuram and resided at Sri Rangam near Trichnapoly, where he worshipped Visnu, in his character of Sri Ranganath. He lived in the south, in the Chola empire, a great reformer, who was the leader of a rival school of thought to that of Shankara. Shankara was a Saivite and a man of intellect. Ramanuja was a Vaisnuite and a man of faith, whose influence spread all over. Ramanuja was a less transcendental thinker than a psychological philosopher. His epithet is significantly the Yoga Indra or Yati Indra, the master of psychological yoga. He speculates on the difference between man and his higher counterpart, the GOD. His dogma is that of SAYUJYATA, connection, but not union, between the Divine, the Gods and Men. He, while maintaining that, B'rhma as principle lies beyond the range of all personal manifestations, emphasises that the Gods are of a higher, that is, less restricted capacity than man, let alone all other earthly beings.

Prior to Muslim invasion, Shankara had successfully achieved the refashioning of Hindu doctrines. Ramanuja further supplemented these and provided Hinduism with a fundamental unity in her philosophic thought. It is undoubtedly on this basis that the reforming movements erected their structures, thereby enabling Hinduism to keep the new sects and cults within her comprehensive framework.

Ramanuja's distinctive teaching was on the existence of a triad of principles : (1) the SUPREME BEING (isvara) (2) SOUL and (3) NON-SOUL. Visnu is the Supreme Being, individual spirits are souls, the visible world is Non soul. All three principles have an eternal existence distinct from each other. He contended that the souls or spirits of men are truly, essentially and eternally distinct and different from the one universal spirit. He held that God is himself both the creator of the world and the substantial cause or material out of which it is formed. He asserted that the world and God stand towards each other in the relation of body and soul, and that body and soul are virtually one. The passage in Mundaka upanishad based on R'gveda (1-16-20) says, 'Two birds - the supreme and individual souls - always unite, of the same name, occupy the same tree (body). One of them, the individual soul enjoys the fruit (consequences of his acts), the other looks on as a witness'. He admitted the dependence of the human soul on the divine and urged the duty of striving after complete, though conscious, union with the supreme (Visnu). With regard to the various incarnations of the supreme Being and the duty of worshipping him, he held that God is present among his devotees on earth in five ways -

1. In Images 2. In divine embodiments (Rama) 3. In full manifestation (K'rsna) 4. In the subtle (Sukshma) all pervading spirit and 5. In the internal spirit controlling the human soul (anta-ratman). Ramanuja, the exponent of qualified monoism has interpreted the Karmayoga taught in the Bhagvadgeeta in his own way. According to him, Karma is equally necessary for a common man as well as a man of knowledge. Performance of Karma preceded by knowledge as means to attain the supreme is taught and then emphasis is given on Bhakti. He declares that when the action are dedicated to God, the obstacles of nescience disappear and when ardent devotion for him arises, then a devotee

get his darshana. According to him, the progress of an aspiration to God by the way of Karma (act), jnana (knowledge) and bhakti(devotion) which are not separate roads but success stages of the same way culminating in the attainment of God is the fundamental teaching of the Geeta.

According to Dr. S. Radhakrishnan, the Geeta is a mandate for action; full active life of man in the world with the inner life anchored in the eternal spirit. The plea of Sankaracharya of the path of knowledge alone is thus not supported.

His followers divided into Veda Galai (Northern school) and Ten Galai (Southern). Northern school accept the Veda while southern have compiled their own Veda (Nalayira : the four thousand verses).

His notable works are Shri Bhasya, Gita Bhasya, vedanta sara, vedanta dipa, Gadatraya and vedartha sangraha. He established many temples and converted many people to vaishnuism.

Madhavacharya; a Kanarese Brahman, also called Ananda Tirtha, was born about the era 1200 AD, at udupi, 60 miles north of Mangalore and was educated in a convent at Anantesvar.

His doctrine is called Duality (Dvaita), as opposed to Shankaracharya's Non duality (Advaita). His school is also called Purna-Projna. He, like Ramanuja, taught there was only one God, whose principle name was Visnu (Hari) and who was the one eternal supreme Being, all other Gods being subject to the law of universal periodical dissolution. He does not believe in qualified absolutism. He rejects the relation of inseparability and the distinction between substance and nonsubstance. He advocates both quantitative and qualitative pluralism of souls and that no two souls are alike. He believes that even in liberation the souls differ in degrees regarding their possession of knowledge and enjoyment of bliss. He does not make any distinction between the body and soul of God. He emphasizes the difference of the liberated soul from God. The soul becomes similar to God in some respects when it is liberated, yet even in these respects it is much inferior to God. Madhava believes that certain souls like demons, ghosts and some men are eternally doomed and damned. They can never hope to get liberation. The doctrine of eternal damnation is peculiar to Madhava and Jainism in the whole field of indian philosophy.

Madhava, the theist, leaving aside the concept of the relationship between the Brahman principle and all its personal manifestations asserts, that the Gods themselves are the highest goal, man can strive to attain in liberation a goal however, which man can never entirely reach. Nor complete identification, nor essential similarity, but at the highest Salokata, nearness in space in a kind of heavenly abode man can hope for. The Gods are the masters and man their devoted and humble servant.

According to Madhava, the supreme Being is to be honoured in three ways - by naming (a child with one of thousand names of Visnu), by worship with the voice (repetition of veda), with the body (alms to the poor & their protection) and with the heart (mercy, love and faith) i.e. in thought, word and deed. The third way advocated by Madhava was by branding (discus on right arm and conchshell on left arm) as memorial of their God on their persons.

Madhava, seeing the irreconcilliable gulf between the finite and the infinite, rejected sankara's attempt to reduce the finite loses its entity. And on the other hand, affirmed (against Ramanya) the absolute transcendence of the infinite over the finite so that there can be no question of immanent identity.

Acharya Nimbarka (Nimbaditya or Niyamananda); a Telegu Brahman, who lived somewhere in the middle or later half of the fourteenth century. His philosophy Dvaitadvaita or Bheda Bheda or Sankasampradays of Vaishnuism is very much indebted to Ramanuja. He continued to explore the immanence of the infinite in the finite and discovered a real distinction between the finite and infinite without compromising the Principal identity of the finite and the infinite. He admits like Ramanuja, three realities God, Souls and Matter, last two being dependent on God. Individual is essentially of the nature of knowledge. The Soul is a real knower, agent and enjoyer. It is dependent on God, is supported by God, pervaded by Him and controlled from within by God. The souls are atomic in size and many in number. A soul is eternal and yet it suffers births and deaths on account of its embodiment which is due to Karma (act) and avidya (ignorance). Liberation is due to knowledge which is brought about by God's grace which itself is due to devotion. The souls and matter have no independent existence and therefore are not different from God. They are limited because of their dependent existence and are different from God who is independent and an unlimited ruler.

Nimbarka believes in identity and difference, which are separately and equally real. The theory of matter and soul as attributes of God is rejected by Nimbarka. Matter and souls as the attributes of God serve no purpose. As there is nothing outside God, they cannot distinguish Him from anything else, nor can they throw any light on God for they do not constitute his essence. Nimbarka also rejects the distinction between the body and the soul of God and the view that matter and souls from the body of God. Nimbarka calls matter and souls as the parts of powers of God.

Nimbarka has written a commentary called Vedanta Parijatasaurabha on the Brahma Sutra, Dashashloki, Shri K'rsna Stavaraja and Madhvamukhamardna.

His chief disciples were Nivasacharya, Aaodumban acharya and Gaurmukhacharya.

Vallabhacharya

Vallabhacharya and his son vitthalnath, early leaders of the Vallabhachari sect and Govardhan, near Mathura, had four disciples each, all of whom were Hindi poets. They were called Ashta Chhap (Eight seals or Diestamps). Their poems were regarded as standards for that dialect of Western Hindi in which they wrote. This dialect was Braj Bhasha (of Mathura, Vrindaban and surrounding country), as compared to Tulsi Das who wrote in Eastern Hindi. Disciples of Vallabhacharya in Ashtachhap were Sur Das, Krishna Das Pay Ahare, Parmanand Das, Kumbhan Das and of Vitthalnàth were Chaturbhuj Das, Chhit Swami, Nand Das and Govind Das, all in the mid or second half of 16th century.

Krishna Das Pay Ahari (Best work Prem Sattvanirup) Nand Das (Panchadhyayi in imitation of Gita Govinda)

Sur Das (1483 - 1563), 'the blind bard of Agra' lived at Gau Ghat, between Agra & Mathura. Reproduced a large number of episodes and passages from the Bhagvata Purana in verse. Sur Sagar, Suravali, Sahitya Lahiri, (in praise of K'rsna), story of Nala and Damyanti (Prose). He composed 75,000 verses. 'Sur is the sun, Tulsi the moon, Kesav DAs is a cluster of stars and poets of today glow worms'.

Chaurasi Varta by Gokul Nath (1568) is devoted exclusively to stories, mostly legendary of the followers Vallabhacharya. It lays a great deal of stress on the erotic side of K'rsna legends.

Radha Vallabhi (a new sect founded in Vrindaban in 1585). In this Radha is placed above K'rsna as an object of devotion. Its founder was Hari Vamsa (Hit Haribans or Hit Ji). Radha Sudha Nidhi was written by him in Sanskrit. In Hindi, his best work was

Chaurasi Pad (Premlata); erotic side of K'rsna and sensuous imagery.

Hari Dasis:

Another sect at Vrindaban is that of Hari Das (End 16th CAD): Teaching closely akin to Chaitanya. His best works are Sadharan Siddhant and the Ras Ke Pad. Vallabhacharya was born in the forest of camparanya in about 1479, a Telugu Brahman who developed the views of Visnusvami, called Shuddhadvaita or pure Non dualism undefiled by Maya. He elevated the transitory realities of the world to the seriousness of divine realities by maintaining the 'Principal' identity of the finity and the infinite while affirming the utter reality of the finite which owes its absolute entity to its being in principle identical with the infinite. Vallabhacharya is the most logically consistent of the Hindu theologians, but his position has not been well understood.

He simply discountenanced asceticism as a mode of commending man to God. He maintained that worship of the Deity need not be accompanied with fasting, self mortification and suppression of the passions, but that the natural appetities were intended to be gratified, and the good things of this world to be enjoyed.

He distinguishes between Jagat or Prapancha and Samsara. Jagat is the real manifestation of God, while Samsara, or the cycle of births and deaths is imagined by the soul on account of ignorance which is five fold:

1. Ignorance of the real nature of the soul.
2. False identification with the body
3. With the senses
4. With the vital breaths and
5. With the internal organ.

When knowledge dawns, ignorance vanishes and with it vanishes the samsara; but the world, the Jagat continues because it is the real manifestation of God. The only means of salvation is Bhakti, firm and all surpassing affection for God with a full sense of His Greatness. It is neither worship, nor knowledge. Affection is its dominant phase. It is the feeling of oneness with God, gained through the grace of God which is one by the purity of heart.

His son Vittalnath and his seven sons, called Gosainji established Gadis at Gokul (Mathura), different districts especially in Bombay, Kutch, Kathiavad and Malwa. Gosain (deviated Gosvamin) means lord of cows-an epithet of K'rsna.

Jiva Goswami (16th Century A.D.) and Baldeva (18th Century A.D.) declared the relation of the finite to the infinite nor amenable to intellectual definition and took refuge in utter surrender of the human mind to the will of God as the only tenable attitude when human vision is blinded by excessive light from all that the infinite implies.

Swami Narayana Sect

Swami Naryana, a high caste Brahman, born at Chapai, near Lucknow, was a vaishnava, who disgusted with the manner of life of the so called followers of Vallabhacharyas. He was against the precepts and practices and licentious habits of the Bombay Maharajas (Vallabhacharya spiritual chiefs). He was a celibate, virtuous, self-controlled, austere, ascetical, yet withal large hearted and philanthropic. He had great aptitude for learning. He was a disciple of Ramanda Swami and was called Sahajananda. His remarkable fascination of manner combined with consistency of moral character, and other qualities singled him out for a leader of an army of devoted adherents. His disciples. Increased so rapidly, that the Brahamana and magnates of Ahmedabad, (where he lived with Ramananda Swami), began to be jealous of his popularity. He erected a temple to NARAYANA (Visnu or K'rsna) associated with Laksmi at Wartal, where he worshipped and preached 'devotion to K'rsna as the SUPREME BEING, with observance of duty and purity of life. The two principal shrines of this sect are at Wartal and Ahmedabad. They have three figures; K'rsna as RanChore (deliverer of evil), an image of Narayana (Visnu, the Supreme Being) and Laksmi, consort of Visnu. In the other temple; K'rsna is in the middle, Radha on his right and Swami Narayana on his left. Swami Narayana, here, is worshipped as an incarnation of Visnu. The doctrines, like its Gods, its idols and its sectarism, are part and parcel of genuine Vaisnuism (purer side of modern Vaisnuism). The SHIKSHA PATRI, followed by the followers, assures the achievement of four great objects of all human desires vis religious merit, wealth, pleasure and beatitude.

CHAITANYA (1485-1527)

Chaitanya was born at Nadia (Bengal) in 1485 in an orthodox brahmin family as the son of Jagan Nath Misra. He was a famous scholar, who gave up his scholarship and took to the way of faith. He became a great bhakta, who went about singing bhajans with his disciples all over Bengal. Caitanya was a great mystic of Visnuism and his influence still exists in Bengal. He lived and practised the eternal truth of Vaisnuism, which reached its heights and became the living religion of the masses. Chaitanya realised in his life and has brought home the fact that mysticism is not to be easily ignored or taken lightly. One of the fundamental problems of Visnuism, is the status and destiny of the individual soul and its realisation with the Supreme Being. Chaitanyas's stress was on 'What is the true nature and ultimate destiny of the individual soul and how can it realise its true nature. His main objective was to determine the REALITY, value and freedom of man, and his only mission was to redeem humanity. He practised the truths embodied in the classics : upanishads, vedanta, Puranas and Gita and preached the path of devotion. His philosophies teachings dealt with problems of ultimate existence of the universe, the nature of Reality, the nature of soul, the nature of the world and the means to liberation. Lord K'rsna and his abode Vrindaban is the ultimate relation of worhsip; the way of devotion of the Gopis in His services is the only ideal path; Srimad Bhagwat is the only authoritative scripture; and love alone is the supreme end of the individual soul.

Chaitnya has been called the prophet and the leader of Vaisvanism. His affiliation to the whole trend of Vaisnava tradition of the past and its influence on him has been varied and abundant.

(S.K. De Early History of the Vaisnava faith and movement in Bengal P1)

In the Bhakti movement, the wisdom of the upanishads as propounded and practised by Chaitanya, in Bengal of medieval period of Indian History.

'Chaitanya ushered a new era in Bengal and laid the basis for Modern Bengal Culture'. He was an apostle of love but also of basic human dignity, to whom humility was as natural as an iron will which never compromised on essentials'

(Majumdar: Chaitanya: His life & Doctrine P X)

Followers of Chaitanya called Gossains, Bhagvatas, Vairagis or other names, worship Visnu in his form of K'rsna, conceived as B'rhma or the supreme spirit. The social importance of his reform consisted chiefly in the complete ignoring of caste. He taught and his followers continue to teach that the original cause of all things was wisdom (of vedas). He is called spiritual, pure, and full of ecstasy. According to him K'rsna, the supreme Being, has three phases : 1. B'rhma, the light of the world that gives vitality to all. The sages try to reach Him by wisdom. 2. Parmatman, he who is sentient, Omnipresent and Omniscient, and 3. Bhagavat or the Personal God, who manifests Himself in the material world. Men try to reach Him through Bhakti (devotion).

'The human soul (Jivatman), according to Chaitanya, is an infinitesimal portion, like a ray, of the Divine Being. God is like a blazing fire, and the sound are like sparks that come out of it[1].

Chaitanya defined Bhakti as an uninterrupted tendency of the heart towards God, just like the flow of a river towards the sea. He preached that it must be the aim of every man to gain K'rsna's love, and Bhakti is the way that leads to it, and that it is the duty of every man to adore K'rsna and to perform good deeds without any expectation of rewards.

Chaitanya treated all followers as equals and said, 'The mercy of God regards neither tribe nor family' Chaitanya taught that the great aim of every worshipper of K'rsna ought to be to lose all individuality and self consciousness in ecstatic union with his God. Incessant repetition of the deity's name, singing, music, dancing or dancing movements brought about intense religious fervour. Chaitanya is a living reality even today, whose religious approach incarnated in Rama Krishna Parmattansa and whose immense influence of K'rsna consciousness, has been manifested today in the 'Hare Rama Hare Krishna' movements.

Repetition of the deity's name (Nam Kirtan) propounded by Chaitanya is the basic practice of this modern international movement (Hare K'rsna Hare Rama).

---

1. Max Mueller : Ram Mohan to Rama Krishna (1952) PP 51 - 53

Chaitanya was revered as the incarnation of K'rsna from his very birth especially because he was in womb for thirteen months and a group of saints including Advaita paid homage to the new born child, soon after his birth, at the end of an eclipse. In his childhood, he resembled the young K'rsna in condescending to boyish sports (K'rsna Leela). He acquired complete knowledge of Sanskrit Grammar and Literature at a very young age. Bhagvata Purana and Bhagvad Gita were his favourite studies at the age of 25, abandoning all worldly connections, he commenced a series of pilgrimages. In his travels during next six years, he visited shrines at Varanasi, Gaya, Mathura, Srirangam and ultimately Jagan Nath at Puri. He appointed his disciples Advaita and Nityananda to look after his followers and himself retired in close proximity to Jagannath temple at Puri and passed last days of his life. Finally his death was mysterious in 1527, when some believe he walked into the sea fancying that he saw a beautific vision of K'rsna sporting on the waves.

He was a remarkable preacher. Crowds gathered round him wherever he went. Many accompanied him in his travels. Even his enemies were attracted by the persuasiveness of his manner and the magnetic power of his eloquence.

CHAPTER - 16

BHAKTI AND BHAKTI MOVEMENT

In Vedic times, Karma (the way of work) through sacrifice and priestly rituals, was practised as the way to obtain salvation (release from samsara i.e. the world of birth, rebirth or bondage). Later Upanishad teachings introduced Jnana Marga (the way of knowledge). Both these methods were restrictive and were limited to brahmins, who could attain moksha (release), The knowledge of Upanishads was for the learned few, Therefore a need was felt in the society for a way for all to attain Moksha and this method was through devotion to GOD (Shakti), open to all, irrespective of caste and creed.

In the popular mind, religion is synonymous with worship or adoration of God. The popular belief in all religions is that God is the foundation and fountain of mercy and His grace is always available to those of faith. Hinduism prescribes a code of righteousness in conduct and moral discipline (DHARMA) for the individual and insists on his acting according to this code, to acquire purity of soul. Mere moral life, is not, sufficient to achieve spiritual satisfaction and happiness. The mind of a devotee should constantly be attracted by and seek solace in God. That is BHAKTI, essentially the attuning of the mind to God. One of the natural instincts of animate beings is to love. If such love is directed towards a permanent entity like God, it is Bhakti, which leads to bliss or permanent unalloyed happiness, a condition of mind by which it is constantly drawn to the Lord of creation. It, therefore, requires concentration of mind. Such concentration has to be cultivated and developed by training. Hinduism provides a number of methods, forms and practices for inculcating Bhakti

(i) By listening to discourses; for the duration of the discourse, the mind of the listener is more or less revetted to God. World wide organisation, International Society for K'rsna consciousness (ISKCON) is based on this method (Bhajans organised by groups of people).

(ii) By recitation of slokas, hymns or songs in praise of God and His glory and seeking His grace. This method of worship, which has been adopted through the ages, has invariable given inspiration and satisfaction to the devotees.

(iii) Practice of participating with devotion in festivals, visiting temples, making pilgrimages, taking bath in holy rivers etc. All these are time tested methods of cultivating Bhakti. Devotees get a high degree of spiritual satisfaction in the temples, where the whole atmosphere is surcharged with piety (particularly in ancient ones).

(iv) The simplest means of worship is NAMA JAPA (repetition of the name of the chosen deity, such as OM NAMA SIVAYE, Narayana, Hare Rama etc. In Hinduism, the divine name represents the deity itself. In this method there is no restriction regarding the time, place, caste, sex or age. In PADMA PURANA, it is stated, 'There is no difference between the holy name of the Lord himself. As such the holy name is as perfect as the Lord himself in fullness, purity and eternity. The holy name is not a material sound vibration, nor has it any, material contamination'.

(v) Image (moorti) puja is a valuable method to attract the mind towards God and keep it steady during contemplation by providing a concrete image before its devotee, a rapport between the devotee and the deity, his ishtdevta (deity of his choice).

The Bhakti (devotion) was based on K'rsna saying in Bhagvad

Gita,'In whatever form you worship me, in that form, I strengthen your faith'. Worship of images in the temples gained prominence, Vishnu, Siva alongwith Sakti became prominent during the Bhakti movement, Avtaras (incarnations) gained importance. Visnu's incarnations as RAMA and K'RSNA took hold of the mind and hearts of the people through epics RAMAYANA and The MAHABHARATTA. This revival in Hinduism grew to such proportions that it spread into distant places like Sumatra, Java, Malaya and Indochina.

The most essential element of Bhakti is reverence and sincerity. Devotion is not measured by the monetary value or worth of offerings. K'rsna says in Bhagvad Gita that a mere leaf, a flower, a fruit or even a spoon of water, is sufficient offering to God, so long as it is done with devotion.

BHAKTI MOVEMENT (1400-1550)

During the transforming period (1400-1550), the various Bhakti movements in Hinduism, fall into three groups viz :-

(i) Those who worshipped RAMA as an incarnation and practised idolatry i.e. Ramananda, Surdasa, Tulsidasa.

(ii) Those who worshipped God under the name of Rama, but rejected idolatry and the doctrine of incarnation viz Kabir, Daau Panthis, Satnamis, Nanak, Malik Muhammad Jayasi.

(iii) Those who worshipped K'rsna (Jaya Deva, Nar Simha Mehta, Vidyapati Thakur (15th C.A.D. Bihari), Umapati (K'rsna songs in maithali & Bengali), Mira Bai, Vallabhacharya, Vithal Nath, Narotam Das (1530, composed Sudama Charitr and Dhruv Charitr), Kripa Ram (1540, composed Hit Tarangini in Braj Bhasha).

Vallabhacharya in his work 'Bhakti Vandhini' consisting of 11 verses says that Bhakti gives strengthening by fixing one's mind on Him while performing one's duties in life. This will give rise to ardent love for God tending to passionate attachment and culminating in arduous love sickness for the attainment of K'rsna. One who possesses this love sickness attains supreme Bhakti culminating in final beatitude (as the God promises in the Bhagvad Gita)[1]. The devotee who is firmly engaged in his worship or deliberations never perishes physically, mentally or spiritually because he is protected by the God Himself.

Gokul Nath Ji, grandson of Vallabhacharya, son of Vithaleshaji (Gujarat), emphasizes the doctrine of Bhakti simple yet benevolent behaviour, inculcation of excellent virtues and noble character in one's life.

Swami Vasudevanandji (Garudeshwara) of Maharashtra (1854) has compared three limbs of salvation (Mukti) viz. Detachment (Virkit), Devotion (Bhakti) and knowledge (Gyapati) to Triveni of three sacred rivers viz. Yamuna, Ganga and Saraswati.

Sri Aurobindo[2] reiterates, 'When a Man has lost his separative personality and has dedicated himself to the supreme God by means of profound Bhakti, he becomes one with Him, attains divine perfection.

Jaya Deva

Jaya deva, who lived at the end of the twelfth century, was born at Kendula, near Bolpur. He wrote and sung songs descriptive of the amours of K'rsna and was one of the best lyrical songsters of India, connected with the Bhakti revival. During his times, those songs were known as Prabandhas, compiled in the famous Gita Govinda. It is a charming lyrical composition and has been translated in English entitled 'The Indian song of Songs'. In these songs Radha pours forth her yearning, her sorrow and her joy

1. Dr. Radhakrishnan S. The Hindu view of Life P 18
2. Sri Aurobindo = Essays on the Geeta P 261

and K'rsna assures her of his love. Gita Govinda is the best specimen of erotic religious lyric of the cowherd K'rsna and is a refined theme of popular song. Jaya Deva's composition of Gita Govinda in Sanskrit was for the dance, like 'Silappadikaram' (Tamil) and 'Padams' of kshetrgna.

Gita Govinda has been a very favourite topic with the artists, in particular with the painters of Rajasthan and Pahari schools. Lalit Kala Akademy (National Institute of Art) has also brought out a port folio of paintings based on Gita Govinda.

Nar Singh Mehta (Nara Simha Mehta) was another musician of the times, who wrote Radha K'rsna lyrics in Bengali. He also composed similar verses in Hindi and Maithali).

Rama Nanda (1400-1470)

The rise of the worship of Rama, which took place about the beginning of the fifteenth century, gave another impetus to Hinduism and its literature, in addition to the long worshipped K'rsna. Owing to the great influence of Ramananda, many others made Rama their principal object of worship. In this period Kabir was the first great teacher who gave the direction of a nonidolatrous theism. From this period (1400 - onwards) and on account of various movements, literature was mostly dominated by religious ideals and almost entirely on the lines which had been laid down by the Vaishnava reformers.

Ramananda was an ascetic who preached that eternal God should be worshipped under the name of Rama, that Rama alone was the source of release from the evils of transmigration and that this should be sought by fervent devotion (bhakti) towards him. He settled at Varanasi and made that the headquarters of the new movement. He was one of the most important Hindu religious leaders in North India, for his own sect and for others who followed in like manner. He did not forbid idolatry, though he criticised it. He preached a vivid faith in the reality of one personal God, spiritual and invisible, whom he called Rama, but no break was made with idolatry, the Hindu Pantheon or the old mythology. Nor did he throw over the system of caste. He acknowledged even outcaste and amongst his personal disciples there have been not only a Sudra, a Jat an outcaste, but even a muslim weaver and a women. Rai Das, his chamar disciple, attained great celebrity as a devotee. His disciple, Pipa, Raja of Gagaraungarh abdicated his sovereignty and became a mendicant. From this on, religious literature started processing in Hindi, as against Sanskrit. Bhakta Mala of Nabhaji (1600) is an outstanding Hindi work of importance in vaishnava movement, in particular for Ramanand's.

Kabir (1440-1518) A muslim weaver was the greatest of the disciples of Ramananda. His birth is disputed as the one from a Brahmin widow. Being an outcaste, he manages to become a disciple of Ramananda. He knew that Ramananda went for bath to the ghat in early hours. So he lay on the steps in darkness, when Ramananda's foot fell on him, he uttered 'Ram Ram'. Since then Kabir gained the discipleship of Ramananda. In preachings, he even excelled him. His teaching and preaching reflected Muslim influence. He uses the name Rama for God (as well as other names such as Hari, Govind, Allah etc.). He has vedantic ideas but rejected the doctrine of incarnations, condemned idolatry and most of the Hindu ceremonies and rites. There was severe opposition of both Hindus and Muslims, who were offended in turn at his denunciation of many of their practices. He was persecuted by Emperor Sikandar Lodi, exiled from Varanasi and ended his days at Maghar (Gorakhpur District, Uttar Pradesh).

Kabir was influenced by muslim sufis and preached the gospel of love of GOD, equality and service to mankind and tried to promote communal harmony. He held that RAM and RAHIM were different names of the same God. His couplets were extremely popular among the masses and are quoted even today. He did not attach any importance to the performance of rituals and ceremonies or to pilgrimages to holy places. Above all he denounced insincerity and hypocrisy. According to him, salvation could be attained by doing good deeds (Karma) and by means of Bhakti (sincere devotion of GOD).

He was equally loved by Hindus and Muslims. On his death, the conflict between Hindus and Muslims, for cremation or burial, could only be settled when they removed the shroud from over his body, and found only flowers, which they divided among themselves.

Kabir Panthis, influenced by teachings of Kabir, have two divisions; one at Kabir Chaura (Varanasi) associated with Maghar (where Kabir died) and the other at Chhatisgarh (Madhya Pradesh). Although the Kabir Panthis have, as a whole, kept free from the worship of images, Hindu influence has, in various ways, found its wayback into the sect. BIJAK, SUKHNIDHAN, AMAR MAL, and KUNDLIYA are the religious books of the sect. Kabir taught Vaishnuism as a form of strict monotheism.

He says:-

'What availeth devotion, what penance, what fasting and worship,

To him in whose heart, there is worldly love

O man, apply thy heart to God.

Thou shall not obtain Him by artifice.

Put away convetousness and regard for what people say of thee.

Renounce lust, wrath and pride.

By the religious ceremonies of the Hindus, conceit is produced,

That if they join and worship a stone, they shall receive salvation.

Saith Kabir, by serving Him I have obtained the Lord. By becoming simple in heart I have met my God.

Many other later vaishnuism seets owe to Kabir the leading ideas of their theology, of the many movements which owe their inspiration to the teaching of Kabir, none is more important than the sect Sikhism. Adi Granth (1604) contains one collection of Kabir's hymns and more than thirty hymns of Rai Das (disciple of Ramananda). The key note of Kabir's teaching was the duty of obeying spiritual leaders. He maintained, in fact, that every man was bound to search for a true and trustworthy spiritual pastor (Guru), and having found one; to make him his master, to submit mind, conscience and even body to his will and guidance[1]. This doctrine of Kabir formed the basis of Sikhism.

Dadu Panthis, founded by a follower of Kabir, named Dadu (1544-1603), a cotton cleaner of Ahmedabad, who spent most of his life in Rajputana. The religious works of this sect are all founded on the precepts and doctrines of Kabir. The followers are really vaishnava theists and worshippers of the one God under some of the names of Visnu. His spirit of forgiveness and kindness was so great that he was called Dadu Dayal. Dadu's teachings contained in 'Bani' in 5,000 verses in 37 chapters dealing with Divine Teacher, Remembrance, Separation, The meeting, The Mind, Truth, The Good, Faith and Prayer etc.

---

1 Williams Monier : Religious life in Ancient India PP 160

Satnamis is another sect founded by Jagjivan Das (1750) Kabir's disciple. They are also vaishnava theisists. They call their one God 'Satnam' and base their doctrine like the Sikhs on Kabir's school of theology. Jagjivan Das wrote Hindi verses "Pratham Granth', 'Mahapralay' and 'Gyan Prakas'. Satnamis adore and True Name (Satnam) alone, the one God, who is without attributes, but the Hindu Pantheon is recognised and the Hindu incarnations are regarded as the manifestations of God. Although Jagjivan Das was a Kshatriya, but the Satnami sect found its followers at the maximum among outcastes.

A few precepts and rules of the sect are :-

'God pervades the universe. He is present in every single thing. The title Lord should be added to every object in which God is present. God is the spring and source of every thing good and evil. Idols must not be worshipped. The ordained religious teacher (Guru) is holy. Distinctions of caste are not to be observed.

Fasts need not be kept. Feed the poor. Wound no one's feelings. When the dead are burned let no one cry or weep; let them only exclaim, 'The Lord gave and the Lord has taken away'[1]. In Rohtak (Haryana), the sect, of Satnami Sadhus, does not mourn or perform any Kria Karm after death[2].

Lal Dasis (Found by Lal Das who died in 1648) in Alwar region, Sadhs (Founded by Bir Bhan in 1658) in Doab area, Charan Dasis (found by Charan Das (1703-1782) at Delhi, Siv Narayanis (Siv Narayan 1734), Garib Dasis (Garib Das 1717-1782 in Haryana; composed Guru Granth Sahib composed of 24000 Sakhis and Chaupais; including 7000 Kabir's Sakhis), Ram Snehis (Ram Charan 1718 in Rajputana) and Pran Nathis (Pran Nath, 18th CAD

---

1 Williams M : Religious life in Ancient India P 179

2 Rose H.A. Religious Life of Indian People P 852

Bundelkhand) are the subsects based on Kabir's teachings (directly or indirectly): the need of a guru and respect due to him, the value of the repetition of the name of God, the supreme importance of devotion (Bhakti), the delusions of Maya (illusion), the value of truth, the duty of living a righteous and sober life, these and a few kinded topics are repeated over and over again, in different ways, in these sects, through smooth and rhythmical verse (Santa ras)

Nanak (Sikhism)

The sect founded by Nanak styled themselves sikhs or disciples to express their close dependence on their teachers of Gurus, a doctrine enunciated by Kabir and of all Vaishnava teaching, which was 'Hear the word of the Guru, the word of the Guru is the guide', much more did Nanak insist on a similar submission. Literally interpreted the term Guru is derived from Sanskrit root 'gri' (to utter words) and Sishya (corrupted into Sikh) in Sanskrit means 'one who is to be instructed, so guru & sikh (sishya) or teacher and taught. So the system may be suitably called Guruism of Sikhism[1].

Of the many movements which owe their inspiration to the teaching of Kabir, none is more important then the religion of the sikhs, which was founded in the Punjab by Nanak (1469-1538). It is said that Nanak, when twenty seven years of age, met Kabir, and the influence of the latter is seen not only in the large number of Kabir's compositions afterwards included - the Granth Sahib, but in the doctrines of Nanak, which are very similar to those of Kabir, and undoubtedly owe a great deal to him, though Nanak stands nearer to Hinduism than Kabir. Nanak made journeys in several directions accompanied by his disciple Mardana, who played the reback while Nanak sang. His hymns and other

1 Williams M : Religious life in Ancient India (1990) PP 161

poetical utterances were in a mixture of Punjabi & Hindi. Although he is nor equal to Kabir as a poet, yet his verse is clear and pithy, and not lacking in poetical excellence. His most famous composition is Japji (a collection of verses which he arranged for their daily use in praise and prayer).

'There is no limit to God's praises; to those who repeat them there is no limit.

There is no limit to His Mercy, and to his gifts there is no limit.
There is no limit to what God Seeth, no limit to what he heareth.
The limit of the secret of His heart cannot be known.
The limit of His creation cannot be known; neither
His near nor His far side can be discovered.
To know His limits how many Vex their hearts.
His limits cannot be ascertained;
Nobody knoweth His limits.
The more we say, the more there remains to be said.
Great is the Lord, and exalted is His seat.
His exalted name is higher than the most exalted.
Were anyone else ever so exalted,
Then He would know that exalted Being :
How Great He is He knoweth Himself.

Nanak,God bestoweth gifts on whom He looketh with favour and mercy'.[1]

Nanak (1469-1538)

The entire teachings of Guru Nanak is but a synthesis of the fundamental priciples of both the religions (Hinduism & Islam).

Nanak was born at Talvandi, near Lahore, in 1469. At an early age he became a diligent student of vaishnava religious

1. Macauliffe : The Sikh religion Vol. 1 translation of JAPJI XXN.

books and in his youth he imitated and example of other incipient reformers, wondering to various shrines in search of some clue to the ladyrinth of Hinduism. His travels included the performance of a haj to Mecca, and on being reproved by the Kazi for lying down with his feet towards the Kabah, he replied, 'Put my feet in their direction where the house of God is not.'

His teaching was mainly founded on that of his predecessors, especially Kabir. He was also a reference who aimed, as other reformers had done before him, at delivering Hinduism, and especially the Vaishnuism of Northern India, from its incubus of caste, superstition and idolatry. He discarded caste system and taught that the supreme being was no 'respecter of persons'. He welcomed all persons of all ranks and castes as his followers God, he said; is supreme Lord overall (Parmeswara). He may be called Brahma, Govinda or anyother name, but his special name is Hari (Visnu). This supreme being does not create the Universe out of nothing, but evolves it out of himself. It is a kind of expansion of his own essence which takes place for his own amusement, such expansion being made up of three Gunas, Sattva, Rajas and Tamas, in perfect equilibrium. These Gunas act like cords to bind the spirit with triple bonds; Sattva (Purity or goodness), Rajas (Passion or activity) and Tamas (darkness or indifference) regarded as equivalent to pleasure, pain and indolence respectively. It is Illusion (Maya) which disturbs this equilibrium and causes the apparent separation between God, the world and the human soul. All this is pure Brahmanism, except in denouncing idolatry, Nanak differed very little from a pure vasisnava; for the taught that in the present age (Kaliyuga) the repetition of the name of Hari is the only means of salvation, notwithstanding the merit to be gained by benevolent works and religious ceremonies and that the knowledge of this name is only to be acquired through a properly ordained teacher, Guru.

Sikhism, founded by Vaishnuvite Nanak later changed to as separate religion through other Gurus Angada, Amar Das, Ram Das, Arjun, Har Govind, Har Rai, Har Kishan, Teg Bahadur and Govind Singh, the last tenth Guru who made it a martial class.

Tulsi Dasa's Ram Charit Manas (Ramayana) was the culmination of the great religious movement of which the great lights that preceeded him were Ramananda, Kabir and Nanak.

Nanak's poetic mysticism (abridged and altered from Prof. Trumpp's version) can be visualised from :-[1]

Namdeva belonged to the Maratha region and was a devotee of Vithoba at Pandharpur. He flourished between 1400-1430 ? As a boy, he showed great devotion but for sometime, thereafter lived an evil life in the company of a band of dacoits. After realisation, he became a great devotee, composed many hymns in Marathi. For his verses in Hindi, he was a noteworthy religious leader in the North. Granth of the Sikhs contains many of his hymns. He was one of the first leaders of the new religious revival (Bhakti movement) in North India.

'At the beginning is the TRUE one,

The TRUE one is, O Nanak/ and the TRUE one also will be, Know, that there are two ways (that of Hindus and that of Musalmans), but only one lord.

By thyself all the creation is produced; by thyself, having created the whole is caused to disappear.

Mutter the name of HARI, Hari, O My heart, by which comfort is brought about; by which all sins and vices disappear; by which

---

1 Quoted from Monier Williams 'Religious life in Ancient India (1990) PP 171
Cf Valmiki, the author of epic 'Ramayana' was also a great dacoit in youth.

poverty and pain cease.

Thou art I, I am thou, of what kind is the difference? Like gold and the bracelet, like water and a wave.

In the seven insular continents, the seven oceans, the nine regions, the four vedas, the eighteen puranas; in all, thou, O Hari, art abiding; in all thy decree, O Hari, is working.

By the perfect Guru, the name of Hari is made firm in me, Hari is my beloved, my king. If someone bring and unite (Him with me), my life is revived...................

'Be united with the lord of the universe. After a long time, this (human) body was obtained. In some births thou wast made a rock and mountain. In some births thou wast produced as a pot herb. In the eightyfour lakhs of (forms of existence) thou wast caused to wander about..................

'Having forgotten all things, meditate on the One Drop false conceit, offer up (thy) mind and body.

An eternal message of hope given in the Bhagvad Gita states:-

'That whenever DHARMA is eclipsed, saints will be born to put down Adharma to defeat evil and to uphold the TRUTH and the good.' So many saints, the preachers of BHAKTI were born all over India, in the south, Meerabai in Rajasthan, Kabir, Nanak in North. In Maharashtra Sant DYANESHWAR and others.

SANT DYANESHWAR

He was the greatest of the saints of Maharashtra, who was born in 1275 A.D. in a brahmin family at apegaon, near Paithon, situated on the banks of river Godavari. He was blessed with Divine knowledge and showed signs of greatness from his childhood. His followers belonged to all castes, as he did not believe in caste system. He condemned rituals, ceremonies and sacrifices in religious worship. His followers called VARKARIS, believe in attaining the presence of GOD through religious songs or Bhajans and prayers. They worship Lord VITHOBA of Pandharpur, whom they believe as the incarnation of VISNU, are therefore Vaisnuites. Sant Dyaneshwar wrote a commentary on Bhagwad Gita in marathi entitled' Dnyaneshwari and also some other religious books in Marathi; AMRITANUBHAVA, ATMANANUBHAVA and BHAVARTH DIPIKA.

SANT NAMDEO

A follower of DYANESHWAR, he believed in the equality of all men. He advised people to follow BHAKTI marga (Path) or the path of deep devotion to God. He created in them a strong desire to protect their religion and a deep love for their motherland. He composed songs in Marathi, but also in HINDI. Some of his devotional songs have been included in GRANTH SAHIB and other religious books of the Sikhs.

SANT EKNATH

Born in 1538 A.D. in a brahmin family at Paithan, was a follower of Sant Dyaneshwara and Sant Ek Nath. He advocated social equality and preached the abolition of distinctions based on class, caste and creed. He did not believe in rituals, ceremonies and other orthodox ways of worship. Through his songs called ABHANGAS, his advice to the people was not to accept any distinction of high and low and taught them true devotion to GOD (Bhakti marag). He also wrote a commentary on Bhagwata Purana entitled ' EKNATHI BHAGWAT'.

SANT TUKA RAM

Born in a vaishya family in 1608 A.D. at Dahu, near Pune, he was deeply religious even in his childhood and spent his time in singing devotional songs in praise of his favourit deity Lord

Vithoba (Visnu incarnate). He believed in and preached Bhaktimarga (Devotion). He preached the virtues of piety, forgiveness and peace of mind. He also gave the people the message of equality and brotherly feeling for one another. He said :-
'He alone is a saint and God dwells with him, who calls the weak and the downtrodden as his own'.

SAMARTH GURU RAMDAS

Guru Ramdas, distinct from Sikh Guru Ram Das, was born on RAMNAVMI (the day of Lord Rama' birth) in 1608 A.D. at Jamb, situated on the banks of river Godavari. A born devotee, he had decided to devote himself to religion and to the worship of Lord RAMA. He made Lord Rama and Hanuman as his ideals. He advised the people that religion is the most precious possession of a man. 'If Faith perishers, then death would be preferable to life' was his message, a necessity of the time as the Hindus were harassed in the worship of their Gods by Muslim rulers of Deccan at that time. Through his great book 'DASBODH', he taught people the ways of a good life.

Gora bai, Chokha Jana Bai and many others thrill the minds of men with their songs on HINDUISM : Bhakti aspect.

The Tamil poet Subramanyam Bharati, visualised K'rsna as friend, mother, father, servant, king, disciple, guru, child, lover, husband and God in his poems. He was a vaisnuvite and preached Bhakti as the path of salvation.

The impact of Islam on Hinduism was two fold. It made the Hindus more orthodox and conservative, Hindu caste rules became more rigid for fear of conversion. The BHAKTI cult which believed in a personal God and which had started in the South in the eighth century A.D., received great momentum under the influence of the sufi philosophers. The Saints of the Bhakti movement de nounced ritualism, sacrifices, fasting etc. enjoined by the BRAHAMANAS. They believed in the equality of all men and the unity of God. They held that through devotion and love, one could attain GOD. Through devotional songs, one could reach the state of ecstasy and Bhajans (religious songs) written and sung by the great saints in different regional languages became extremely popular.

All the saints of the Bhakti movement were inspired by the philosophy of the Upanishads and wanted to simplify Hinduism and purify it of its ritualism. They carried the message of love and devotion in regional languages and thus enriched their minds. The Bhakti movement had two social effects also. First, it denounced the Hindu Caste system and secondly it tried to raise the status of women in society and restore to them the place of honour and respect, which they enjoyed in the VEDIC AGE. Bhakti movement gave an impetus to liberal reformatory movement in Hinduism.

BHAKTI, devotion to personified God occupies a place of pride in all three main schools of philosophy in Hinduism viz the Advaita of Sankaracharaya, the Visista of Ramanujaacharaya and the Dvaita of Madhavaacharaya.

CHAPTER - 17

FLORA IN HINDUISM

'With a Hindu, all organic life is sacred. Even plant life is to be respected, and must not want only be destroyed.' The Hindu was taught to worship and rever the tree, in the belief that it would influence his own personal being. The tree which offers shade, gives fruit, a valuable source of food, a tree of the field is man's life. It is not surprising, therefore, to find a tree cult as far back as Vedic times, and trees or rather the spirits which inhabit them, invoked as deities.

Nature, elements of nature, have always been worshipped since the Vedic times. Fertility of crops and human beings was considered by the primitive people, to be influenced by the powers invested in the trees. To such trees, offerings were made at seed time and harvest. It was a step to invest them with all sorts of divine attributes, as the waving of their leaves to primitive minds clearly showed that they held spirits. Groves of trees, have been looked upon form times immemorial, as the home of Gods. Primitive tribes dared not cut down forest trees, for the fear of wrath of the inhabiting spirits in them.

'Evergreen trees are regarded by some devout Hindus as types of eternal life, and the forest tribes bury their dead in trees and believe that the spirits of the dead inhabit them:[1]

There are many sacred trees, which have been referred to in the PURANAS and have been reverred by the people since protohistoric period. More ancient and important of the trees belong to Fig species.

---

1. Blackham R.J. : INCOMPARABLE INDIA

THE PIPPAL

PIPPALA or ASVATTHA tree (Pipal), botanically termed Ficus religiosa, is a holy fig tree, held to be the most holy. It is said to be pervaded by the TRINITY (B'rhma, Visnu and Siva). Representations of Pipal appear on many seals and painted pottery of Indus valley culture. It is believed that spirits delight to sit in the branches of this tree and listen to the rustling of leaves. It has a divine personality, occupied by the essence of God B'rhma. It is so holy that no Hindu would venture to tell an untruth or deviate from the strictest rectitudes conduct, while standing under a pipal tree. Uncanny movement of its leaves causes 'awe' among village folk. In BHAGVADGITA ,K'rsna says, 'I am ASVATTHA among the trees'.

The most famous of pipal trees is the sacred pipal at Gaya, under which BUDDHA sat, when he gained wisdom. No doubt, the old tree of Buddha's period (BODHI DRUMMA) does not exist anymore, by succession of trees has been secured by planting new shoots inside the old decaying stem, as we see at present.

In about 300 B.C. Asoka the great, transferred an offshoot of Bodhi tree to Sri Lanka (Aniruddha Pura), in a golden vase, in which it was transported by sea to Sri Lanka. It was received by King TISSA, who planted it and it still exists there after 2000 years.

Braham Purana[1] legend about Pipleswar Pilgrimage substantiates the benevolence of Pipal tree, and also of river Saraswati with her presiding deity Goddness Saraswati. In this legend, Daddichi rishi, his wife Lopa Mudra and their son Piplashan, have been described. Pipleswar pilgrimage is an reverence to Piplashan Rishi. The legend is that at one time, after gaining

1. BRAHAM PURANA PT I .46

a victory over the Asuras (demons), Gods and deities did not find anymore use of the weapons. Since these weapons were not likely to be used, carrying these was considered as burden some by them. So they thought of keeping them in safe custody. They, then went on the banks of Bhagirthi Ganga and came to the Ashram of Daddichi rishi (saint). After exchange of reverence, Goda stayed in his ashram. In due course, they expressed the intention of their visit. They said that as Rishi Daddichi was the only one, who had the expertise of all weapons and that his ashram was safe, the wished to deposit all their weapons with the Rishi. Daddichi hesitated, his wife also reluctantly suggested not to take the risk. Ultimately Daddichi agreed and all weapons were accepted. Gods took leave of the Rishi and went away.

As the disputes between Suras (Gods) and Asuras (demons) were always there and demons were powerful and cruel, Daddichi apprehended danger in retaining the weapons. So he, by his divine powers, stored all weapons in his body frame. By the passage of time, Gods visualised invasion from the demons. So, they approached Daddichi and requested him to return the weapons. Daddichi replied that all those weapons had been installed in his body and those could only be procured from his bones and his internal body. He further said that he would give up his life by virtue of his Yoga qualities and then weapons could be retrieved by the Gods. Then Daddichi, sitting crosslegged, under meditation, gave up his life. Immediately, then Gods requested Swashta to extract the weapons out of the body of Daddichi. Swashta expressed his inability to extract weapons from the body of a Brahmin. Then Gods requested the cows to lick the body of the rishi, so done, Swashta then extracted the weapons and the body was taken away to rishi's abode.

In due course, Lopa Mudra, rishi's wife returned. She was pregnant. She lamented at the death of her husband and wished to curse the Gods. Since she had no power to curse them, she decided to give up her life and submerge in Agni (fire). Then she gave birth to an infant, placed the infant under a Pipal tree and breathed her last. Before her last breath, she said, 'Whoso-ever is born in this world, that all is mortal. All those who are very pious, give away their life for the sake of Gods and perceptive Brahmins.'

The infant, nourished by Pipal tree was named PIPLASHAN. By the passage of time, he attained youth and mighty power. He took a vow to take revenge against those who were the cause of the death of his parents. He under went severe asceticism and worshipped God SIVA. Gods and divinities were frightened because by the powers attained from worship of Siva, Piplashan could gain powers enough to massacre Gods. So they, approached B'rhma, who advised them to go to God Siva. Siva, on hearing the problem of the divinities, advised them to go to SURYA and that under his care and in his domain, they would face no risk. Gods then prayed to Siva to calm down Piplakshan. Siva said to Piplakshan, ' O Piplad, your dead father Daddichi cannot come back. These gods have, produced you to perform divine duties, since your father was a friend of Gods, incomparable to anyone else in the world and was merciful. Your mother was also very pious, virtuous and a faithful wife. Both of them are now in paradise (Swarga). You have also been awarded with great respect. These divinities are afraid of you and you are the only one who can safeguard them. No deed is more virtuous than that.' Explaining the necessity of benevolent action, Siva advised him to calm down and in solace undertake good work. Piplad was convinced, obediently he agreed to do as ordained by Siva. Thus Gods and divinities became free from fear and all of them praised Lord Siva. On request from Piplad, Siva gave Piplad a chance to see his parents in Swarga. His father Daddichi blessed him to have a wife and children, and then disappeared. Deities then appealed to Piplad to terminate the evil of revenge and that he would be benedicted, because at that time ferocious ANAL had appeared in his mouth. B'rhma expressed his inability to cool down that Anal because that was AGNI, a synthesis of all five elements (Prithvi, Water, Air, Fire and Sky). On further request of B'rhma other divinities, worshipped Agni and on their prayers, that Fire turned into Badwa river and merged in Ganges. Agni, then in a horrible form appeared and advised deities to learn that among all elements, water is superior most. So to call down Anal (Fire), it was essential that Agni should reach the waters (sea). On wishing to know how that could be done, Agni advised that if a virtuous virgin could take me in a nutshell (golden Pot) to the sea, then his progress could be cut down.

Hearing this, Gods and deities prayed to the virgin Saraswati.Gods addressing her said, 'O Saraswati, May you take this Anal (fire) on your head and take it to the sea.' Saraswati replied that she alone was incapable of undertaking such a hazardous job. If there were four more virgins, she could then easily take that to the sea. The deities then prayed to GANGA, Yamuna, Narmada and Tapti separately. Then Saraswati with the help of other four divine rivers carried that Anal fire to the sea, where gradually that fire (Agni) became a part of the waters. Piplad (Piplakshan) rishi married the daughter of Gautam rishi. His sons settled there. Since then that place has become a holy place for pilgrimage, the PIPLESHWAR pilgrimage, where Lord Siva is the reigning deity.

BANYAN TREE

The next most worthy notable example of tree worship is the Banyan tree, also called Vata, Vad, botanically Ficus indica. It is sacred to Kaal (TIME). The name Banyan seems to have been given, because the merchants (Banyas) used to worship it. Like Pipal, Banyanis also supposed to enjoy immortality. The planter of this tree prays, ' May I abide in heaven as many years as this tree continues growing on the earth.' The propagation of Banyan is a common knowledge. MILTON in PARADISE LOST supports its immortality :-

'The fig tree as this day to Indians known
In Malabar or Deccan, spreads her arms,
Branching so broad and long, that on the ground
The besided twigs take root, and daughters grow
High over arched and echoing walks between.'

A Banyan tree, on the banks of Narbada river near Broach, called KABIR VAD, has grown every year, by sending down roots that it can provide shade to about 7000 persons. This tree had grown out of a twig, used by Kabir as tooth brush. The Banyan has received homage in Hinduism through many ages, and its many stems may be regarded as the home of Gods and spirits. An undying Banyan tree in Allahabad fort, mentioned by Hieun Tsang (630 A.D.) has a legendary tale that RAMA, Sita and Lakshmana, took refuge under it, while, in exile.

The anthropomorphic worship of the Banyan is represented on a Buddhist sculpture from Malwa and is pictured as the 'Wishing tree'.

BEL (Bilva, Vilva, wood apple, botanically Aegle marmelos):-

Leaves of Bel tree, supposed to possess cooling properties, grateful to the God Siva, are offered in prayers and placed on Siva Linga and Nandi (Siva's bull). Triple form of Bel leaf is consecrated to Siva with his triple functions (creative, preserver and destroyer).

Some other trees held sacred are :-

ASOKA, botanically Jonesia asoka; a plant sacred to Siva.

AMRA (Mango) asserted by brahmins as an incarnation of the God of love. Its leaves are used in worship and also adored on entrance doors on ceremonious occasions. Its wood is used in yageyas (Havan).

NIMBA (Neem), BAKULA (Mimusops elengi), AMALAKI (Emblic myrobalan) are also sacred trees, worshipped by certain tribes.

ARKA (Sun plant) is sacred to Surya and ACACIA to Goddess SAMI, who is venerated to remove guilt and as the destroyer of enemies.

SACRED SHRUBS

Among the sacred shrubs, the divine plant SOMA comes first. It is also called AMRITA or Ambrosia. Some plant produces milky fermented liquor, called SOMA, which was an integral part of Vedic sacrifices, where it was drunk by the priests in token of its acceptance by the Gods. Like the sap in trees and the blood in animals, Soma juice was considered to be the vital fluid in all beings, just as Agni was the vital spark. Soma plant, originally belonged to the Gandharvas (celestial spirits), for it grew in the mountains, where the Gandharvas dwelt. It was given by them to the Goddness Vach, (one of Indra's wives) Goddess of waters and called 'the melodious cow, who milked forth sustenance and water.[1] SOMA, because of its power personified by Indra, in due course, became to be known as a primeval deity, all powerful, healing all diseases, bestower of riches and even the supreme God himself. The whole ninth book of R'gveda is devoted to the praise of SOMA deity, one time Bacchus of India.

This plant, botanically known as Sarcostema viminalis or Asclepias acida, a kind of creeper with a succulant leafless stem, which was indigenous in the ancient home of Aryans, as well

---

1 Ions V : Indian Mythology

as in the soil of India, and Persia, supplied an invigorating beverage supposed to confer health and immortality, and held to be the vital sap which vivified the world. Hence its juice became an important ingredient at every sacrifice, and was the subject of constant laudation in numerous Vedic hymns.

Some creeper plant, believed to be found in heaven only, has been pointed out by the late Dr Burnell, to be found in Southern India, and is still used by those orthodox brahmins in the Maratha country who attempt to maintain the old Vedic worship.[1]

TULSI (Basil; Ocymum sanctum) is the most venerated plant in Hindu homes in the modern period. It is not only sacred to VISNU and Lakshmi but also is pervaded by the essence of these deities and is itself worshipped as a deity. It is regarded as metamorphosis of SITA (Rama's wife) or as RUKMINI (K'rsna's wife).

In whatever light regarded, TULSI is the object of more adoration than any other plant in modern Hinduism.

A prayer to Tulsi is :-

"I adore that Tulsi, in whose roots are all the deities, and in whose upper branches are all the VEDAS.' In Sanskrit the verse is:-

Yan - Mule sarva tirthani yan madhye sarva devatah

Yad - agre sarva Vedas ca Tulasim tam namamy aham.'

In India, as well as in Sicily, Tulsi is venerated for its sanitary properties and a remedy against the poison of snakes. It is found in the courtyard of almost every respectable Hindu household and venerated as a domestic divinity. Reverential circumambulation

1. Quoted by Monier Williams in RELIGIOUS LIFE IN ANCIENT INDIA.

(Pradakshina) is done round the tulsi plant by women for securing long life for the husband and a large family of sons.

During the month of Karttikeye (October), the ceremony of marrying Tulsi to K'rsna or Black Saligrama pebble (symbolic of K'rsna) is performed; very ceremoniously by Vallabhacharya maharajas.

'Forget not the fragrance of the Basil
in marrying, in burying, in living'.

PARIJATA PLANT

Parijata plant is a divine plant of Indra's swargs(heaven). It has been a cause of conflict between Gods and the demons. ANDHKA, a demon, son of Kashyapa muni and Diti, who had thousand arms and heads, thousand eyes and thousand feet, was charged with the crime of an attempt to seize the Parijata tree from the heavens. To combat against him, the trinity of Gods created Trinity of Goddesses[1]. The plant was then restored by K'rsna. Since this plant is no longer available on the earth, its religious importance remains unknown, but it must be so sacred that Gods made it their own.

GRASSES

Among the various varieties of Grass, DRUVA GRASS is sacred to Ganesha. KUSA and DARBHA, botanically poa cynosuroides, is the holiest of all grasses. It sanctifies the soil, forms the most sacred of all seats, cleanses everything it touches, purifies the impure and when wound round the fingers, it makes them fit to engage in the most solemn rites.

1. Singh Dr. C.L. & P.N. HINDU GODDESSES (Crest Publications) 1994

FLOWERS : LOTUS

Lotus flower, not worshipped as such, but has gained great importance in Hinduism, because of its association with B'rhma (Born in lotus), Lakshmi (coming out of ocean with a lotus in hand) or Lakshmi (floating over the water on the expanded petals of a lotus flower). This is constantly alluded to in Indian poetry.

FRUITS

Of all the fruits COCONUT (Narkal) is recognised as the fruit of the Goddess of prosperity.

SITA PHAL (Custard apple) is the fruit considered sacred, as the fruit of SITA, Rama's Shakti.

Trees, shrubs flowers and fruits, as described herein, have come to be regarded as sacred in the habitations of Gods and an oath taken beneath such trees and in the name of such flora, become binding in faith. Hinduism, the nature loving faith, regard trees as types of eternal life. Though tree worship cult has enormously changed in the modern concept, yet this cult has not been totally vanquished. Rural folk still adore Pipal and Banyan trees, Tulsi plant is worshipped in most of the Hindu houses. Though the trees worshipped previously, do not receive as much adoration in the modern times, yet due regard is still paid and no Hindu will disregard their sacridity.

CHAPTER - 18

FAUNA AND HINDUISM

In the eyes of the orthodox Hindu, every animal is more or less sacred and inviolable. Association of great heros and saints with animals is not confined to India only. Evengeists were associated with animals, for instance St: Mark with a lion; St: Luke with the OX and St: John with the eagle. It is difficult, for a believer in Hinduism, to draw a line of demarcation between Gods, men and animals. If men depend on animals, so also are the Gods. Most of the Hindu deities are described as associated with or attended by their own favourit animals, which they sometimes use as vehicles (Vahana). As for instance B'rhma (swan); Siva (Bull-Nandi); Karttikeye (Peacock), Indra (Elephant); Yama (Buffalo); Kama (Parrot); Ganesh (Rat); Agni (Ram); Varuna (Fish); Durga (Tiger); Visnu (Garuda); Saraswati (Swan, Peacock).

Metempsychosis has a strong hold on the Hindu mind, as such a Hindu has no difficulty in believing that a beast, bird or reptile, at any moment may develop human faculties and function. Even a noxious insect, therefore, may enclose the soul of some person, who was a saga, saint or an orator. It is on this account that the excellent stories about talking animals and their sayings and doings, everywhere current in India, are the generality of some Hindus, not mere fables, but true narratives. A beast or bird may on special occasions speak with a human voice, engage in long arguments, acquire profound learning, and be troubled with a sense of right and wrong, without violating any law of organised life, or outraging any of the usual ideas of probability. At the recent World Life Conference, New Delhi (14.12.1994), Mr Justice Krishna Iyer laid stress on Animal world order, animal energy and man's dependency on it and on learning the language of the animals.

Because of the belief in animals in various aspects, no man, woman or child among the Hindus will venture to kill an animal of any kind. Animals of all kinds, of every description, live on terms of the greatest confidence and intimacy with human beings. They share the earth with men. Animals of all kinds rove over the fields, build nests and freely move all over. Bulls walk about in the streets with grace, sit under the shady pipal trees and are fed when in the vicinity of a house. Monkeys domesticate over roof tops, in temples and are prohibited to be killed. Parrots, sparrows, pigeons hop about the houses, fearlessly and daringly.

THE COW, BULL, OX

In the forefront among animals comes the cow. An orthodox Hindu speaks of the cow as his mother. Belief in the sanctity of this animal increased even under the teaching of Arya Samaj founded by Swami Dayananda. Cow is a very useful animal, in particular to the brahmins, some of whom make milk as their sole diet.

The mother cow is the tangible form of the Mother Power. Many hymns in the Vedas and PURANAS, have been devoted to the magnanimity of the cow. Almighty has produced the mother Cow's power (Sakti) as an aid for the nourishment of the human being. With the creation of the universe, the benedictory intention of the Supreme God was that the created humans should progress, one for each other. MANU said, 'The oblation given in yageya (sacrificial fire) is an offering to God Surya (Sun), who imparts sunlight. From sunlight is produced food grain, by which the world is preserved' (AGNI PURANA : Gomata Vidya). For the satisfaction of even Surya, the oblation with the aim of achievement, is through Yageya only. The milk juice producer cow is the one, who imparts potentiality to the Yageya, because in the whole process of yageya, the use of Cow's excreta, milk, curd, ghee are essential. To cool down the blazes of Agni (fire), putting ghee is the only solution. The legend about KAMDHENU cow has already been given in the chapter on Visnu, under his avtara Parsurama.

In addition, the cow family comes into our great help in everyday life. With the help of the oxen, tilling the soil can be done easily. Food is thus produced. Cow's urine and dung is used in plastering the courtyard in the house and the place is made sacred. By giving a cow in charity, a man gets rid of many sins. By leaving astray Bulls, nature's expansion, reproduction is a virtuous gain. This charity accords satisfaction to one's ancestors. BHAGWATI SRUTI ordains against cruelty to ADITI formation faultless cows. 'Aditi is the mother of Gods'.

R'gveda (8.101.15) : 'As the presence of B'rhma is essential for a yageya, so is the cow a necessity for her milk, ghee, for such an auspicious occasion.' The yageya depends on tow essentials; one a brahmin to chant the hymns (Mantras) and second; oblation of Cow's milk, ghee etc. Therefore the brahmin and the cow have been made of one class (family). That is why for the welfare and protection of these two, God has to incarnate again and again.

In MAHABHARATTA (Anushasana Parva), the cow has been given as much importance as the mother earth. Like the powerful earth, the cow's power nourishes the world. The earth maintains the human beings, the ones who progress by the GRACE of Gods on account of sacrificial yageyas by men; but the yageye cannot be performed without cow's produce. So like mother earth, mother cow is always a potential.

Kalidasa, with reference to Dilipki cow service, compares the cow as a manifestation of BHAGWATI DEVI and lays stress on her likewise worship. He prays to cowas if to ADITI Goddess. The classical literature describes the cow, as the cause of all

Gods and that all Gods have an abode in her.

In fact, both the cow and the earth circumbulation is as rewarding as of the other. This is clear from Ganesha and Kartikkeye legend : Once Parvati mother of the two said, ' The one who goes round the world and comes back first, will be married to BUDDHI Siddhi.' Peacock borne Kartikkeye immediately ran forth; but heavy bodied and mouse borne Ganesha, wise Ganpati circumambulated the cow and became the Lord of Buddhi Siddhi.

In K'rsna's activities, the importance of cow worship has been exalted. K'rsna himself worshipped the cow; almost in every daily action. From times immemorial, cow has been worshipped as a mother's power (Matri Sakti). This has been elaborated many a times in the PURANAS. The whole of SUR SAGAR,by saint poet Sur Dass, is full of ever binding relation of K'rsna with the cows and cow herds.

The mother cow is the one, which imparts immortal natural juice for the world. PURANAS describe the emergence of KAM DHENU (cow) as one of the fourteen jewels, extracted out of the churning of the ocean. There are many tales in the Puranas, in which the rishis have sermonned the rewards achieved by service to the cows. Maintenance of the cows in the ashrams of Gautam Rishi and Vaisistha rishi, bear evidence to this concept.

In ancient scriptures, the cow has been praised as a complete SAKTI (energy). The Divine power and importance of Bhagwati has been narrated as a cow manifestation. A legend describes that once Siva (Sankara) committed some offence against the rishis. The rishis cursed him. Siva saught asylum under SURABHI in the world of cows. He prayed, 'O mother Surabhi, you are the creation, stability, destroyer of evil, divinity bestower by your juice, strength nourisher for the welfare of the world, the mother of Rudras and sister of Adityas (Gods), you are the Ash (swaha) in the yageya and the SWADHA for the ancestors.' B'rhmand Purana, Padma Purana, Skanda Purana, Bhabhishey Purana and many other scriptures have described the power of the cow, in visible and invisible manifestation.

The cow cannot be equated with any other animal, as holy Ganges has no equivalent in any other river. In the RAMAYANA, in the conversation between ANGAD and RAVANA, Angad has called those people 'imbecile', who call the cow and the Ganges, as ordinary animal and a river. GITA ,GANGES the COW (including oxen) and GAYATRI, are the basic elements of Hinduism.

SERPENTS

In matter of worship in Hinduism, serpents come next to the cow. It is believed that snake worship was the earliest form of religion prevalent among men in all parts of the globe. Serpents, either have been or still are objects or worship in Egypt, Persia, Kashmir, India, China, Tibet, Sri Lanka, Babylonia, Phoenicia, Greece, Italy, Lithuania and among the Kalmuks and many uncultured tribes of Africa and America. It is generally agreed that the chief factor in the universality of this phase of superstition is the dread inspired by a mysterious creeping creature, silent and stealthy in its movements, apparently quite unprovided, with the most ordinary means of offence and defence, yet possessing most deadly of all known destructive weapons of almost instantaneous death. A large majority of these animals are quite innocuous. Inspite of their evil qualities, there is evidence of actual demoniacal possession.

The beautiful markings, spiral movements and striking aspect of many species of innocuous snakes are suggestive of only pleasant ideas. Their beauty markings are ascribed to Divine beauty and beneficence, coiling of the body and annual rejuvenescence (renewal of the skin), symbolize immortality and the never ending cycles of eternal time.

Ancient writings of India, as well as VEDAS and Aryan immigrants, provide no authority for such diversified conception of serpent nature. However, like other aboriginal cults, incorporating every superstitious idea, the cult of snake worship has continued to this day, particularly in Saivism and Visnuism.

GARUDA

Garuda is the vehicle of Visnu, Visnu's attendant, the Divine Garuda is half man and half bird. The head, wings tailons and beak are of an eagle, the limbs and the body are of a man. His face is white, wings red and his body golden. At birth, he was so dazzlingly brilliant that he was taken for AGNI and was worshipped. Garuda is an incarnation (not among ten) of Visnu, a King of vultures, who fought Ravana, while he was carrying away Sita, in the Ramayana epic.

Garuda is the son of Kashyap rishi and Vinata, daughter of Daksheya. Garuda like the K'rsna form of Visnu, is the destroyer of serpents, which typify sin and evil.

Garuda was born with a great hatred for evil and roams about the world devouring the bad, though his patents forbade him to eat brahmins. He is also famous for his relentless hatred for snakes, which he inherited from his mother, who was at odds with Kashyap's chief wife Kadru, the mother of serpents. The two wives and an argument over the colour of the horse Uchchaisravas, produced during the churning of he milk ocean. The loser of the wager was to become a slave of the winner. Kadru won and imprisoned Vinata in netherland, guarded by

---

For details, refer:-

Ions V: INDIAN MYTHOLOGY

Williams M : RELIGIOUS LIFE IN ANCIENT INDIA.

serpents. Garuda sought to release his mother, but the serpents demanded as ransom a cup of the God's ambriosia (AMRIT: immortality awarded juice). Amrit was in the mountains,guarded by fire. Garuda, because of his brightness drank up many rivers and extinguished the fire. Next obstacle was a revolving wheel, but Garuda made his body small and slipped through. Facing two fire spitting snakes was the next stage. Garuda blinded them with dust and cut them to pieces. He, then turned back and shattered the wheel. He took up the cup of AMRIT and flew back to the Nether region. Gods pursued him and Indra struck him with his thunderbolt. Garuda fought Indra and the later was defeated. Garuda took up the cup and reached the domain of serpents. On his arrival, the mother was released. Serpents were unlucky, because as they were about to drink the Divine juice, Indra attacked and snatched the cup away. The spilt juice was licked up by serpents. The juice was very strong which divided their tongue. So the serpents have a forked tongue. Another mythological legend states that serpents demanded the moon as ransom. Garuda was able to snatch moon, but in the struggle between tortoise, elephants and Garuda, destruction of some brahmins life was in danger, forbidden to Garuda by his parents. However Garuda reached the Nether region with the moon. The Gods, though defeated, sought a compromise with Garuda in return for the moon; Garuda was to become the vehicle of Visnu, to become immortal and to have a seat higher than Visnu. So the compromise fructified and Visnu rides a Garuda, but Garuda's emblem flies over Visnu's chariot.

Images of Garuda can be seen in the galleries of some Vaisanava temples. In some country districts, villagers are in the habit of invoking Garuda's protection against snakes, every night before goings to sleep.

MONKEY

The importance of the monkey (ape) in Hindu mythology, is on account of homage to HANUMAN in the RAMAYANA, whose appearance resembled that of an ape. (In fact, Hanuman was an aboriginal tribal chief, who helped Rama). The veneration, in which apes and monkeys of every kind are held throughout India, is on account of everybody's knowledge of the RAMAYANA. All monkeys are believed to be Hanuman's relations, though they were objects of worship long before his time. Vrisha Kapi of R'gveda (x.86) point to a very early veneration of apes, arising, perhaps, from their mysterious resemblance to men. The monkeys, in habits, are quite as ungodlike in the regions, where they are worshipped. The mischievous nature of the monkeys is tolerated and their sacred character shields them from harm.

In Hindu mythology apes and monkeys are as intimately connected with the worship of VISNU, as bull is of Siva.

There is a temple in Varanasi, called 'Monkey temple'. The deity there is Goddess Durga and not Hanuman. A goat is sacrificed in honour of the Goddess and the monkeys all around witness and take interest in the ceremony. Intelligent monkeys, with true simian, mock human curiosity. These monkeys in the temple, as elsewhere in Ayodhya, Vrindaban and other pilgrimages, are daily fed by pious persons. Who frequent the temples. To feed one monkey is a highly meritorious act and to injure one, would be the most heinous of crimes. A monkey, killed accidentally or intentionally can cause a public riot in a Hindu locality.

The importance of monkeys, in Hinduism, is due to HANUMAN, the monkey God, who is worshiped as the model of a faithful and devoted servant. A description of this special patron of wandering acrobats, has already been given in the chapter on Minor Deities.

BEARS

Bears are not worshipped in Hinduism, but because of their king JAMBAVAN and his role in the RAMAYANA and his death at K'rsna's hands, the bear is held auspicious.

Jambavan, the King of bears, has been described, as the wise and powerful soul, who was created as a bear by B'rhma[1], whose father was VISNU, in the previous birth. He was a very wise consellor and had been honoured by a boon from Rama that he should be vulnerable only to his own father. In[2] the RAMAYANA, when it was learnt from Garuds, that Ravana had abducted Sita, whose kingdom was across the sea, the question arose as to who could go across the ocean, survey the place and find out the hideout of Sita. Jambavan, the wise bear king, then in conversation, found none had the confidence to go across the sea and comeback. At that time Jambavan said, 'I am old now and do not have the strength as before. Do you not know that when noosing Bali, God had enlarged his body, I circumbulated Rama seven times in two minutes.' Angad volunteered but showed his doubt of a safe return. Then the wise Jambavan said, ' You are all capable, but Angad is the force 'commnader, so how could he be sent'. He further said, ' O' Hanuman, listen to me, there is no other strong like you, why are you quiet ? O' the son of VAYU (air), your strength and speed is like that of the wind, you are the house of wisdom, patience and knowledge, No work is difficult for you. Your very birth is for assistance to Rama.' Hanuman, happily appeared in his mighty body and asked advice from Jamabavan, who said, ' You just go, see Sita and comeback with the news. Then Rama with his power and GRACE, accompanied by monkey force, will go and

---

1. Ramanathan Lady S : THE RAMAYANA : Notes
2. THE RAMAYANA : Kishkinda Kaand

bring back Sita.

Later when during the war, Rama cut off Ravana's head and limbs with his arrows, still Ravana was not killed. More heads and limbs appeared on him. Seeing this, the monkeys got furious and they all attacked with trunks of trees, but Ravana, catching hold of the trees, smashed back the monkey army. Ravana was very happy on his achievement.

When Jamabavan saw the falling monkeys, he rushed forward, along with the army of bears. They, in the formation of rocks and trees, shouted on Ravana. Ravana was enraged and started befelling the bears. Seeing the devastation of his army, furious Jamabavan struck Ravana in the chest by his foot. Ravana fell down from his chariot. He was still holding many bears in his hands, so Jamabavan struck again and Ravana was carried off by his troops in an unconscious state. All monkeys and bears went back and reported to Rama. Jamabavan brought up the rear of the Monkey army during the march on Lanka by Rama.

Jambavana's role in the RAMAYANA, is well known and quite popular, but his role in a K'rsna episode is little known. the episode is:-

'During K'rsna's role as prince at Dwarka, one of the Yadvas SATRAJIT, practised such rigorous austerities in honour of Surya, the SUN GOD game him a magic jewel Syamantaka, which everyday produced eight loads of gold, and protected its wearer against evil, wild animals, fire, robbers and famine. The condition for the wearer was that he should be a virtuous one and would bring disaster to the wicked. K'rsna asked Satrajit to give the jewel to him, but the latter refused. Sometimes after the jewel was stolen and K'rsna was accused of it. Satrajit's wicked brother PERSENA wore the jewel one day and went for hunting. He was killed by a lion, who carried away the Syamantaka, but

Jamabavan in the cave saw it. Jamabavana killed the lion and got the jewel.

K'rsna, to get rid off the accusation, was in search of the jewel and he learnt that Jamabavana had got it. K'rsna, in a single combat killed Jamabavana. As Jamabavana had the boon not to be killed by anyone, except his own father, Jamabavan was surprised, but when he learnt that he was not killed by anyother than his own father (Visnu) in K'rsna incarnate, he begged forgiveness and gave the jewel to K'rsna and married his daughter Jambavati to K'rsna. The jewel was given back to the virtuous Satraji, who gave his daughter SATYABHAMA to K'rsna as a wife.

TIGER

Goddess KALI rides a tiger, Siva wears tiger skin round his girdle, tiger is spread as a seat for the saints and ascetics. A whole host o tradition and superstition has gathered round this king of the animals.

In some parts of the hills, when a man is killed by a tiger, no one will visit the spot until a priest has gone through a series of antics, representing the animal in his fatal spring, which end by taking up from the ground a mouthful of the blood stained earth.

In north Konkan, a tribe called WARALI, worship Vagobha, the tiger Lord for protection against snakes.

THE ELEPHANT

In Hindu mythology, belephant AIRAVAT was the sacred elephant of God INDRA. Elephant is believed to be supporting the ends of the universe. Ganesha with an elephant head is the God of good luck. In 1813, a white elephant caught in Travancore, was believed to indicate a prosperous reign for the young maharaja.

'The earth is not only spported by SESHA, thousand headed king of serpents, represented as supporting Patala (Nether region), but also on the vast heads and backs of eight male and eight female elephants, who all have names and distinct personalities. They are called the ELEPHANTS OF EIGHT QUARTERS.

When anyone of them shakes its body, the whole earth quakes (RAMAYANA 1.41).

Sometimes they are described as indulging locomotive propensities, and roaming aboout in the neighbourhood of their stations.

Elephant is not worshipped, but wherever one passes, people run around in order to get some feed for the elephant.

THE HORSE

Satarudriya hymn of the Yajur Veda (xvi.10), describes reverence to the horse and the lord of horses, has been addressed to Siva. The auspicious occasion of Dusehra festival is a special occasion for decoration of horses with garlands; so also when conveying a bridegroom to the brides's house.

The muthical horse 'UCCAIHSRAVA' (high eared) produced during the churning of the ocean, as the prototype of the whole race of horses, is generally considered sacred to Indra. ASVA MEDHA, the horse sacrifice was a very ancient ceremony. R'gveda hymn 162, 163 Mandala I was used at this rite. It was held to be the chief of all animal sacrifices, and in later times, its efficiency was so exaggerated that a hundred horse sacrifices entitled the sacrificer to displace Indra from the domain of heaven. Indra, therefore, always endeavoured tp capture the horse before its immolation. (RAMAYANA 1.13).

After the yageya, Rama let loose the horse as Asvanedha.

The horse was caught by Lova and Kusha, living in the ashram. Sita asked them to let loose the horse, buit the boys insisted that the owner should come and ask for it. Eama came in response to the brave action of the boys and wished to meet their mother, but Sita did not like to face him and submerged in the cracked earth. Rama took back the boys. who later ruled; Lova at Lahore and Kuhsha at Kasur.

THE DOG

The dog, in Hindu mythology, is connected with Siva, A sect existed who worshipped MALLARI, as (Lord of dogs); Rudra is the lord of dogs. In Siva's character as Kirata or mountaineer, a dog is connected with Him(Rudra). Hence in the Satarudriya hymn of Yajurveda (xvi.1), addressed to Rudra in his hundred aspects and surrounded by his countless host of attendants, Rudra is addressed as the Lord of dogs in the expression, 'Reverence to dogs and the lord of dogs', The name 'KRITA JNA', 'the grateful one' is applied equally to Siva and to dogs. In western India, it is customary to feed dogs as a sacred deity on a certain day in each month. Feeding GUDD (jaggery) to a black dog on Saturday is considered auspicious, to ward of evil.

In the BALI HARANA (Kaka Bali) ceremony, performed everyday by religious Hindus before dinner, a prayer is said to Yama's two watch dogs, and offering of food is placed on the groundfor the dogs, crows etc. The reign of the death, presided over by YAMA, the road to Pitris(ancestors) in the upper sky, is guarded by two four eyed watch dogs called SYAMA,(dark) and SABALA or KARBURA (spotted).'R'gveda x.14.10-12.

This road to upper sky, is believed to be the one, on which the spirit travels in form of smoke, when a body is burnt.

On the other hand. in some passages of the epic poems, dogs are described as unclean animals. Panini II.1.42 uses terms of reproach for dog cookers.

Dog is not an animal for worship, but by nature of reverence for natural creations and in order not injure any soul, dogs get their feed here and there.

OTHER ANIMALS OF IMPORTANCE IN HINDU MYTHOLOGY

SWAN (Hansa -Goose) is sacred to B'rhma, also to Saraswati.

FISH TORTOISE AND BOAR, are worshipped as avataras (incarnations) of Visnu, into which he infused his essence with the object of delivering the world or aiding it in certan special exigencies. Their forms have already been described in the chapter on VISNUISM.

Fish are kept in tanks and fed as a religious duty.

Tortoise, held sacred, are found in waters near the temples. They swarm in rivers and are fed by pilgrims. Pushkar lake, near Ajmet, unique for its only one B'rhma's temple, has many tortoise, Alligators and crocodiles (makar) which are regularly fed by the pilgrims.

CROCODILES, alligators(makar) are held sacred, sometimes to KamaDeva. In earlier days, children were thrown in the Ganges to be devouvered by the crocodiles.

The CAT, is sacred to Goddess SHASHTI, who is supposed to use it as her vehicle, For killing a cat, the penance for such a crime , is an offering of a model cat made of gold.

PEACOCK is sacred to SARASWATI, but of greater relevance to Kartikkeye ('Subramanyam). as their conveyance. On account

1. WILLIAMS M. RELIGIOUS LIFE IN ANCIENT INDIA.

of its importance in India, it has been recognised as the 'National Bird'[1].

It is certain that every form of fetishism and Totemism of worship stone, tree or animal, as well as every variety of polutheistic and pantheistic superstition, have sprung up spontaneously and flourished vigorously on Indian soil and identified in Hinduism; but the continuous changes and reforms, have always pushed out the bad practices. Animal worship, since the ancient times, has received adoration, on various accounts:-

1. Because, like an elephant or a lion, it happens to ossess superhuman strength and courage.

2. Because it is believed to be an incarnation of a deity viz tortoise, Fish, Boar.

3. Because it is regarded as a totem or representative of a tribe or family (Totem- from dodaim, signifies the patron or typical animal of a tribe.

4. Because it is the conveyance of the deity of his choice for worship.

Animal worship, has to be assessed by the working of one or other of the motives, gratitude, fear, or awe, operating separately.

In modern Hinduism, except the Cow, Bull Nandi of Siva and to a great extent Serpent, worship, no other animal Is worshipped, except as per the natural behaviour towards all creation, animate or inanimate, any Hindu will not cause inury, even to an ant (Ants are fed everyday in Jainism).

CHAPTER - 19

PEFORMIST MOVEMENTS

The antiquity of a religion, which is often appealed to as a proof of its truth, like everythig else also grows old and can seldom defy four thousand years. The older it is, the more likely it is to have become effete in human hands and unfit for new times, and to require either reformation or entire abolition, to make room for a new and better form of faith[1]. Hinduism has always been incorporating reforms in its Religion in conformity with the circumstances and the society. Brahmosamaj, Arya Samaj and Rama Krishna Missions came to be established, as reformist movements.

Brahmo Samaj and Raja Ram Mohun Roy : (1774-1833)

In the last century, another great teacher Raja Ram Mohun Roy arose and founded a reformed Theistic sect (Brahmo Samaj), based on a belief in the unity of the godhead, the brotherhood of man and direct communion with God in the spirit.

The sect has split up into three groups differing more in their ritualistic than religious views. 'The Adi Samaj, the oldest and most conservative section, clings more closely to Hindu beliefs and to the system of caste, the Nabidhan Samaj or 'New Dispensation', is more advanced, and seeks to assimilate what it finds best, nor only in the sacred books of Hinduism, but in those of Islam and Christianity. The third section, the Sadharan Brahmo Samaj, is the most liberal in its views, as shown in the rejection of caste and of all that is ordinarily regarded as essential to `Hinduism'.

1. Max Muller : Biographical Essays (1884)

The Brahmo Samaj remains Hindu in a sense, because it refuses to sever its connection with India, or to acknowledge European authority in matters of religion. But the Brahmo Samaj could not have come into existance but for Ram Mohun Roy's friendly and intimate acquaintance with European christians and unitarians.

The new attempt to reform Hinduism in the 19th century was definitely influenced by Christianity & western thought. Raja Ram Mohun Roy, a great man and a great scholar, connected with abolition of Sati, knew Sanskrit, Arabic and many other languages and had studied various religions carefully. He was opposed to religious ceremonies and pujas and such rituals, and he pleaded for social reform and women's education. He founded Brahmo Samaj, a small organisation, confined to English knowing people of Bengal. It had great influence. The Tagore family took to it. Poet R.N. Tagore's father Maharishi Debendra Nath Tagore was the prop and pillar of the Samaj. Another leading member was Keshab Chandra Sen.

Dwarka Nath Tagore, Prosonno Kumar Tagore and others helped Ram Mohun Roy in the establishment of the first theistic church at Calcutta in 1828. Prayer meetings were held every Saturday evening and consisted of 'recitation of vedic texts. 2. reading from the upanishads 3. delivery of a sermon and 4. Singing hymns. The beginning of January 1830, inaugurated a new era in the history of Indian religious thought. A new phase of the Hindu religion took shape, essentially different from the past ones. European education and Christian ideas had their influence, but were independent Hindu views, thoughts and spiritual teaching.

Dwarka Nath Tagore, father of Maharishi Devendra Nath

Tagore, visited France in 1844. His visit created a great sensation in acquainting the public with 'Hinduism'. On account of him, a new interest was roused in India for the study of the vedas.

Raja Ram Mohun Roy studied all the major religions of the world and found a spiritual core common to all. He was therefore moved to organise a religious society devoted to the essence of every religious faith. He denounced all forms of polytheism and idolatry, and advocated purging Hinduism of these elements. In seeking to formulate a universal religion, he gave up many of the general beliefs of Hinduims, such as the doctrine of the transmigration of souls. Hinduism now took on a dynamic role. There was less insistence on the worship of images and of many Gods. Like all reformers, Raja Ram Mohun roy continued to stand for a universal religion based on the fatherhood of God and the brotherhood of man.

Max Muller says ' I know of no other instance in the whole history of religions that equals the honesty and self denial of the members of the Brahmo Samaj in their throwing down and levelling the ramparts of their own fortress, and opening the gates wide open for any messengers of truth. Their honesty will appear all the more creditable when we remember that they were by no means inclined to discard the vedas altogether, but only declared that reverence for the Deity prevented them from claiming any longer anything like Divine workmanship or penmanship for the whole of it[1].

Raja Ram Mohun Roy, the founder of Brahmo Samaj was born in 1774 at Radhanagar (Murshidabad - Bengal) in a high caste Brahmin family, worshipers of Visnu. Having studied Persian and Arabic literature, he took to studies in Sanskrit. He betook himself to the simple vedic system and the vedanta as expressed

---

1. Max Muller : Biolographical Essays (1884)

in the upanishads. Faced with opposition at home and in family, he visited Varanasi and Tibet. In Tibet he studied Buddhism and had discussions with Buddhist priests. Raja Ram Mohun Roy was, thus, the first earnest minded investigator of the science of comparitive religion that the world has produced. He studied Kuran, old Testament, New Testament, Buddhist Tripitaka, but asserted that he had found nothing in the works of anyother country, Asiatic or European, equal to the scholastic philosophy of the Hindus.

He awakened attention to the absence of all vedic sanction for the self immolation fo widows (Sati). In the R'gveda, the command to a widow is to return to her home after having performed the last duty to her departed husband. This command during the course of time was falsified to interpret that she should enter into the womb of fire to follow her husband to a better world. Raja Ram Mohun's pioneer efforts to reform Hinduism by abolition of the tradition of Sati, was promulgated as a statute throughout British India, in 1829.

Adi Brahmo Samaj

Debendra Nath Tagore (1818) was a saint like son of Dwarka Nath Tagore. His principle was 'we are but humble seekers of the Truth and humble workers in her cause. We must work and labour each in his own sphere and according to his own light, regardless of consequences. The crowning and fruition of our work rests with God alone, and we may repose our trust in Him for success. Truth will triumph in the end' (Satyam eva Jayati). As a founder of Adi Brahmo Samaj (1839) also called Calcutta Brahmo Samaj Tagore discarded hymns and Brahmanas, made careful selection of important passages from upanishads and published them as 'Brahma Dharma' (the law of the Brahmas). The primitive religious doctrines of the upanishads were reduced to an elaborate system of philosophy by Badarayana. the vedanta philosophy declares more consistently that the world is phenomenal. It is not what it seems to be, but it would not even seem to be, unless it reposed on the Divine, which alone is really real. That Divine, in order to be what it is, or what it ought to be, conceived to be, must, according to the vedanta, be free from all limitation, it must be subjective, not objective or perceptible by the senses, devoid therefore of all qualities. Even our unreal world could not exist unless there was at the back of it a something real, and, if we claim any reality for ourselves, we can only do so after surrendering all that is phenomenal in ourselves, all that is changing, perishing and mortal. Only then can we find and recover our true being, where alone it can be found, namely in the Divine, invisible, but ever present, absolute power, the uncreate, the eternal and never changing Being, whom we all God. This was that ultimate Reality called B'rhma (Ultimate, unknowable, the great reality, the Hidden, the Abyss, the silence, the fullness, the Eternal life).

Every member in this Samaj, also called 'Truth Investigating' or 'Truth teaching Society', had to take a vow for seven solemn declarations viz. 1. to abstain from idolatry, 2. to worship no created object, 3. but to worship through the love of God, and 4. through doing the works dear to God, 5. the great God the creator, the preserver, destroyer, the causer of emancipation, the partless, the one only without a second, 6. to lead holy lives and 7. to seek forgiveness through abandonment of sin. Prayers, invocations, hymns and meditations were promulgated for use in the daily services.

Adi Brahmo Samaj allowed a great latitude in regard to the maintenance of old national customs and a friendly demeanour towards encouragement of the national religion. This was not acceptable to new young members who felt that a more complete reform was needed before the samaj could deliver itself from all complicity with degrading social society. So then came Keshab Chandar Sen's Brahmo Samaj of India (1861).

Ramatanu Lahiri (Ramatanu = body of Rama) born in 1813 is generally considered as the Nestor of Brahmo Samaj (Brahmo in Bengali). He denounced caste as a great social and moral evil and silent submission to superstitious customs as reprehensible weakness. He discarded the Brahmanical thread. Later in life, he was attracted to the new Brahma Samaj, and became a close friend of Keshab Chander Sen.

Keshab Chander Sen, born in 1838 was the third great Theistic reformer of British India. Although he was born in a Vishnuvite family and brought up in an atmosphere of Hindu superstition and idolatry, yet his education at Presidency College, Calçutta, inculcated in him a collision with scientific truth. His attitude towards all religious became one of absolute indifference. As a member of Adi Brahmo Samaj, he was ambitious of penetrating to the very springs of social life and altering their whole course. The first change he advocated was that all who conducted the services in the mandir should abandon the sacred thread which distinguished the Brahmans and higher castes from lower ones. Second step was the alteration of the Sraddha (worship of deceased ancestors). Next was the remodelling of the ritual at the ceremonies of birth (Jata Karman = Name giving) and cremation of the dead. A solemn and impressive form of initiation into the Brahma faith was substituted for upanoyana (initiatory rite of Brahmanism) Education and elevation of women was advocated.

He fobade child marriage, as an ever present source of weakness and improverishment, destructive of all national vigour, and fatal to the development of national thrift and economy Polygamy (more than one wife) was discouraged. He was the first to introduce the remarriage of widows into his family. He was against semblance of idolatrous worship, all orthodox rituals, all noisy music, display and unnecessary expanse at marriage ceremonies. Debendra Nath Tagore was his strong supporter in his Brahmo Samaj of India (1864); but when Keshab Chandar Sen performed a marriage ceremony between two persons of different castes in 1864; Devandra Nath fell apart and found Sadharna Brahmo Samaj (schismatic) in 1878. Immediate cause of the breakup was the marriage of K.C.Sen's daughter (under fourteen) to the young Maharaja of Cooch Behar (under sixteen).

The Sadharana (General)Brahma Samaj came into existance in May 1878; with a view to remove the serious and manifold evils resulting from the then state of things, and to secure the representation of the views and the harmonious cooperation of the general Brahma community, in all that affects the progress and well being of the theistic cause and theistic work in India, as against the unilateral administration of K.C. Sen. A.M. Bose and Pandit Sivanath Sastri were its promising leaders but lacked the eloquénce, ability, rligious genuis of K.C.Sen and literary culture of Protap, Chandar Mazumdar and Raj Narain Bose.

Monier Williams has described the essential points of Brahmo Samaj, who believed in 'the fatherhood of God' and 'the Brotherhood of man' as follows[1] :-

God is the first cause of the universe. By His will He created all objects out of nothing and continually upholds them. He is spirit, nor matter. He is perfect, infinite, all pwerful, all merciful, all holy. He is our Father, Preserver, Master, King and Saviour.

The soul is immortal. Death is only the dissolution of the body. There is no new birth after death; the future life is a continuation and development of the present life. The men that now live are the embryos of the men that are to be.

---

1. Williams Monier : Religious Life in Ancient India (1883 - Rep 1990)

The true scriptures are two - the volume of nature and the natural ideas implanted in the mind. The wisdom, power and mercy of the Creator are written on the universe. All ideas about immortality an mortality are primitive convictions rooted in the constitution of man.

God Himself never becomes man by putting on a human body. His divinity dwells in everyman and is displayed more vividly in some. Moses, Jesus Christ, Muhammad, Nanak, Caitanya, and other great teachers, appeared at special times and conferred vast benefits on the world. They are entitled to universal gratitude and love.

The Brhma religion is distinct from all other systems of religion; yet it is the essence of all. It is not hostile to other creeds. What is true in them it accepts. It is based on the constitution of man, and is, therefore eternal and universal. It is not confined to age or country.

All mankind are of one brotherhood. The B'rhma religion recognises no distinction between high and low caste. It is the aim of this religion to bind all mankind into one family.

Duties are of four kinds : (1) Duties towards God such as belief in Hm, love, worship and service (2) Duties towards self such as preservation of bodily health, acquisition of knowledge, sanctification of soul (3) Duties towards others such as veracity, justice, gratitude, the promotion of the welfare of all mankind. (4) Duties towards animals and inferior creatures - such as kind treatment.

Every sinner must suffer the consequences of his own sins sooner or later, in this world or the next. Man must labour after holiness by the worship of God, by subjugation of the passions, by repentance, by the study of nature and of good books, by good company and by solitary contemplation. These will lead through the action of Gods' grace to salvation.

Salvation is the deliverance of the soul from the root of corruption, and its perpetual growth in purity. Such growth continues through all eternity, and the soul becomes more and more godly and happy in Him who is the foutain of infinite holiness and joy. The companionship of God is the Indian Theist's heaven.

The united prayer of the samaj was :-

'Lead us, O God : from untruth to truth, from darkness to light, from death to immortality. O : thou Father of truth, reveal thyself before Us. Thou art merciful, do thou protect us always in thy unbounded goodness. Peace, Peace, Peace'.

Many other theistic bodies, more than 170, were established in different parts of India viz. Veda Samaj in Madras (1817), Prarthana Samaj in Bombay (1867).

Prarthana Samaj under the leadership of R.G. Bhandarkar and Justice Mahadev Govind Ranade, swept Maharashtra in the latter half of the ninteenth century. It advocated the worship of one God, Western education and revival of the tradition of the Maharashtrian saints like Nam Deva, Tuka Ram and Ram Dasa. Ranade advocated that without equal emphasis on all branches of human activity, the progress of mankind would be lopsided and would not achieve the desired results. As such his reformist zeal affected every human activity social, economic, educational and religious.

The manual used by the followers of this Samaj contains selections from the vedas, upanishads, christian Bible, Kuran and Zand Avasta. Hymns are sung in Hindu fashion to the accompaniment of Vina. Prayers consisting chiefly of invocations of the superme Being, praise and adoration of his attributes, but without confession of guilt, and the hands joined in reverence. The sermon at the end aims at honest striving after a pure soul stirring theism. The old vedantic pantheism influence persists.

Arya Samaj and Dayananda Saraswati

Dayananda Saraswati (1824-1883), a Gujerati Brahmin, was a liberal minded man, who initiated a great reform of Brahmanism. He also was willing to surrender his belief in the divine revelation of the Brahmans, though he retained it in full strength with regard to the vedic Hymns. He published large commentaries on the vedas. He was a strong opponent of idolatry as wll as of both pantheism and polytheism, but contended that the four vedas were a true revelation and that the hymns to Agni, Indra and Surya were really hymns to one God. He advocated the remarriage of widows, supported the movement in favour of raising the marriagable age of boys and girls, and showed himself free from many prejudices as to caste, food and all the rest. His name better known in Europe also, from the time that he fell into the net spread for him by Madame Blavatsky. But this lasted for a very short time. In his book 'Satyarth Prakash', he declared that he was not an independent thinker but a follower of the vedas; that the four Samhitas texts of the vedas were to be received as a primary authority in all matters relating to human conduct, that the Brahmans, beginning with the Satapatha; the six Angas or limbs of the veda, beginning with Siksha; the four up vedas; the six Darsanas or schools of Philosophy and the 1130 schools of vedic teaching (Sakhas) : One thousand for Samveda, one hundred for Yajurveda, Twentyone for R'gveda and nine for Artharvaveda[1] were to be accepted as secondary authority in expounding the meaning of the vedas, and that adoration, prayer,

1. Patanjali Mahabhashya 1.1.1.

and devotion were to be offered to one God only, abstracted from all idea of shape and form, and without any second, as per the vedas. However, influence of this powerful disputant became greater and greater, till at last his opponents, the orthodox and unchanging Brahmans, were suspected of having poisoned their dangerous rival. Another rumour is that because he managed to stop the stipends of dancing girls granted by Maharaja of Jeypore, the dancing girls poisoned Dayanands's food by the help of a Brahmin cook. He died suddenly, but his followers, under the name of Arya Samaj, form still a very important and growing sect in India, specially in Punjab, Delhi and Haryana, that keeps aloof from all European influences and has many more adherents than the Brahmo Samaj.

Arya Samaj was founded by Swami Dayanand Saraswati in 1875. Its clarion call is 'back to the vedas', under the conviction that the religion of the vedas is the oldest and purest of all religions. He stressed the revealed truths of the vedas and called for a return to the ancient purified Aryan way of life. It also rejected many of the later growths of Hinduism and combated caste. It was a reform movement influenced by Muslim and Christian thought, but it became an aggressive movement, rival and opponent to Islam. It was an attempt to convert the defensive and static Hinduism into an aggressive Missionary religion. It was meant ot revive Hinduism. It was Hindu nationalism raising its head. It is largely confined to middle class.

Dayanand Saraswati, the founder stressed that there was no mention in the vedas of 'widow burning', or 'child marriage' or the enormously hurdensome custom of 'dowry' and so he opposed all of these. He found no prejudice against women and no degradation of them in the vedas, so he taught respect for women.

He founded respect for integrity, for worldly activity and for education. Since performance of vedic rites had to be followed by a strict formal procedure, a certain separateness from all non Hindus was advocated. These thoughts are the fundamentals in Arya Samaj.

Rama Krishna Missions

Rama Krishna Parmahans (1833-1886) born at Kamarpukar (Hooghly - West Bengal) on 20.2.1833, was a semi-educated priests in a temple (Dakshineswara) at Calcutta. He was a devout Hindu and believed in the traditional way of worship but at the same time, he had a liberal and unorthodox approach to other religions. He mixed freely with Muslims and Christian priests and believed that all religions led to the same goal, the realisation of God. He never claimed to be the founder of a new religion. He simply preached the old religion of India, which was founded on the veda, more particularly on the upanishads and was systematised later on in the sutras of Badarayana, and finally developed in the commentaries of Sankara and others. He worshipped the Gods of men viz. Vishnu, Siva and others. Steeped in the Shaivite devotionalism of Bengal, Rama Krishna experienced frequent ecstatic trances and vision of the Goddess Kali, whom he worshipped as the Divine Mother with fervent devotion. The purely human devotion and love which he expressed for his Divine Mother, is sometimes most startling (Partaking food with Mother Kali), but one feels all the time that, if he could express it, he is groping for that God head which he must find in himself or in his self before he can find it in the self of the whole world, in the self even of the old idols. He came to believe that all the traditional Hindu devotional movements, whether Shaiva, as experienced by him, or vaishnava, were all in fact worshipping the same Divine Being. Later this idea was extended to all religions. He preached this international audiences, he taught that whatever the forms of their worship, all religions were really worshipping highest and truest vision of this one supreme Being was the Divine Mother; the Goddess Kali. He defended image worship and most of the traditional forms of Shaivite devotion.

Every human heart has its religious yearnings, it has a hunger for religion which sooner or later wants to be satisfied. The religion taught by the disciples of Ramakrishna came to these hungry souls without any outward authority.

The life of Ramakrishna is interesting. In boyhood he was named Gadadhara (Visnu, the holder of club). His father Khudi Ram Chattopadhyaya saw Visnu in his prophetic dream. He possessed supernatural powers, power of speech (Vaak Siddhi) i.e. whatever he told, good or bad, came true. He was a great lover of God. The mother of Ramakrishna Chandramani Devi was an ideal pattern of simplicity and kindness. They were great lovers of Rama and worshipped him.

The young Ramakrishna used to repeat the whole of the religious operas and dramas, the acting, the music and everything, after hearing them once. He had a melodious voice. He was a good judge of the merits and defects of the statues or images of Gods and goddesses. At the age of six, he was well versed in the Puranas, Ramayana, the Mahabharatta and Srimad Bhagvad Gita, by hearing them from the Kathaks (bards). At the age of sixteen, he was sent to school but soon left it saying that he would never care for that kind of learning, the sole aim of which was to gain a few pieces of silver, or a few maunds of rice and vegetables and that he yearned to learn something which would raise him above all these, and give him as a recompense God Himself.

Rani Rasmoni, a lower caste, established a temple of the Goddess Kali at Dakshineswara in 1853, where Ramakrishna succeeded as priest to his brother; but he would not partake the food cooked in the temple and so cooked his own. He began to look upon the image of goddess Kali as his mother, the mother of the universe, living, breathing and taking good out of his hand. He was married to Saroda Devi or Saradamani Devi, who was only five years at the time of marriage. At the age of 17 when she returned to Ramakrishna, he told her that the old Ramakrishna was dead, and that the new one could never look upon any woman as his wife. He said that even then he saw his mother, worshipped her with flowers and incense, asked her blessings, (like a child from a mother) and then became lost in a deep trance. The wife was content by only allowed to live near him, cook for him and serve him. She looked upon her husband as an incarnation of God Himself, and tried to forward the work of her husband. Undaunted, cheerful as ever, he entered into samadhi at 10 PM on 16 Aug 1886 and never returned. 'Ramakrishna understood that in the Absolute, there is no thou, nor I, nor God, nay, that it is beyond all speech or thought. As long as there is the least grain of Eelativity left, the Absolute is within thought and speech within the limits of the mind, which mind is subservient to the universal mind and consciousness was to him his mother and God.

Ramakrishna would have remained unknown as a religion reformer, if his Gospel was not propagated by men like Keshab Chander. Sen and Swami Vivekananda. Ramakrishna Missions were established in several cities of the U.S.A. and Europe as well as in India with the object of interpreting vedic philosophy to the people. Side by side with religious activities, the missions carry on reformist and humanitarian activities.

RAMAKRISHNA MISSIONS (THE VEDANTIC SOCIETY)

Followers of Rama Krishna Parmahans, hold to three fundamental beliefs :- (i) Human nature is Divine (ii) The aim of human life is to realize this Divine nature and (iii) All religions are essentially in agreement. They believe that all religions lead to the goal of betterment of human life through spirituality. Thus a Vedantist will give reverance to a multiplicity of Gods and to a variety of religions/saints. To him, each is an aspect of ONE B'rhma, an unchanging reality, which is beneath the illusionary universe and which is consciousness itself or existence itself. B'rhma, is atman(soul) and thus the nature of mankind is Divine.

Vedanta society, which has a number of centres with a membership of over 1500 in America, has three monastries and two convents in America. These members have their guidance from UPANISHADS, the BHAGVADGITA and the teachings of Shankaracharya. The society is dedicated to summarizing and preserving the teachings of Rama Krishna. Vedantist temples are fairly simple and display some images of Hindu deities and a picture of Ramakrishna. The worship is restricted to chanting prayer and address by the presiding swami. Scripture reading and Indian music is allowed. Vedantists seek primarily to enlighten, NOT to convert.

SWAMI VIVEKANANDA (NARENDRA NATH DUTTA) (1863 - 1902)

A disciple of Ramakrishan Parmahans, he championed the greatness of Vedantic philosophy. His talk at the Chicago conference of world religions in 1893, made the Westerners realize the greatness of Hinduism for the first time. He visited U.S.A. in 1893 and then lectured there for ten years. He was a learned scholar of Hindu philosophy and an equally famour orator and preacher. He propagated, far and wide, his Guru's message of universal brotherhood and essential 'ONENESS' of all religions. He advocated Hindu Muslim unity. He took pride in ancient Hindu culture without belittling religious philosophies of other faiths. He asserted that Vedantic philosophy was the essence of all religions. He believed that man had the capacity to raise himself spiritually by the practice of meditation and prayer to GOD, Rama, Hari, Allah and Christ were names of the same supreme reality.

Sister Nivedita, an American lady, became his disciple. Swami Vivekananda, very eloquently and forcibly, preached the gospel of nationalism. This was not in any way antimuslim or antiany other religion, nor it was the somewhat narrow nationalism of Arya Samaj. None the less Vivekananda's nationalism was Hindu nationalism and it had its roots in Hindu religion, culture and philosophy.

ANNIE BESANT AND THEOSOPHICAL SOCIETY

Madam H.P. Blavasky, a Russian lady and Colonel H.s. Olcott, an American founded Theosophical society in U.S.A. in 1875 with headquarters at Newyork. colonel Olcott established this society at Adyar, near Madras in 1886. Mrs. Annie Besant, an Irish lady, who came to India in 1893, established it as reformist movement in India.

Theosophy means 'A system of philosophy professing to attain intimate knowledge of GOD by spiritual joy'. the theosophists tried to revive the principles of the ancient Hinduism, Buddhism and Zoroastrianism. They believed in the doctrine of the transmigration of the soul and preached the universal brotherhood of man. The Theosophical society glorofied Indian religions, mainly Hinduism and its philosophy. As this movement was led by foreigners, it helped Indians to recover confidence in their own religions and traditions.

The work of Theosophical society under the leadership of Annie Besant is remarkable in religious, social and political fields. Modern India owes much to this society as well as to its great leader Mrs. Annie Besant.

Summarily, these reform and progessive movements in Hinduism tried to fit in, as far as possible, the new scientific and political ideas, derived from the West, with their old religious notions and habits. They were not prepared to challenge and examine fearlessly these old notions and habits, nor could they ignore the new world of science, political and social issues which lay around them. So they tried to harmonise the two by trying to show that all modern ideas and progress could be traced back to the old sacred books of their religions. This attempt was bound to end in failure. It merely prevented people from thinking straight. Instead of thinking boldly and trying to understand the new forces and ideas, which were chaning the world, they were oppressed by the weight of ancient habit and tradition. Instead of looking ahead and marching ahead, they were all the time looking back furtively. It is nor easy to go ahead, if the head is always turned and looks back.

Religious and social reformers like Raja Ram Mohun Roy, Swami Vivekananda, Swami Daya Nanda and Mrs. Annie Besant, regenerated Indian society and thus prepared the ground for national awakening. Their movements, though primarily religious, were at the same time national - religion inspired nationality.

CHAPTER - 20

MODERN HINDUISM

Hinduism, the oldest of the great religions existing today, is, of course, the product of India, so also is its sister religion BUDDHISM, which, now, has spread all over China, Japan, Burma, Tibet and Sri Lanka. In religion, of course, India was the fountainhead whether it was Hinduism or Buddhism[1].

Hinduism has always had an astonishing toughness and resiliency in meeting challenges in the past. In the varieties of its approaches to these contemporary issues, Hinduism is reaching for its own solutions. Although Hinduism has been suppressed from time to time, particularly during the reign of Aurangzeb (1658-1707); 'When the Hindus were forbidden to construct new temples and to repair the old ones. Encouraged by the orthodox policy of the emperor, many fanatic provincial governors demolished many Hindu temples. Aurangzeb reimposed the hated Jaziya in 1679 A.D. on the nonmuslims. Restrictions were also imposed on the celebrations of the Hindu festivals like Holi and Diwali. The tax on pilgrimages was also reimposed. The Hindus were forbidden to carry arms[2]. Inspite of all this, the truth prevailed and Hinduism flourished. Jawahar Lal Nehru rightly said, ' Men may come and men may go, and governments and empires may lord it a while and then disappear into the past; but the old tradition continues, and generation after generation bows down to it[3].

'Hinduism, quite apart from the religious teachings, lays down

---

1. Nehru J.L : GLIMPSES OF WORLD HISTORY
2. Fuste J & Mehta : INDIAN HISTORY AND CULTURE
3. Nehru J.L. GLIMPSES OF WORLD HISTORY

social codes and rules about marriage, inheritance, civil and criminal law, political organisation, and indeed almost everything else. In other words. They lay down a complete structure for society and try to perpetuate this by giving it religious sanction and authority[1]. Hinduism is a literary based system of living and there can be no doubt that ancient India was a home of learning. Dr F.W. Thomas[2] said ; 'There is no country (except India), where the love of learning had so early an origin or has so lasting and powerful an influence : (Hinduism). The Hindus have acquired their present religious culture through thousands of years, practice of their customs and manners as enjoined in their religion and through their temples. The different observation of rituals, ceremonies, festivals and what more, the seemingly mere entertainments at temples have actually been prop and mainstay of faith and helped sustain their undying religion through the vicissitudes of ages. The construction and general atmosphere of temples are such that every piece of architecture, every painting is a symbol of Hindu religion.

If India is a nation, it is because of its Hindu culture, which is the life line of India. Hinduism, a wide open ocean of religious thoughts, brings in synthesis in the changing times. That is the nature of this religious culture. One thinks of a devout Hindu performing his morning prayers by the Ganges; one hears the blowing of the conch shells and the ringing of bells in the temple; One is amazed to see the crowds of worshippers in countless temples. Seeing the RATH yatra, one is surprised. The colourful Diwali, Holi and Dussehra festivals, drawing millions, exhibit the faith of the people in Hinduism. Infinite are its rituals, modes of worhsip and innumerable its myths, symbols, ceremonies, sects and systems, but with all its diversity, it is a popular, flexible, and at the same time, orthodox religion, open to reforms, accommodating the needs of the society and even changing with the times;

---

1. Ibid
2. Thomas Dr. F.W. : Quoted in Blackheim : INCOMPARABLE INDIA

a living religion, that was, that is, and that will be. AUROBINDO[1] had anticipated such a Sanatan Dharma (Primordial religion) wherein Vedas, Vedanta, Bhagvad Gita, Upanishads, philosophy, Puranas, Tantra and even Bible and Quran should find a place.

Hinduism is a continuous unity of devotion and objectivity; of attachment and detachment, retaining the broad perspectives of rationality, as explained in Bhagvad Gita:-

Thus action is B'rhma, who is one
The only, All pervading; at all times
Present in sacrifice. He that abstains
To help the rolling wheels of this great world,
Glutting his idle sense, lives a lost life,
Shameful and vain ....
Therefore, Thy task prescribed
With spirit unattacked gladly perform,
Since in performance of plain, duty, man
Mounts to highest bliss[2].

RAMAYANA and the MAHABHARATTA bring us together. These scriptures, in epic form, with followers all over the world, are the symbols, the identifications of Hinduism.

AIMS OF HINDUISM

Hinduism aims at the protection of the existence of everyone (SARVA BHAVANTU SUKHEEN). Everyone, who takes birth in this world, has some duty to perform and that he should be given an opportunity to achieve his goal. Materialism believes, 'The one who will earn, will eat'; but Hindu says, 'The one who is born,

1. AUROBINDO : PANCHJANEYE NOV/1993
2. Journal of Oriental Society of India 1947

will eat and the one who eats, will also feed others'. Self earning and eating is natural, snatching from others and eating is mutilation; but self earning and feeding others is CULTURE. This is the measure of evaluation of culture. Hinduism code of life aims at social welfare of all, particularly the weak ones, the old, handicapped, children and such others, who cannot earn for themselves. (VIVEKANANDA)

PRINCIPLES OF HINDUISM

Four cardinal principles of Hinduism are:-

(i) Struggle for existence

(ii) Existence of Supreme power

(iii) Non exploitation of Nature

(iv) and has no faith in illegal impure rights of individuals.

Hinduism, as a religious organisation had four goals to be achieved. First was DHARMA or virtue, the fulfillment of one's own specific duty according to class and stage.

Second was ARTHA, economic and political success. Hinduism is the only religion that imposes religious obligations to become as rich and powerful as possible.

Third goal was KAMA, pleasure. Hinduism is one of the few religions, that commands the religious person to enjoy life and to seek his own pleasure as part of an overall religious and human fulfillment. Kama includes all forms of aesthetic enjoyment; painting, sculpture, music, poetry, dance, drama and social pleasures. Nateyesastra, Kamasutras are the literary authorities.

These three goals have to be practised in hormonious balance, none excluding anyother. In case of confilict, demand of DHARMA (duty) should be preferred.

The fourth goal was MOKSHA or release from the human condition, in exclusion of the first three goals. This came from Buddhism and Jainism.

In Hinduism, all four are offered side by side. The unity of Hinduism is neither doctrinal, nor ethical, nor mythological. It is a practical unity.

Hinduism has faith in NATURE and considers nature as his mother, motherland, mother of cows, mother of sacred plant TULSI and the mother of Ganges. It regards and gives due reverence to the creation of the nature viz Pipal tree, Banyan tree, feeding milk to the snakes and giving sugar to the ants. A Hindu worships all creation of the nature and that is the reason which prohibits him from exploitation of the nature.

in Hinduism, the supreme being is the impersonal B'rhma, a philosophical Absolute, serenely blissful, beyond all hamperings either ethical or metaphysical. That the world is temporary, worthless illusion (Maya). UPANISHAD says :-

'ISHAVASEYMIND SARVA YATIKANCH JAGATIYAN JAGAT

TENAKTEYEN BHUJHENTHA : MAGRIDH : KASEYE SVIDHAMNAM

It means that whatever is there in the world, it, all is God's (Isvara's) utilise it with an intention to sacrifice and don't accu mulate it.

In Hinduism, a person may follow any of the three optional methods for salvation : The intellectual way of knowledge (Jnana marg) concerning pantheism; The emotional way of devotion (Bhakti marg) to any favourite deity or the practical way of work (Karma Marg). A combination of Jnana marga and Karma marga is the teaching of the Bhagvad Gita.

UNIVERSALITY, EQUALITY AND AFFECTION

Hinduism aims at the development of the universe through individual to individual, Swami Dayananda, the founder of Arya Samaj, said, 'One should not be content with his own progress, but should consider the progress of all, as his own.'

Hinduism is a universal human religion, which wishes the prosperity of all; the well being of all creatures; then how can it be opposed ot its fellow religionists. Every one, according to Hinduism, is equal and the one encourages the other to make this life progressive. Because of human outlook, many philosophers, saints and priests have praised it and have condemned communalism and untouchability as non classical and non religious.

According to Nobel Laureate Rabindra Nath Tagore,' Any religion which dishonours humanity, that is false. A religion which makes a man blind, the one which shuts the mouth, such a religion can only be forced on unitelligent and unscrupulous people. Now enforcement of such religion should be prohibited.' (R.N. Tagore was a staunch Hindu).

Lokmaney Tilak said.' There is no basis for unscrupulousness in religion. The door of almighty (Isvara) is not closed to anyone, and if that closes, then God is no God, this is my conviction'.

In the VEDAS, there are innumerable hymns (mantras), which incite all persons to feel equality and thus practically pass life together. All these hymns aim at the welfare of all. There is no trace of casteism or of high and low.

R'gveda (10.52.6) 'O man, be you, be busy in wordly affairs, but gain knowledge in so doing. Save the enlightened paths of wisdom, develop the deeds of those, who undertake knowledge and action. Be thyself a good man and inculcate Divine qualities in devotees, your kin and all.'

R'gveda (5.60.5) 'Among the men, there is none high, none low, they are equal bretheren. They should all make effort to attain wordly and godly divinity.'

MAHABHARATTA (Sha. P.A. 188) 'There is no difference between the castes, (no castes were differentiated by God, no separate religions were his creation). The whole creation is by the one and the same God alone.'

Shakspear rightly said,'What is in a name? That which we call rose By anyother name, would smell as sweet.'

R'gveda (10.191.2) 'O men, you all move in unison, talk to each other, Your minds in equality may gain knowledge. As the ancient intellectuals have been worshipping the ceator God, so should you, The thoughts of all people should be likewise. Thier meetings, conferences, should be of like thinking. Their minds and brain should aim at likewise thoughts.

R'gveda (10.191.3), 'O man, I almighty God (Parmeswara) make you of similar thoughts, all equal and bestow upon you likewise food and thoughts for sacrifice.'

R'gveda (.10.191.4), 'Therefore, O men, your minds should be likewise, So that you all, in unison, can dwell together.'

Atharava Veda (12.1.12), 'O friends, let us all together, enjoy fragrant and nutritious food'.

Atharva Veda (12.1.45), 'This Prithvi (earth) maintains all those speaking different languages and bearing different thoughts, all alike as members of one family residing in one house. 'Accordingly the separationists should learn a lesson from the Vedas.

Atharva Veda (3.30.1), 'Bestow your love to one and all alike; like a cow who feeds all new borns, irrespective of all other considerations'.

Atharva Veda (3.30.3), 'No brother should be jealous of another, no sister should bear jealousy towards another. You all, as fellow beings, should follow the path of Truth by sweet words.'

Atharva Veda (7.52.1), In a prayer to Mitr's (Divine illuminaries), one prays, 'May there be love between ourselves and love for others; award us the quality of living in equality together.'

CASTEISM IS NONVEDIC

MAXMULLER was asked; 'Is there any provision of modern castes in the Vedas? He replied, 'The clear answer is NO'.

In YAJURVEDA (30.5.22), 172 occupations have been mentioned, but there is neither the name of a caste nor of any discrimination between them'.

SANKHEY DARSANA (Karika 5.7) It is evident that all human beings are of one caste. According to Hinduism, all men in the world are of one caste viz Human caste. Vaisheye, Brahmin, Kshatri, Thakur, Barbar and such others, which are termed castes, are really not castes; they only represent a certain functionary/occupation. This is why Hindu scriptures do not discriminate between those, who adopt different occupations, they all belong to ONE religion, the Primordial religion, later named Hinduism.

JATIGAUTAM NAYEYE DARSANA (2.2.70), 'The ones, whose process of birth is the same, they are all of one caste. 'It means that all those whose birth, age, living and reproduction systems are similar; they all belong to one caste, which includes men, monkeys, eagles etc. Pandit shiv Shankara in Akriti Jyoti Linga says:- 'All those creatures, whose figure is alike, they all belong to one caste.'

According to the RAMAYANA (Uttarakand 30), 'All men were

of one form and one language. There waas no difference in their thoughts (religious) or philosophy or in their characteristic features.'

According to MANU SMRITI (1.88.91) and Bhagvad Gita (18.42.44) :- For the progress of the society and for the performance of different functions (occupations), men were divided into four classes (orders), This was a work system, which later changed into Caste system. Upto the Mahabharatta period, work system was in vogue, but it disintegrated later, during the Brahamanical period.

BRIHARNAYAK (3,4-11-13):- The qualities and behaviour of men keep on changing; so the work system of classification of human beings was accordingly altered. The four caste system is of a very late duration. According to Yagey Valkaney rishi, 'Initially man was of one order; according to the needs of the society, from one it became two, from two to three and from three to four.

The MAHABHARATTA (Shantiparva 188.10) and BHAGWAT PURANA (9.14) support the above work system classification.

Swami Vivekananda said:- 'I agree that initially there was an arrangement according to qualities and type of work. For cultural development, the upward step is the division of men, which should be according to their qualities and culture. Our aim is to make the Shudras as Brahmins'. How and when this work system division changed into casteism, is difficult to trace, but it is very clear that in Hindu scriptures, there is no mention, nor recognition of orthodox castes. Therefore the present casteism is completely Non Vedic, Non recognisable undesirable and anti Hinduism, impracticable and undivine. Modern Hinduism of castes, is Brahamanical supremacy and not basically Hinduism religiously.

ELEMENTS OF STRENGTH IN HINDUISM[1]

Belief in one supreme, omnipresent, non material spiritual reality underlying all phenomenon.

Belief in a knowledge of, and union with, the Divine as life's goal.

Belief in a sure future life, with appropriate retributions for deeds done.

Belief in the solidarity of the society into which one is born, something divinely instituted, and superior to the individual.

Ability to make religion thoroughly permeate the life of its flowers.

Ability to hold together so many groups, for so manycenturies, within a social unity, by means of a common religious faith.

Modern HINDUISM, is the outcome of centuries, ever changing according to the times, the society and ever eager for universality, equality and brotherhood. Kipling rightly wrote :-

'The ends of the earth were our portion,
The ocean at large was our share,
There was never a skirmish to windward
But the leaderless legion was there.

The relevance of Hindu universalism is to an age, in which nations are armed for mutual annihilation. The successful application of the religiophilosophical teachings of Hindu seers and scriptures will help humankind to overcome the worst crisis facing it in this nuclear age and will lead to restructuring the world on, the all embracing principle of equality and universalism.

---

1. Hume R.E. : THE WORLD'S LIVING RELIGIONS 1927

Hindu scriptures represent notable stages in the progress of the Human mind towards spiritual and religious evolution. One writer speaks of the BHAGVADGITA as the HINDU BIBLE, wherein the TRUTH is manifested that the pure in heart, of whatever creed or race, shall see God. A few excerpts from BHAGVADGITA are quoted here:-

Modern Hinduism

The concept in GITA, is in seeking refuge in God, does not at all annul the responsibility of man to act on his own in his ontological freedom to reach the fullest development of self hood:

GITA has a message for all men without being the scripture of any sect. In the succeeding centuries, the founders of religious cults betrayed both K'rsna and authentic religious sensibility'.

'To explain the mystery of human life in its intricate relationship with Nature and with Primordial energy from which, all creation emanates'.

'Certitude can be rewon by integration of knowledge (Vijayanana) and intuition, insight or wisdom (Jananna). It makes it imperative for man to integrate knowledge available in his time with his intuition and to draw his conclusions without dogmatism.'

'Wisdom cannot be taught, each one has to find it for himself '

Bhishma tells Yudhishtra, 'The code of right being cannot be derived only from the Vedas, it must be arrived at by personal experience, through awareness of the World, and through reason'.

Gita is an epic poem, which could mirror the world in the variety and complexity of its characters, their interactions, the objective transformation of circumstances they led to. It is episodically very rich. It is a transcription of life. It suggests that GOD, man and

Nature constitute a chord, and none of the three notes has the ring of TRUTH without the accompaniment of the other two. GOD created man and Nature (World), but granted them autonomy, but it is only when MAN chooses to act in accordance with God's design that there is harmony and redemption. The sole redeemer or betrayer of man is his own self and NOT God.

Bhagvad Gita (Chapter ii,P.70) on self control sermons:-

'The self restrained man, who moves among objects with senses under the control of his own self, and free from affection and aversion, obtains tranquility. When there is tranquility, all his miseries are destroyed, for the mind of him whose heart is tranquil, soon becomes steady. He, who is not self restrained, has no steadiness of mind; nor has he, who is not self restrained, perserverance in the pursuit of self knowldge. There is no tranquility for him, who does not persevere in the pursuit of self knowledge, and whence can there be happiness for one who is not tranquil? For the heart which follows the rambling senses leads away his judgement, as the wind leads a boat astray upon the waters'.

'He sees truly, who sees all actions to be in every way done by Nature alone, and likewise the self to be not the doer.' (Ch xiii)

CHAPTER - 21

SYMBOLS IN HINDUISM

In the texts on Hinduism and in its literature, many symbols are frequently used. A symbol may be as simple as a trident of Siva, but the holding of trident has a meaning, which is not generally thought of, with the result that ambiguous notions are made regarding Hinduism. Therefore some of the common symbols, generally met with in literature, have been explained briefly in this chapter.

Different kind of symbols and images have their distinct sanctity. There are those which exist spontaneously and are of their own nature pervaded by the essence of the deity. These are called SVAYAMBHU. These are either not carved at all, or very slightly moulded into shape. They are merely rough stones or rocks supposed to have descended direct from heaven or to have appeared miraculously on the soil. They are most sacred of all material objects of adoration, and when discovered, temples are built on them. Such are LINGA and YONI, related to Siva.

Other symbols held sacred, but not as much as Svayambhu are certain small pebbles found in rivers and polished by the action of water. Such pebbles represent LINGA (Siva) called Bana Linga or Vanalinga apparently of white quartz, found in Narbada river.

Black pebbles representing VISNU, K'rsna, called SALAGRAM (ammonites imbedded in the stone) are found in river Godavari.

A third form are the masonary sculptors carved images. These are very common and generally seen in temples. These came into worship during Brahamanical period.

Some common symbols, which one sees almost everyday, alphabetically as :-

BRANDING : Branding of chests, arms and other parts of the body; In Saivites, it represents the weapons and the symbols of Siva (trident, linga).

In Visnuites, symbols branded are discuss, the club and the conchshell.

SYMBOLS PERTAINING TO B'RHMA

OM TAT SAT : All meditations begin with this. It reminds us of only ultimate reality, B'rhma, which is the highest intelligence and is Supreme BLISS.

FOUR HEADS : Signify that B'rhma, has created the entire universe in all four directions.

SATCHITANANDA : B'rhma is satchitananda, which means that which exists (SAt), has pure intelligence - consciousness (Chit) ; and pure joy-Bliss (Ananda).

OM : The symbol of B'rhma, encompasses in itself the whole universe, the past, present and the future and goes beyond TIME. It is the essence of all that is sacred in Hinduism. A detailed description follows.

OM (AUM), pronounced as Oh-M, the single syllabled incantation called PRANAVA (something that pervades life or runs through breath: Prana), is a symbol of the ABSOLUTE.

The mystic syllable 'OM' is known as the Pranava. It is the symbol of the B'rhma. This sacred word encompasses in itself the whole universe, the past, present and the future, and goes beyond the periphery of TIME itself.

From the Vedic times, until the present day, the word 'OM' has been taken as a symbol and as an aid to meditation by spiritual aspirants. It is accepted both as one with B'rhma and as the medium, the Logos, connecting Man and God. The entire history of the syllable is in the revelations of the Vedas and in the declarations of the Upanishads.

Being the symbol of B'rhma or the universal soul, it is the very essence of all that is sacred in Hindu thought. It is used at the beginning and end of the prayer, during the practice of yoga, in fact at all times when the thought of B'rhma pervades One's being. There is a verse in the Vedas: 'Prajapatr vai idam agra asit' i.e. In the beginning was Prajapati, the B'rhma: 'Tasya vak dvitiya asit', viz With whom was the word, 'Vag vai paramam B'rhma' i.e. And the word was verily the supreme B'rhma. The idea of the WORD belongs to Hinduism, although later in the fourth gospel of New TESTAMENT, it was repeated: 'In the beginning was the word and the word was with God and the word was God'. This sphota (word) has its symbol in the word. 'OM'. Thus in the 'Maitriyana Upanishad', after it has been said that there is one B'rhma without words and a second, a word 'B'rhma, we are told that the word is the syllable 'OM'. The sound of OM is also called PRANAVA.

The very central theme of 'MANDUKYA Upanishad' is the Syllable 'OM' through which the mystery of B'rhma is gathered to a point. The text of the Upanishad first treats 'OM' in the terms of the upanishadic doctrine of the three states of waking, dream and sleep, but then passes on to the fourth (Turiya), thus transporting us beyond the typical upanishadic sphere into that of the` later 'Classic Advaita Vedanta'. Speaking of 'OM' TAITTIRIYA upanishad says, 'Thou art the sheath of B'rhma' that is 'OM' is the container for the supreme and, therefore invoking 'OM' is invoking the supreme B'rhma.

'OM' represents the self, which is the supreme Non Dual Reality. The self is known in four states (waking, dreaming, sleeping and Turiya). All these states are represented in the three sounds of 'OM' (as A U M) and the silence that follows and surrounds the syllable.

The sound 'A' represents the waking state; the sound 'U' represents the dream state and the sound 'M' represents the deep sleep state. The waking state is superimposed on the 'A' sound because it is the first of the three states of consciousness and so is the sound 'A' ; the very first of the letters of the alphabet in all languages (Hindi, English, Urdu, Gurumukhi etc), the first known quantity in algebra and the first hypothetical person or example. Dream comes second among the three states of consciousness because it occurs between the waking and the deep sleep states. So 'U' being next to 'A' in order of sounds represents the dream state. 'M' sound of 'OM' is superimposed as the deep sleep state. It is the closing sound of the syllable, just as deep sleep is the final stage of the mind in rest. A small pregnant silence is inevitable between two successive OMs. On this silence is superimposed the idea of the fourth state called 'Turiya'. This is the state of perfect Bliss when the individual Self recognises its identity with the supreme. In 'OM', the sounds A, U, M are called mantras or forms; there is also in AUM the common principle called the Amatra OM, that which signifies the thing in itself, running through and pervading the three fold phenomenon of the three states. As we remember all our experiences in all the three states, there must necessarily be a single common factor which was a witness of all the happenings in all the three planes. There must be some entity within ourselves, who is present in the waking world, who moves and illumines the dream, who is a distant observer in the deep sleep world and yet which is not conditioned by any of these three realms. This entity is the fourth state

TURIYA, the real, the changeless, the intelligent principle.

The syllable 'OM' symbolises both the spheres; (a) the phenomenal visible sphere of the 'Jagat' (world) wherein the manifestations of time and space appear and perish, and (b) the transcendent, timeless sphere of the imperishable being, which is beyond, yet one with it. Thus all the four states together comprise the totality of this manifestation of ATMAN- B'rhma as a syllable. Just as the sound 'M' manifests itself, grows, becomes transformed in its vocal quality and finally subsides into the silence that follows, similarly the three states of components of being, ultimately merge to the homogeneous silence of the fourth Turiya. The other three states are transformations of the one experience, which constitute the totality of its modes.

Swami VIVEKANANDA said:- 'This 'OM' is the only possible symbol which covers the whole ground, and there is none other like it. The sphota is the material of all words, yet it is not any definite word in its fully formed state, That is to say, if all the particularities which distinguish one word from another be removed, then what remains will be sphota. Therefore, the Sphota is called the NADA B'RHMA, the sound B'rhma. Now every word symbol intended to express the inexpressible sphota, will so particularise it that it will no longer be a sphota. That which particularizes it the least and at the same time most approximately expresses its nature, will be the truest symbol thereof; and this is the 'OM', and 'OM' only; because the three letters A, U, M, pronounced in combination as 'OM' , can alone be generalised symbol of all possible sounds. The letter 'A' is the least differentiate of all sounds. Again, all articulate sounds are produced in the space within the mouth - beginning with the root of the tongue and ending at the lips - the throat sound is 'A' and 'M' is the last lip sound; and 'U' exactly represents the rolling forward of the impulse which begins at the root of the tongue, continuing till it ends in lips. If properly prounced, this 'Om' will represent in itself the whole phenomenon of sound production, and no other word can do this; and this therefore, is the fittest symbol of the sphota, which is the real meaning of the 'OM'. And as the symbol can never be separated from the thing signified, the 'OM' and the sphota are one. And as the sphota, being the finer side of the manifested universe, is nearer to God, and is indeed the first manifestation of Divine wisdom, this 'OM' is truly symbolic of GOD.

'OM' thus represents the entire manifested world and the unmanifest, and also that which lies beyond both the manifest and the unmanifest, the B'rhma, which is the changeless substratum for the changing objects of the world of experience.'

Just as a living body has no vitality when the life giving breath is not flowing through it, so too a Mantra has no life in it without the addition of 'OM', the 'PRANAVA', which means that something which pervades life, or runs through PRANA (breath).

We have said before that OM is the container for the supreme and the sheath of B'rhma. This aspect has been diagrammatically explained by Swami Chinamayanada:-

OM is the ATMAN (ourself, our real nature-omnipotent and omniscient)

ATMAN is enveloped by sheaths of matter.

ATMAN gives semblance of life to the different sheaths. It envelopes all and none envelops it. As per SRUTI, it is all pervading.

The sheaths are :-

Outermost Food Sheath, which is the existence of Knowledge and action. This is subtle and pervasive.

Next Upper is VITAL AIR Sheath, which controls all organs of action called PANCH PRANAH in Vedanta. This is more subtle and pervasive than Food sheath.

Next Upper is MENTAL Sheath, which is the mind sheath and entertains doubts, joys, sorrows, desires and the like. It is still more subtle and pervasive than Air sheath.

Next above is INTELLECTUAL Sheath, which is the determining factor. Whatever the mind sheath entertains, the decision is by intellectual sheath. This is still more subtle and more pervasive than Mental sheath.

The innermost is BLISS Sheath, which is positive joy in deep sleep state of consciousness. This is the most subtle and pervasive of all sheaths.

The first four are in waking state and the last 'BLISS' exists during our deep sleep state of consciousness. In this the man experiences a joyous condition, positive joy. This is the interpretation and the true meaning of OM.

OMKARA or Pranava mantra, the most solemn invocation known to the Hindus, is composed of the letter AUM, the union of three gods; A (Visnu), U (Siva), and M (B'rhma). In the vedas, it is used to denote all the Gods. It is also said to typify the three holy fires, the three steps of Visnu etc. Frequent meditation upon it and constant repetition of it ensures release from worldly existence.

DEVI-DURGA : The tiger symbolises the ego and arrogance, the man has to subdue.

GANESHA: Ganesha on the mouse signifies equal importance of the biggest and the smallest creatures.

IMAGES : SIVA LINGA; distinctive organ of the male sex, delegated creative power, which needs no dress, food, decoration, sleep and requires to be cooled down by BEL leaves and water from ganges.

VISNU: Complete image of a well formed human being as K'rsna Rama and soon.

NECKLACE : SAIVITES: The necklace worn may be a rosary of Rudrakshas, or formed of teeth of the dead bodies or a sling of serpents round the neck.

VAISNUITES : A necklace of TULSI wood beads or of a LOTUS seeds (Kamalaksha)

ROSARIES (JAPAMALA) : Saivites: Simple string of 32 or 64 rough berries of the Rudraksh tree (Elaeocarpus ganitrus).

Visnuites : 108 beads of the wood of sacred TULSI shrub.

SARASWATI:SWAN is to remind the chaff from true knowledge, just as the swan removes the water from milk before consuming.

PEACOCK of Saraswati symbolises that the ego is to be suppressed.

SIVA (RUDRA)

: THIRD EYE in his forehead and a moon's crest above it, marks the measuring of TIME by the months.

: SERPENT, round his neck, denotes the endless cycle of recurring years.

: SKULLS second necklace, with numerous other serpents, symbolises the eternal revolution of ages and the successive dissolution and regeneration of the races of mankind.

: TATANKA in left ear and KUNDLA in right, denote half man and half female (Ardhnarisvara), an ideal union of man and woman.

: COMPLEXION: His dark complexion identifies with the dark destroyer TIME (KAAL).

: BLUE THROAT is from the stain of the deadly poison, which would have destroyed the world, had not Siva in compassion for the human race undertaken to drink it up, out of the churning of the Ocean.

: NANDI; white Nandi typifies generative energy, symbolises the soul of man (JIVA), yearning for Parmatma, the great soul and GOD.

SIVA : DEER SKIN and TIGER SKIN, are of those magical animals produced by rishis, when their wives were attracted by Siva's beauty.

: ELEPHANT SKIN, sometimes worn by Siva. is the skin of that elephant which belonged to a demon named GAYA. whom he conquered and slew.

: TRIDENT (Trisul) denotes his combining in his own person; the three attributes of creator, destroyer and regenerator.

: WAR LIKE WEAPONS; such as were engaged by him in battles against demons PURA, TRIPURA, ANDHAKA and others.

SWASTIKA

Swastik is a symbol, which has been of great importance since the ages and is as much revered today, as it ever was.Prehistoric stone carvings seals of Indus Valley civilisation, symbols of Jainas, Buddhas and Hindus and folk art are all appear to have come to one nucleus in the shape of a Swastik. Swastik represents the tradition of this country and of the TIME, which is a speciality in India culture and gives the impression of some eternal spirit. It was known to the Hindus, not only from Vedic or historical period, but from much earlier prehistoric times. One of the earliest Swastika carvings can be seen in Banyaberri Caves in Pachmahri (Madhya Pradesh) where the worship of Swastik was by an offer of an umbrella. Indus Valley seals show Swastika, turned upwards and also downwards. Women with no upper cloth. used to cover their breasts in Swastik shaped cross. Two headed ADITI(mother of Gods) has been represented in a Swastika symbol. Swastika has been represented in many folk art forms as 'SATHEYEYE', 'SATIYEYE, 'SATEYE' and 'SATHEYE'.

ORIGIN : From SHATPATH BRAHAMANA, it is learnt that there was an independent Goddess named 'SWASTI', who was worshipped as a manifestation of all the four VEDAS or as a symbol of tradition, she has also been identified as 'BAGH DEVI '.In due course, Swasti in union with Baghdevi, merged in Saraswati and its symbol SWASTIKA became knowledge, wisdom and happiness bestower. Four arms of Swastika indicate the four VEDAS. As the LORD of four directions, Swastik is also considered as a symbol of the SURYA (SUN).

Dr. V.S. Aggrawala in 'BHARATIYE KALA' says,' This four directioned form of square universe, is related to SURYA. This consists of four directions and the SUN is in the centre. This is the most sublime, good omen for the welfare of the humanity and the universe'.

Dr. V.C. Srivastava in 'SUNWORSHIP IN ANCIENT INDIA' states, ' previously Agni, Indra, Varuna and Soma, were recognised as masters of the four directions, later this was replaced by LOK-

PALAS. Later BIRUDHK, Nagas, Yakshas united with different directions and the combination of all these as 'SWASTIK(became more developed and popular.

IMPORTANCE: From Maharashtra. down to South there is a tradition of making coloured 'Alpana' in front of entrance doors. In these, Swastika is universally designed. In those regions, where Ganesha is worshipped, Swastika is still more adored, because in such regions, Swastika is identified as a manifestation of Ganesha.

Swastika has also been recognised as Vedanta Chatushpad B'rhma, but the creation is only in one Pad (foot), other three are unknown, In the PURANAS Swastikas has also been identified with four faced B'rhma. Where there was a count of FOUR, there itself the importance of SWASTIK increased.

In some regions, Swastika is recognised as a form of a SUPARNA, the first and third representing the head and tail, and fourth as two wings of a flying bird Suparna.

The Khatti sect Aryans had, long back depicted a form of ADITI, mother of SUPARNA, as having two headed flying bird.

THe calligraphists claim that SWASTIK is a combination of ऊ of Devanagri script, म of BRAHMI script and a foot of Nandi bull (Siva's). In YOGA literature, SWASTIKA is twisted and recognised as the basis of body formation.

In ancient times. in the city planning and military arrays, Swastika form was considered as an IDEAL.

All crossings, even today, are of Swastik formation. Both are considered as indicative of speed and movement.

Thus from prehistoric times, SWASTIKA has been revered in different forms, all through the ages, in Hinduism.

SAKTI (SHAKTI)

Cosmic energy in its dynamic form.

TILKA (Pundra, Nama or Gandha) on the forehead:

SAIVITES : Three horizontal strokes (tripundra) made with the white ashes of burnt substances (Vibhuti) represent the destroying character of their God SIVA.

VAISNUITES : An upright mark (Urdhava pundra) made with bright red, yellow and white colouring substances (the white called Gopichandana), represent the foot print of their Human and Humane God Visnu,

VISNU : Most of the symbols pertaining to God Visnu, have already been described under the chapter Visnuism, but LYING VISNU on many headed COBRA ANANTA in the ocean means:-

ANANTA : Cosmic energy

OCEAN: Ananda or endless BLISS and grace

CHAKRA: maintains DHARMA (righteousness).

In Hinduism rites and practices, in its vast literature, in the symbols and emblems, in its hymns, its worship, in its art and architecture, whatever is there, has been introduced after serious consideration and every bit has a meaning, aimimg at the highest TRUTH, righteousness and the best ways of living.

CHAPTER - 22

HINDUISM IN A NUTSHELL

Hinduism, continually growing, is like a sacred banian tree, whose thousand ramifications find their way into walls, old buildings and even enrooting down in the ground, which form fresh centres of growth and vitality.

To become a Hindu, one must be born a Hindu, yet Hinduism is continually growing within itself.

Hinduism was the first to give spiritual emphasis to ecology and environment, considered modern problems.

Hinduism is a rare faith with few Do's and Dont's.

Hinduism is a living, practical religious system, due to its flexibility and dynamics. It accommodates the change in man and the society.

Hinduism is a system of living and not an orthodox religion.

Hinduism adopted and assimilated the religious beliefs of all the primitive tribes and peoples with whom the early Hindus came into contact. There was no conversion or use of force.

Conversion to Hinduism least as compared to another religion has never been through force or wars, nor as a result of bigotry or by temptations to the weak and the trodden, nor by promising to confer any spiritual benefits.

BELIEFS

Hindus believe that creation is without a beginning and that it is eternal (endless).

* B'rhma, the universal soul, is immanent, within and about

us, as also transcendent, outside material existence, transcending TIME and space, Individuals may die, but the Universal soul is deathless. The life does not die.

* God, the great power pervades the entire universe. It may not be seen but it exists and pervades all life and all things animate and inanimate.

* A basic belief of Hinduism is the law of KARMA (activity); action; the law of cause and effect.

* Law of Karma, makes Hindus believe in fate and not fight. Karma is not a fatalistic doctrine, but a logical theory, which explains differences in our births and temperaments and guides us in moulding our future lives.

* TRUTH, all encompassing, is unchangeable. Law of society may change from age to age. Slight deviation from Truth is Untruth. Hinduism, itself is based on TRUTH and the pursuit of Truth.

* The UPANISHADS reveal some of the greatest TRUTHS, ever known to mankind.

* The path to the Divine is TRUTH. Victory lies only with Truth. Untruth can never win. (Manduka Upanishad).

* Self control, implies control of the five senses, the mind and the spirit.

* One of the virtues enjoined in Hinduism, is that like overeating and excessive drinking; loose talk and harmful gossip, should be avoided.

SCRIPTURES

* The VEDAS are the very soul of Hinduism, DHARAMSASTRAS are like the body, subject to decay

and change with the times.

* The MAHABHARATTA codifies the ideal conduct for man and woman, king and the commoner.

* The RAMAYANA teaches what ideal behaviour should be, subtly yet effectively.

* Hinduism, unlike any other religion, has a wealth of scriptures, to guide both the initiate and the scholar. Time to time commentaries have kept it up with the times.

* CHARAKA, the greatest of ancient Hindu physicians, was possibly the first to speak of a code of Ethics for the physicians, to treat patients without thought of gain or reward.

* Hinduism imparted initial knowledge of HERBAL Medicine, surgical instruments, plastic surgery; as also of archery, use of weapons and missiles.

* Science of Music, Dance and Dramatology was first standardised by Hinduism.

* GRAMMAR and PHONETICS and ETYMOLOGY are the awards of Hinduism.

* Arithmetic, Algebra, ZERO, INFINITY and Decimal system, so also ASTRONOMY are the inventions in Hinduism.

* Literature has been glorified by Hinduism metres in PROSE and POETRY.

SOCIAL ASPECTS

* The destruction of evil by GOOD, either by oneself or by Divine intervention, is a constant theme of Hinduism.

* Very few religious faiths have such a tolerant approach,

as in Hinduism. Religiously, socially and politically, it has been the most tolerant.

* Hinduism is practical enough to permit social change and scientific progress, yet highly philosophical and sublime, aiming at ethical perfection.

* Hinduism is unique in that it accepts that the rules of society change with every age, and therefore the laws, or the Dharma SASTRAS, must change from time to time. Hindus area pacific people, who tolerate derision of their religious practices.

* Hinduism is unique because it differentiates between duties of man and man, as also between the duties to be followed at various stages of one's life.

* Hindus are not isolators, they donot worship the image or the figure, but consider the ICON as a symbol of GODHEAD.

* There is no religious sanction in Hinduism, to the concept of UNTOUCHABILITY.

* Hinduism has many signposts showing the different spiritual paths available to different types of people.

* Hinduism offers the widest choice in regard to the form in which GOD could be worshipped, the manner of worshipping and also in regard to the degree of involvement in his devotional activities. There is no rigidity.

* Hinduism aims at UNIVERALITY, SUBLIMITY and FRATERNITY: The UPANISHADS say, 'VASUDHAIVA KUTUMBAKAM' , which means the whole world is my family.

Swami Vivekananda said, "We have a philosophy, the capability, but not power for action. We have principles of Vedanta, but no capacity to put them into practice. In our religious scriptures, the human being in the world is equal, but in our dealings, we create discrimination. Communalism creates narrowism, inequality and isolationism.

ATHARVA VEDA (6.40.3) "There should be none unfriendly in the South in the North, in the West or in the East.

ATHARVAVEDA (19.15.6) "According to Vedas, the man should be surrounded by friends, in all the four directions.

ATHARVAVEDA (1.31.4) Hinduism wish well for all human beings. 'Bless the Mothers, the Fathers, the Men and the whole Universe'.

YAJURVEDA (36.18) 'O Lord, the remover of evil from the minds of all I fast unto Matriye today, so that all living beings should look towards me with friendship, because from today, I have become friendly to all. We all should look towards each other in a friendly manner.' It means that Hinduism is completely the one of equality and affection. There is not a trace of communalism in it.

YAJURVEDA (16.4) 'May the whole world be free from Disease and be of healthy mind'.

YAJURVEDA (16.48) 'Let the whole society be healthy and free from disease'.

* SANKARA ACHARYA, a great mystical Hindu seer, anticipated many today's theories in Primal energy (SAKTI), the atom (ANU), vibrations of the universe and the physical and psychic world around us.

HINDUISM IS UNIQUE THROUGH AND THROUGH

APPENDIX

GAYATRI — GYATRI MANTRA

Gayatri indicates the infinite REALITY, the B'rhma. Gayatri is a particular method of mediation, symbolically represented by Goddess GAYATRI, as a goddess with five heads and ten hands and holding nine weapons in all the hands, except one. Five heads represent five bhutas or the five basic elements, we find in nature, i.e. Earth, water, air, ether and fire. Ten hands signify the ten directions (In addition to eight geographical directions, upwards and downwards make ten in Hindu mythology), which signify the proper regulation and utilization of cosmic energy for the benefit of human beings. The nine weapons represent the nine planets symbolically representing certain specific attributes of these planets.

GAYATRI MANTRA, also called SAVITRI mantra, dedicated to the deity SAVITR (Surya- Sun God). It belongs to R'gveda, found in third mandala in the sixtieth Sutra as the tenth mantra. The seer of the Mantra is saint Vishwamitra. In addition to R'gveda, it is also seen in Yajurveda (both Shukl and K'rsna). Gayatri mantra has been recognised as one of the oldest Divine hymns.

After the R'gveda Sutras, came the Agamas, which laydown theological disciplines and doctrines for the worship of particular deities. Each agma claimed the Gayatri as their own; and they declared that Gayatri is presided over by Visnu, Siva or Sakti, after Agamas, the SAKTAS gave the idea that Gayatri is the infinite Goddess and made her a feminine deity, GAYATRI DEVI, the mother of the Vedas.

GAYATRI MANTRA

Gayatri mantra is :- 'Om Bhuh Bhuwah Swah
Om Tat Savitur Vareneyam

Bhargo Devasya Dhimahi
Dhiyo Yo Nah Prochodyat'

This mantra is never enchanted for the purpose of material gains, physical or otherwise. Its very invocation concludes with an appeal to the pure consciousness to illumine more our heart; it is a prayer unto the self to unveil itself and come to manifest as PURE WISDOM in our life.

Om Bhuh Bhuwah Swah means :-

OM (AUM) : In Gayatri mantra, in pronouncing, the meditator can visualise the three worlds, 'as arising from, existing in, and disappearing into AUM. He can subjectively identify them with the waking, dream and deep sleep, conditions of consciousness, transcending which extends the realm of the infinite; the entire world.

BHUH : Bhuh indicates the permanent, the all pervading one that exists at all periods of time, the most auspicious, ever free self, of the nature of pure existence in all forms, is invoked by this term.

BHUWAH : Bhuwah suggests the pure consciousness due to the etymology of the term. Bhuwah from 'Imagines (Bhawyati) suggests the awareness that illumines (Prakashyati) our thought.

SWAH : Swah suggests 'One's own essential Reality, because all (Sarve) well (sushti) courted ardently (wiyeman) is our ownself.***

The Gaytri Savitri mantra in Vedic metre, is the most important mantra written out in this metre and, therefore, by tradition this mantra has come to be known as GAYATRI. It is generally

***Adi Sankara's own annotations upon the Gayatri mantra, quoted in Swami Chinmaynanda's TUNE IN THE MIND.

constituted of three lines of eight syllables each. The three lines of Gayatri (Savitri- Savitar) mantra are as follows:-

'Om Tat Savitur Vareneyam
Bhargo Devasya Dhimahi
Dhiyo Yo Nah Prochodyat'

On literal analysis, the meaning of the letters in the Mantra, the presiding deity of the letter, its power and functions, have been tabulated below. For the proper enchantment of the letters in the mantra, different parts of the body should be touched simultaneously with the syllable, as given below:-

Letter	Deity	Part to be touched	Shakti (Power)	Functions
Tat	Ganesha	Toe	Success	Riddance of meloncholy, Development of widsom
Sa	Narsinha	Feet	Gallantry	Manlihood, bravery, Heorism, enemy destruction.
Vi	Visnu	Ankle	Preservation	Maintenance of the living, protection of dependants.
Tu	Siva	Knees	Honesty	Self scarifice, emancipation, detachment, self confidence.
Va	K'rsna	Heart	Yoga	Active, detached action beauty, simplicity.
Re	Radha	Sacred parts	Love	Affection, riddance of jealousy.
Nya	Lakshmi	Testicles	Wealth	Wealth, position, honour, deserving substances.
Ma	Agni	Waist	Penetrating	Heat, light, increased competency, brilliancy.
Bha	Indra	Nabhi (umblicus)	Defence	Protection against evil spirits, enemies and thieves.
Rgo	Saraswati	Stomach	Wisdom	Increase in intelligence, purification of thought, cleverness, farsightedness, mental stability.
De	Durga	Chest	Suppression	Victory over obstacles, suppression of cruels, and massacre of enemies.
Va	Hanuman	Heart	Loyalty	Dutiful, fearlessness, and celibacy.
Sya	Prithvi	Neck	Subtlety	Pardonable, capacity to bear load, tolerance.
Dhee	Śurya	Face	Soul	Light, increase in health.
Ma	Rama	Jaws	Dignity	Invisible, steadiness, maintenance of decorum, friendship.
Hi	Sita	Tip of the Nose	Asceticism	Immutable, piety, modesty, melodiousness.
Dhi	Moon	Eyes	Peace	Excitement/pacification, agitation, blessing.
Yo	Yama	Eyebrows	Time	Fearlessness from death, utility of time, agility, awareness.
Yo	Birhma	Top of the head	Production	Reproduction, Increase in progeny.

Contd...

Letter	Deity	Part to be touched	Shakti (Power)	Functions
Nah	Varun	Frontal lobe	Godly	Sentimentality, respect, sweetness.
Pra	Narayan (Visnu)	Back lobe	Ideal	Ambition, virtuous qualities, good behaviour, bright character.
Cho	Heygrieve	west of face	Courage	Enthuisasm, bravery, fearless ness, capacity to face difficulties.
Da	Swan	North of head	Patience	Bright action, self consolation, far sightedness, and cooperation.
Yath	Tulsi	Above the head	Service	Truth, chastity allegiance, self satisfaction, and removal of troubles of others.

In short, Gayatri mantra can be translated as:-

'Endowed with all attributes, Creator, the husband of Goddess of Lakshmi, ever joyful, creator of everything, embodiment of all activities who control our intelligence, that power which pervades the entire Cosmos, which embodies universal bliss, which happiness and knowledge are desired by everyone, that power, I meditate.' *

The present belief of the brahminsis that if one has chanted Gayatri Mantra, he has chanted the Vedas.

Gayatri mantra should be chanted in the morning at the junction of night and day and in the evening before sunset, each time atleast ten times.

If one gets frightened in the dark, immediately Gayatri mantra chanting is advised.

On starting for any important and great work, if a man detects some bad omen, he must immediately sit down and chant eleven times the Gayatri mantra.

By chantment of Gayatri mantra, the devotee means, 'May my intellect be steady without agitations, May it be clean without the dirt of passions. May the light of consciousness come to shine forth a brilliant beam of its radiance through my intellect.' May my perception of the world be clear, my discrimination subtle, my judgements correct and quick, My comprehensions of situ ations and beings precise and wise.'

---

1. Venkatesha T.S. GAYATHRI 1990.

SELECT BIBLIOGRAPHY

1. AIYER V.G.: Chronology of Ancient India 1982
2. Awasthi B.M. : QUEST OF KNOWLEDGE 1974
3. AYACHITS. M. : ASPECTS OF RELIGION 1974
4. Blacker J.F. : a b c of Indian Art 1975
5. Beswick E : THE HINDU GODS 1993
6. THE BHAGVAD GITA
7. Bush Richard etel : THE RELIGIOUS WORLD 1980
8. Chinmayananda : MEDITATION AND LIFE
9. Christananda : THE PHILOSOPHY OF INDIAN MONO-THEISM 1979
10. Cunningham A : THE ANCIENT GEOGRAPHY OF INDIA 1871
11. Deshpande U. : THE GLIMPSES OF INDOLOGICAL HERITAGE
12. FAZAL ABUL : A-IN-I AKBARI
13. FUSTE J & MEHTA I.R : INDIAN HISTORY AND CULTURE 1978
14. Gorham C : ETHICS OF THE GREAT RELIGIONS OF THE WORLD 1904
15. Harshananda S : HINDU GODS AND GODDESSES 1992
16. Hume R.E. : THE WORLD'S LIVING RELIGIONS 1927
17. Ions V : INDIAN MYTHOLOGY 1988
18. Jaganathan S: HINDUISM 1984
19. JEVONS F.B : COMPARATIVE RELIGIONS 1985
20. KALYAN : SPECIAL SAKTI NUMBER 1961 (Hindi)

21. KASHINATH : NEED TO REVIVE ATHEISM IN INDIA 1992
22. Mahajan V.D. : ANCIENT INDIA 1992
23. THE MAHABHARATTA
24. Meena V : THE TEMPLES OF SOUTH INDIA
25. MIRANDA P : AVATARAS AND INCARNATION 1992
26. Mukherjee R.K. : THE FLOWERING OF INDIAN ART 1964
27. Murty K.S. & Dasgupta : THE DIVINE PEACOCK :UNDERSTANDING CONTEMPORARY INDIA 1995
28. Nehru J.L. : THE GLIMPSES OF THE WORLD HISTORY 1982
29. THE PURANAS.
30. RAJGOPALAACHARYA C : THE RAMAKRISHNA UPNISHAD 1955
31. RAO N : THE HERITAGE OF VEDANTA 1968
32. Ramanathan L : THE RAMAYANA 1992
33. Roy G : CAITANYA'S APPROACH TO GOD REALISATION 1986
34. Radhakrishnan S : THE HINDU VIEW OF LIFE 1927
35. Sharma C.D. : A CRITICAL SURVEY OF INDIAN PHILOSOPHY 1979
36. SAMBUDDHANANDA S : VEDANTA THROUGH STORIES 1971
37. Sanyal R.K. : THE HINDU IN SEARCH OF GOD 1995
38. Singh C.L. : PAINTINGS OF SIVA IN INDIAN ART 1990
39. Singh C.L. & P.N. : THE HINDU GODDESSES 1995
40. Stent D. : RELIGIOUS STUDIES 1983
41. Subbamma M. : HINDUISM AND WOMEN 1992

42. THE UPANISHADS

43. Vallett G. : DISCOVERY OF INDIAN HERITAGE 1993

44. THE VEDAS

45. Vivekananda S: THOUGHTS ON THE GITA 1978

46. Williams M. : RELIGIOUS LIFE IN ANCIENT INDIA 1990

INDEX